BAJA BOOK IV

The Complete Guide To The Baja California Peninsula

GINGER POTTER

Fourth Edition, Completely Revised

BAJA SOURCE
1945 Dehesa Rd.
El Cajon, California

Photographs for Baja Spacemaps© from NASA Earth Resources Technology Satellite.

Illustrations by Hope "Esperanza" Bartmess.

First edition copyright by Tom Miller and Elmar Baxter, 1974.
Second edition, copyright by Tom Miller and Elmar Baxter, 1979.
Third Edition, copyright by Tom Miller and Carol Hoffman, 1987.
Fourth Edition, completed revised, copyright by Ginger Potter, 1996.

Library of Congress Catalog Card Number 95-94715
Potter, Ginger M.
    Baja Book IV: A complete guide to the Baja California Peninsula.

ISBN 0-9644066-0-8
Printed in the United State of America.
Published by Baja Source, Inc., 1945 Dehesa Road, El Cajon, CA 92019. Write, call or fax for free catalog. 619-442-7061

DEDICATION...

This book is dedicated to my dad, Mike McMahan, for without him to introduce me to Baja I would not know it today. Baja became his mistress, he spent every minute he could exploring and enjoying this marvelous peninsula. In 1953, he co-authored a best selling book, Baja California, and then went on to write two more Baja books; There It Is: Baja and Adventures in Baja. He created the first 5 editions of the colorful large Baja wall map now seen everywhere on the peninsula (and on the back cover of this book). My dad and I took many trips down the peninsula together. He shared his favorite surf fishing spots with me. Back in the 60's before anyone else got there, we hauled 'junque' out of Baja's famous junk beach, Malarrimo. I taught my dad, at age 83, to ride an ATC so he could get farther down the beach "where the fish were." In 1990, dad passed away. He is buried in Loreto.

ABOUT THE AUTHOR...

I come from a family of Baja enthusiasts. My husband, Chuck, and I love exploring and fishing in Baja. In 1966, we spent our honeymoon driving along the Pacific coast of Baja from Punta Canoes to Boca de Marrón. In 1972, we put a house trailer in at El Tomatal, an isolated fish camp 40 miles north of Guerrero Negro. We enjoy our times at the trailer, but we are more likely to be found exploring unknown places and seeking the new adventures that Baja continues to offer.

Our family began traveling to Baja when I was a child. Every year, during Easter week all of my relatives camped together in a canyon on the beach some 13 miles south of San Felipe. We called the place Easter Camp. Altogether there were about sixty of us and this tradition continued for over forty years. Here is where I first learned to drive and years later our daughters, Terri and Reina, learned to drive, all of us in dune buggies on the same bumpy, dusty Baja roads.

At the age of 9, on a sportfishing boat out of Orange Landing, I caught my first albacore. It was an awesome experience, dad telling me what to do and the fish doing the opposite. Between that experience and my efforts to learn surf fishing at Easter Camp, I've been hooked on fishing ever since. Today, because there seems to be no more albacore, I prefer surf fishing - and hardly a day goes by when I am in Baja that I don't get a line wet.

Over the years I've developed an avid interest in the history, plants, and geology of Baja. As a young child I learned to identify the elephant tree, the cardón, the smoke bush, the mesquite tree and many others. From Easter Camp, we would go foraging in the desert looking for ironwood for the fire. It was during these trips that I had my first introduction to the botany of Baja.

In college, I was struggling with a geology final and my brother, Pat, with a minor in geology, spent hours filling my head with great information about our earth. I got an "A," thanks to him. But I also received something else, for soon after, I saw in Baja what I had learned from my brother. Besides igneous, metamorphic and sedimentary rock, Baja geology reveals earthquake faults, fossils, minerals, etc. I am sure my new husband thought his new wife was absolutely brilliant as I rode alongside him there in the car on our honeymoon identifying all the formations and expounding for hours on what I knew about mother earth. Obviously, I now realize the rest of the world has all the geological features Baja has, but they are more prominent in Baja.

History was never my forte but exploring the missions, getting to know the people, the ruggedness of Baja, developed my interest.

Beachcombing, surf fishing and exploring the many isolated and undisturbed places in Baja is very interesting to me. I had the opportunity to be involved in the international whale count during the 1980's under the supervision of Dr. Raymond Gilmore of the San Diego Museum of Natural History. I have driven the peninsula many times, end to end and side to side, before the highway and on the highway and I know the roads. Currently, I operate "Baja Source", a company exporting and distributing American merchandise to all of Baja.

4

Chuck and Ginger Potter with an afternoon high tide catch of spotfin croaker. These fish were taken from the surf near Tomatal.

ACKNOWLEDGMENTS...

Tom Miller created the original Baja Book. Baja Book I and Baja Book II were written with Elmar Baxter in 1974 and 1979. Baja Book III was written with Carol Hoffman in 1987. The book format and the road-log with the space maps are Tom Miller's creation. He was truly Mr. Baja. When Tom passed away, I elected to take over the job of keeping "The Baja Book" going and when I am gone, hopefully, someone else will continue to keep it going.

Tom Miller and Ginger Potter at the grand
opening party for the Discover Baja Travel Club.

This edition of the Baja Book came to completeness through the efforts of many experts on Baja: Gene Kira *the* Baja Fisherman; Mike Bales the trailer-boating specialist; Kirk and Jan Brown who lead hundreds of RVs to Baja; John Minch the geological expert on Baja; Norman Roberts whose love for Baja lead him to be an expert on the plants of the peninsula; Harry Crosby who ultimately put the Jesuit history of Baja in order correctly; W. Michael Mathes for explicit correction of the section on the Dominican and Franciscan history; Andromeda Romano-Lax who travels Baja's outer coast by kayak; John and Terry Burkhart of the Flight Log. Oscar Padilla for current insurance information. Louis Semon of U. S.. Customs.

My husband, Chuck, (who's cooking skills increased tremendously while I wrote this book) for his patience in taking that side road again to double check the mileages, and for working so hard at keeping our truck and *my* dune buggy in "Baja shape" so I wouldn't have problems on those frequent trips when I went down to Baja alone.

Ray Bradley for taking and double checking my tedious notes on our many trips up and down the peninsula.

Vello and Margaret Sork for their Canadian point of view.

Pat Smith for editing my terrible English.

The Delegados of the districts of Baja California for information enabling me to create the city maps.

Maleni Sorhouet, tour guide for the whale-watching trips from the Malarrimo Cafe in Guerrero Negro, for much of the information on the whales and the salt mines at Guerrero Negro.

Many thanks to Chris and Alleen Jensen, full time residents of Mulegé, for their assistance in verifying portions of the book.

Thank you to all of my friends in Baja who encouraged me to put this book together and to those of you who assisted me in my research.

Last, but of prime importance, I acknowledge Hope "Esperanza" Bartmess for her unique illustrations. She, too, is a lifelong Baja enthusiast and has the "feel" of Baja in her art.

Hopefully you will find first hand, useful information on everything covered in this book. Baja seems like such a small place in this big world but there is so much more to it than meets the eye. I hope you will discover for yourself what Baja has meant to all of us and that you will return to Baja again and again.

IMPORTANT NOTICE AND DISCLAIMER...

The Baja Book IV is a general road and recreation guide to Baja California. Although every effort has been made to make this book as accurate as possible, there may be unintentional errors in the information provided. herein. Prices and other information are representative at the time of publishing. For legal purposes the maps, scales and headings provided in this guide must be considered approximate.

All drivers, owners and passengers of any vehicle using the Baja Book IV are explicitly forewarned that some hazards or obstructions may not have been shown or described, and anything depicted herein is subject to change due to acts of God, political decisions and/or other circumstances beyond our control. Do not drive at night and drive slowly as the Baja highway was not built for high speed travel; it was built for economic development.

This guide may be used only with the understanding that the information contained herein is subject to unintentional errors and/or omissions and that the publisher and author cannot and do not, make any warranty, express or implied, as to the ultimate accuracy, safety or completeness of this information, nor shall they have any responsibility or liability for any person or entity in connection with any actual or alleged losses or damages caused by the use of the material in this book. Travel at your own risk. Use caution and have a wonderful time exploring Baja.

CONTENTS

INTRODUCTION... 11

Chapter 1
PAPERWORK AND PREPARATION
YOUR TOURIST CARD.. 12
PERMITS 12
HUNTING LICENSES... 13
FISHING LICENSES.. 13
INSURANCE.. 14
FERRIES TO MAINLAND MEXICO... 15
DOLLARS VS. PESOS... 15

Chapter 2
GETTING TO BAJA
BY COMMERCIAL AIRLINE 17
BY PRIVATE PLANE.. 18
BY CAR, OR RV 18
RV TRAVEL TIPS 19
RV CARAVANS TO BAJA... 21
ROAD CONDITIONS 22
ARRIVING BY SEA.. 27
BOAT PERMITS.. 27
BAJA BY BUS 27

Chapter 3
SURVIVAL TIPS
THE LAW IS NOT THE SAME 28
ENTERING MEXICO.. 28
RETURNING TO THE U.S. 29
AGRICULTURAL INSPECTIONS... 31
GROCERY SHOPPING IN BAJA.. 31
CLOTHING 32
YOUR CAMERA.. 32
YOUR PETS.. 33
TRAVEL CLUBS.. 33
TIPPING 34

Chapter 4
UNDERSTANDING BAJA

GEOLOGY 35
PLANTS...38
MISSIONS 44
A DIFFERENT CULTURE..50
HOLIDAYS...51
FAMOUS COMIDA 52

Chapter 5
CITY MAPS

TIJUANA..58
ENSENADA..60
SAN QUINTIN...62
GUERRERO NEGRO 64
SAN IGNACIO 66
SANTA ROSALIA...68
MULEGE...70
LORETO..72
CONSTITUCION...74
LA PAZ...75
SAN JOSE DEL CABO 78
CABO SAN LUCAS...80
SAN FELIPE 82

Chapter 6

ROADLOG 85
100 Pages of mile-by-mile roadlogs

Chapter 7
ENJOYING BAJA

WHALE-WATCHING 87
FISHERMAN'S PARADISE..94
YOUR BOAT AND BAJA...101
CAMPING..102
BEACHCOMBING..105
SEA KAYAKING IN BAJA 106
SURFING...107
WINDSURFING 108
DIVING 109

Chapter 8

RESOURCE GUIDE 110

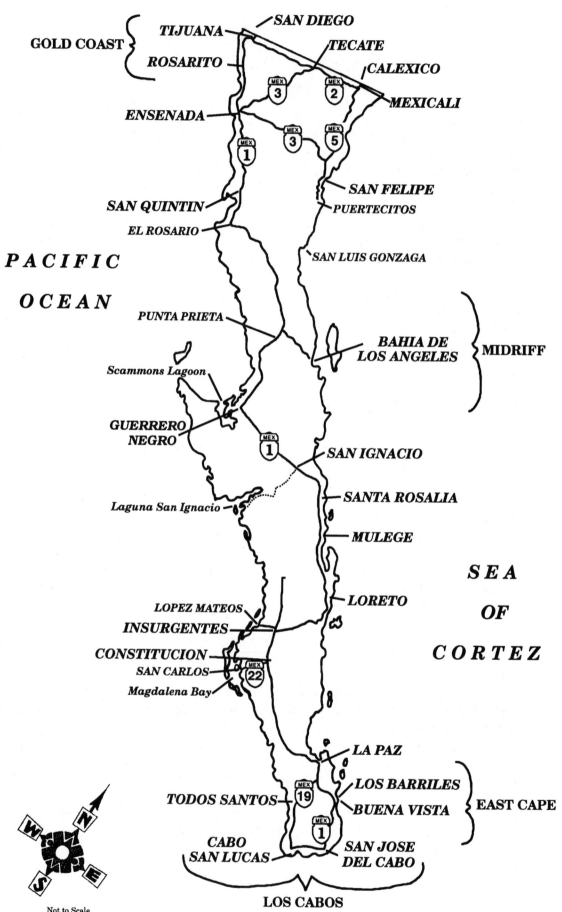

INTRODUCTION

Baja has 2000 miles of beautiful, rugged coastline, with hidden coves, white sandy beaches, rocky bluffs and crystal blue waters teeming with life, all waiting for you to enjoy. If you're hoping to just relax and do nothing, want to fish 'til your arm drops off, explore isolated beaches, surf on a lonely south-facing beach, kayak, windsurf, whale-watch, bird-watch, beachcomb or stargaze on a clear night - this is the place.

The two states of Baja, Baja California Norte and Baja California Sur are separated at the 28th parallel just north of Guerrero Negro. The peninsula is about 800 miles long and varies from 75 to 125 miles wide. There is only one paved road going the length of the peninsula and this is México 1. Annual rainfall is minimal but it usually rains in the northern and southern parts of the peninsula more than in the middle.

People have coined names to different areas of Baja. The "Gold Coast", so named because the land became as valuable as gold when the tourists came, extends from north of Rosarito Beach to a few miles north of Ensenada. The "midriff" is the narrowest area of the gulf or Sea of Cortez. The "East Cape" is the area from La Paz south along the coast to San José del Cabo. "Los Cabos" is the term used to describe the area from San José del Cabo to Cabo San Lucas.

Driving down the 1000 mile paved highway one can stop and enjoy watersports on both sides of the peninsula. For the passenger car, hotels are conveniently spread out over the length of the peninsula allowing for short or long days of travel. For the motorhome, RV parks are also conveniently located throughout the trip. Airlines fly into the major cities and car rentals are available.

The economy of Baja hinges on the tourist dollar. You will be well received and catered to. There is a good roadside assistance program in case you have a problem on the road. American goods are available in the larger cities. Many of the people speak English, especially those you will come into direct contact with. The Department of Tourism has offices in all major cities to assist you in case of a discrepancy. In general, food and accommodations will cost you less than in the United States but if money is not your concern there are also some expensive world-class hotels in Cabo San Lucas.

This book covers preparing for your trip (including the necessary paperwork required), what you're allowed to take and bring back, survival within a foreign culture and some suggestions on how to enjoy yourself while you are in Baja. Descriptions of Baja's unique features include a chapter on the geology, plants and missions. A complete and detailed Roadlog gives you kilometer by kilometer descriptions of what to expect as you travel. City maps are provided for your convenience in finding your way around within the various towns and cities. Lastly, a complete, detailed Resource Guide is listed for planning your vacation of a lifetime.

Welcome to Baja!

Chapter 1

PAPERWORK AND PREPARATION

YOUR TOURIST CARD...

A Mexican tourist card, (visa) is necessary if you go south of Ensenada or stay more than 3 days in Baja. Identification required to obtain your visa can be any one of the following; current passport, birth certificate, naturalization papers, affidavit of birth, military discharge papers or armed forces ID card. These tourist cards can be obtained from the Mexican National Tourist Council, one of the offices of the Mexican Consulate, travel agencies that service México, Mexican auto insurance offices or the travel clubs. (See Resource guide in the back of this book.)

When you cross the border you can have your visa validated inside the secondary inspection area (on the right immediately after crossing) or at the office of the *Delegación de Servicios Migratórios* in Ensenada (exact location is noted in the Roadlog and on the Ensenada city map). Your visa can be validated for up to 180 days. Should you need to renew your visa while in southern Baja you can do so in Santa Rosalía and La Paz. It is possible to request an extension upon proof of financial solvency.

Another type of visa, "visitante rentista" or FM-3, is good for a 1 year stay in México and for multiple entries during that same time period. These may be obtained at any office of the Mexican Consulate General. In San Diego the office is located at 610 A St., San Diego, CA 92101. Applicants must apply in person between 9 and 12 noon. Be early! You will need to have with you a valid passport and a notarized letter from your bank stating that you are financially solvent and showing your income level. The "minimum solvency level" changes but for reference purposes in 1995 it was $1800.00 U.S. per month. Also required are 2 passport photos, front views, black and white matte finish. There is a charge for the FM-3. Applicants can be U.S. citizens or from any one of 18 other countries.

This type of FM-3 will not allow you to take your furniture into México duty free nor will it allow you to work while in México.

PERMITS REQUIRED...

If the vehicle you are taking into México does not belong to you, you must have with you a notarized letter from the registered owner granting you permission to take the vehicle into México. This applies if you have a loan on your car and the legal owner listed on your registration is someone other than yourself.

If you have children with you who do not have both parents with them they will need a notarized letter, signed by both parents, stating that it is all right for them to be with whomever they are traveling. This includes having a notarized letter from one spouse if the child is traveling with the other.

Vehicle permits: If you plan to stay within Baja California you will not need a vehicle permit. If you intend to take a ferry to the Mainland you will need to temporarily import your vehicle. An 800 number for information on importing your vehicle into México is in the Resource guide. If you need information on getting this permit in La Paz see the section on "Ferries to Mainland México" in this book.

A current U.S. drivers license wil be sufficient for brief trips. If you end up staying in Baja permanently (a lot of people do) then you will need to obtain a Mexican drivers license.

HUNTING LICENSES...

Quail, dove, duck and geese hunting in Baja should be fantastic, there are certainly a lot of game birds. The Mexican government has instituted many new rules and regulations in the last few years which makes it a costly, bureaucratic and time-consuming ordeal to get everything done correctly. One problem has developed in that it seems the same rules don't apply to Baja as they do to mainland México and nobody has written down this second set of rules. If you are an avid hunter and want more information, call the Mexican Hunting Association in Long Beach at 1-310-430-3256. They can also provide information about the Mexican hunting clubs available (in Baja) for quail, dove, duck and brant shooting.

FISHING LICENSES...

All passengers, including children, aboard a boat that is actively fishing must have in their possession a Mexican fishing license. This applies to fresh or salt water. (Believe it or not , there are some trout streams in the Sierra San Pedro Mártir.) The cost for this license is reasonable and can be purchased for varying lengths of time. These licenses are available from the Mexican Department of Fisheries, phone in San Diego is 619-233-6956. Some of the travel clubs and Baja Outfitters, conveniently located at the border just before you cross into Tijuana, also sell fishing licenses..

There are limits on certain fish, check for current information before you go south. At the time of this writing, anglers may catch a total of 10 fish per day with no more than 5 of one species and no more than 5 members of the tuna family, 2 roosterfish or dolphinfish (dorado), 1 sailfish, marlin, swordfish or black sea bass. Totuava are endangered and should not be taken. Fish are still quite plentiful along the coasts of Baja. The government has set limits for anglers and for commercial fishermen. If the rules are followed by everyone, the fishing in Baja will endure. If you love the sport, treat this precious resource with loving care. Catch and release has really caught on in Baja.

Boats are not allowed in any of the coastal lagoons during January through March because the whales are visiting at that time of year.

No fishing license is required for surf fishing. But if you don't have a license, someone will ask if you would like to go out fishing with them in their boat so it is best to have one. If you intend to carry fish back to the U.S. you will be required to show your license if stopped and searched.

INSURANCE...

The following article contains information provided by Oscar Padilla Mexican Insurance Services, Inc.

Automobile insurance in México is a must. Your American insurance will not be recognized in México. Whether you choose basic liability or full coverage you will find the rates are reasonable compared to our U.S. rates. You can buy your policy for the length of your trip or by the year. A Mexican automobile insurance policy covers five specific risks. They are:

1. Collision, upset and glass breakage.
2. Fire, lightning, total theft, hurricane, hail, strikes & riots, cyclone, earthquake, volcanic eruption, flood, explosion, and landslide.

(Note: Risks 1 & 2 pay up to the limit of current value of vehicle.)

3. Property Damage Liability.
4. Bodily Injury Liability.
5. Medical Expenses.

You must have liability insurance if you drive a vehicle in México. If you are pulling anything, it must be on the policy too. Insurance coverage applies to the described vehicle in the policy. It does not follow the named insured. This enables the coverage to apply while any licensed individual is operating the described vehicle.

If you have an accident, you need to report it to your insurance agency prior to leaving Baja. When you receive your policy you will receive a list of phone numbers in the major cities. Should you have an accident in the "outback" and your vehicle is still driveable, you will find most agencies have facilities in Ensenada where you can file a claim and they can photograph the damage. If your car is not driveable you should see that it is towed to a federal impound location and that you get a receipt for the vehicle. One such impound yard is at the intersection of México 1 and the turnoff to Bahía de Los Angeles and there are others located throughout the peninsula. The "Green Angels", those wonderful roving trucks provided by the government, can assist you with any problems you may have. Whatever you do, don't leave your vehicle unattended along the highway, it will be cannibalized.

Your insurance is void if you are found to be under the influence of alcohol or drugs at the time of an accident.

México has traffic laws very similar to the U.S. The application of their laws is what makes the difference between México and California. The law in México is based on the *Napoleonic Code* where guilt prevails over the assumption of innocence. In the U.S. the law is based on the *English Common Law* where innocence prevails over the assumption of guilt.

In the event of an accident in México all parties are detained until it is determined who is responsible. If someone is seriously injured or killed the responsible driver will be incarcerated and eventually large fines will be imposed. If just minor damage has occurred the responsible driver will have to pay for the damages. Assessment of damages is normally handled by the officer in charge at the police station.

It is a good idea to have an extra copy of your insurance policy along. Should you get into an accident they may want a copy of your policy.

For a current quote on the cost of Mexican insurance contact Oscar Padilla at 800-258-8600.

FERRIES TO MAINLAND MEXICO...

If you plan on taking the ferry from Baja to mainland México you should make your ferry reservations well in advance, perhaps 3 or 4 weeks, and then confirm them one or two days in advance at the ferry dock. During the winter you may have to make reservations 6 weeks in advance. A vehicle importation permit is necessary to take your vehicle into mainland México. To get this you need three copies of each of the following; vehicle registration, driver's license and tourist card. If your vehicle registration shows any other name on it than your own (leasing company, finance company) you will need to have in your possession notarized permission from that person (or entity) to take the vehicle into México. If you're in La Paz you can get your import permit by taking these papers to the ferry terminal office of the Secretary of the Hacienda and Credito Publico, (SHCP, commonly known as the "Hacienda") located east of town at Pichilingue. Here you will also be asked to post a bond to guarantee your vehicle will exit México within 6 months. This bond can be put on your credit card, paid in cash or be in the form of a letter of bond. You will receive your window decal and your permit that you will turn in when you purchase your ferry tickets. In La Paz the ferry ticket office, Sematur, is located in town at the corner of Guillermo Prieto and Cinco de Mayo, it is at this office where they measure the length of your vehicle to determine the fare. The fare may be paid in pesos, U.S. dollars, or with Mastercard or Visa. At this point you may want to consider getting accommodations for the trip, different ferries offer different options. You will not be allowed to return to your vehicle once it is parked on the ferry. If you have a cat or dog it must be left in the vehicle.

If you have further questions regarding your permit call 900-452-8277 in the U.S. before heading into México.

The Santa Rosalía ferry leaves on Sundays and Wednesdays at 8 am and arrives in Guaymas at 3 p. m..

The Mazatlán ferry from La Paz, Pichilingue terminal, leaves on weekdays at 3 p. m. and arrives at 9 am.

The Topolobampo ferry leaves La Paz, Pichilingue terminal ,weekdays at 8 p. m. and arrives at 6 am.

In México, reservations for ferry transfers may be made by calling: Santa Rosalía: 91-115-20013; La Paz: 91-112-53833.

DOLLARS VS. PESOS...

It is a good idea to carry enough pesos to pay for your expenses when you travel in Baja. With planning you can arrange to exchange your dollars with most U.S. banks before you go or you can buy pesos at one of the many money exchange places (Casas de Cambio) along the border. After arriving in Baja you can exchange money at the banks or in the larger towns at the money exchange booths. Many banks have short hours, usually 9:00 a.m. to 1:30 p.m. and they take advantage of all holidays so plan ahead. Banks in Baja can have very long lines so try changing your money on Tuesdays or Wednesdays early in the day when the lines are generally shorter. At the time of this writing the peso is fluctuating a small amount everyday. It is a good idea to check the bank exchange rate before you buy your pesos. It is probably not a good idea to buy large amounts of pesos at any one time.

On August 31, 1976, President Echeverría made the decision to allow the value of the peso to float on the international market. The fixed exchange rate of 12.50 pesos to the dollar fell immediately to about 20 pesos to 1 dollar. Over the years numerous devaluation's took it to 3000 to 1 where it stabilized for a few years. Among other things this created havoc with the calculators and computers because there just wasn't enough room to enter all the zeros. In 1993, they dropped 3 zeros and printed new currency and made new coins to reflect the change. The old currency was supposed to be phased out of circulation by 1995, however, things don't always happen as planned and this currency is still in circulation. In late 1994, they started issuing a smaller size of bills and have included a 500 peso note and other new denominations in this series. Should you encounter all three currencies at once it takes some getting used to. An old 1000 peso note is equal to 1 nuevo peso (new peso), 10,000 equals 10 nuevos pesos and so on. The new bills are printed with the words "nuevos pesos" and the old ones are not but they look identical otherwise. The newer smaller size bills are, likewise, similar in appearance . It is possible to have in your hand at one time, three different bills equaling twenty pesos each.

On December 20, 1994, President Zedillo devalued the peso again. From about 3.3 pesos to the U.S. dollar it went to 7 to 1 in a very short period of time. If you happen to be in Baja when the peso is fluctuating wildly keep in mind that there can be a big difference in the rate to buy pesos and the rate to buy dollars. During the first few weeks after the 1994 devaluation the difference was about 20%. A few days after the first devaluation, when the exchange rate was fluctuating wildly, it was 4 to 1 to buy pesos and 5 to 1 to buy dollars. During this time the best way to buy pesos was with your Visa or Mastercard at the cash machines. These transactions received the best rate available in México for that day. During a major devaluation some real bargains are to be had if you can get a good rate in buying pesos and get to the stores before they mark their prices up. One place you will really want to have pesos is at the gas stations as their exchange rate is generally much lower than other places.

Visa and Mastercard holders can obtain cash advances in pesos at Bancomer branches throughout Baja. You will receive the current exchange rate and there has been no commission. You might want to prepay cash on your credit card prior to your trip so you can avoid the high interest rates.

There will be a "value added tax" added to most of your purchases. This tax is included in gasoline prices. Shopkeepers are supposed to post a sign telling you whether or not this "IVA" tax is included in their prices.

Credit cards, in particular Visa and Mastercard, can be used in Baja. Most hotels, motels, larger markets and restaurants accept them. The places that accept credit cards are paying 6% to their banks to handle these transactions. Gasoline credit cards are not accepted anywhere in Baja. Travelers checks are generally accepted everywhere.

Chapter 2

GETTING TO BAJA

Baja has been called México's "Diamond in the Rough", the "Forgotten Peninsula" and "Yesterday's Land". Until just 25 years ago you needed a map, a compass and a lot of luck to find your way, without mishap, to land's end at Cabo San Lucas. Baja received world wide attention when, in 1967, the first Baja 1000 race occurred. This tortuous race spanned the full length of the peninsula, received worldwide attention, and made people aware of Baja's existence. In the late 1940's, Erle Stanley Gardner began writing books on Baja. These books were filled with amazing pictures and stories of rugged adventure. In 1962, after writing four books on Baja he wrote The Hidden Heart of Baja and revealed his discovery of the now famous Indian cave paintings in the mountains of central Baja. Although he was not the first to discover the paintings, he was the first to make the site known to the world. The archaeological world took notice and scientists came from far away to study and photograph.

In 1953, when my dad, wrote Baja California, a story of his 6 week journey down the treacherous one lane dirt road to Cabo San Lucas, his book quickly became a best-seller and made some of the more adventurous sit up and take notice. A new frontier was revealed and the sale of four-wheel drive vehicles rose as more and more people ventured south. In those days, 80 miles travel in a day was making good time. Of those who braved this rugged trip, many were enamored and came back again and again. Baja's mountains, her seas, her plants and her history were mostly unknown and unexplored. For anyone with the slightest leaning towards an adventuresome spirit, Baja awakened this spirit and they returned.

Baja is truly different from its mother, México. Baja is isolated and this isolation has kept it safer and cleaner.

Today, Baja is accessible by road, by plane, by sea; her doors are open to all who care to come. Since 1973, with the completion of a highway running the length of the peninsula have come many new visitors. Huge airstrips now dot the land. Yet there is still much unspoiled rugged beauty to be enjoyed. The advantage we have today is that we can enjoy more of Baja through the study of others before us, and we can get there much faster.

BY COMMERCIAL AIRLINE...

There is good commercial airline service from Los Angeles to Cabo San Lucas, La Paz and Loreto. In winter time the rates are generally much higher so if you plan ahead you can save as much as fifty percent on air fare. When the flights out of Los Angeles are booked you can sometimes catch a flight from Tucson to La Paz or Cabo San Lucas. Flights to Loreto are very expensive currently; however there are plans for a new service at reduced rates.

Sometimes there are reduced rates if you fly from Tijuana to La Paz and Cabo San Lucas but don't plan on parking your vehicle at the Tijuana airport without paying an exorbitant amount for parking. There is a bus from the Tijuana border, San Ysidro crossing, to the airport that is very reasonably priced; however, you should allow an hour and a half for the ride. I have flown to Hermosillo to get to La Paz and saved money by adding this additional 40 minutes to my flight time. All flights suggest you be at the airport at least one hour ahead of time to confirm your reservations. During peak seasons schedules change so call the airline one day prior to confirm your flight time and date as they don't always advise you of the changes. At the airport you will be asked to "push the button" that determines whether your luggage will be searched. It is a random red light - green light signal and they use the same set-up at the international border when you cross. When you cross the border have your airline ticket in hand to avoid questions about your luggage. You will need your passport or other acceptable form of ID and a visa when you enter Baja by air. Check the weight limit for your luggage when you buy your tickets, it is strictly enforced and you will be charged for overage.

BY PRIVATE PLANE...

Private pilots have been flying to Baja for a long time. This form of travel to Baja is quite pleasant and safe. Current information on airport conditions and the availability of fuel can now be obtained.

Rules and regulations? Sure they have them here too. They are not much different, but as with entering any foreign country there are documents to present. Once you know what is expected you'll be pleasantly surprised to find the Mexican airport officials are unfailingly courteous and helpful.

Runways are located at many of the nicer spots in Baja. Many of the hotels on the gulf side of the peninsula have their own runways, some right at the hotel door. If the runway is beyond walking distance transportation is available for someone to pick you up. All hotels with Unicom monitor 122.8. Use Unicom to call for someone to pick you up. A few of the hotels have catered exclusively to the private pilot for many years. Today one can 'hotel hop' down the peninsula seeking the best fishing, the best weather or just the adventure.

Flying down the gulf from Mexicali the DME/VOR navaids run out. GPS and Loran work...but guess what? Look out the window. Keep the water on your left and the land on your right. You can't get lost. Did you come all this way to watch those instruments so you know how fast, how far, how much wind? You can do that at home. If you don't look out the window, you will surely miss something wonderful. Baja has a beauty all her own, especially from the air.

If you are a pilot and would like more information on flying in Baja contact John and Terry Burkhart at the Flight Log, P. O.. Box 2465, Fullerton, CA 92633, 714-521-2531. These folks have been flying in Baja for many years and lead groups down for whalewatching and various activities.

BY CAR, OR RV...

México 1 (the Baja highway) was completed in 1973. This 2 lane paved road stretches and winds over the length of the peninsula for just over 1000 miles. In places it is quite narrow and in places there is no shoulder. The road winds through and around jungles of cactus, beautiful green oases, mountains and towns, revealing stark naked landscapes, lush tropical palm groves, awesome geology, weird plants, an ocean and a sea. The scenery is fantastic, the countryside is clean and appears untouched throughout most of the peninsula.

Many people drive their regular passenger cars, staying in the various motels and hotels along the way. Motorhomes are typical traffic on the road and many RV parks accommodate this type of travel. Whatever your mode of transportation, it is important than you plan each days travel so as to not get caught in the dark of night. Cattle and other large animals feed along the road and they are difficult or impossible to see at night. In some places there is no white line, further impeding night travel. Warning signs are inadequate in places and potholes are almost impossible to see until you get right on top (or in) one, furthermore you will probably encounter vehicles with only one or no headlights!

Traveling during the daytime you will find the traffic can be fairly light and you may drive for miles without seeing anyone. Baja has no railroad so you are going to see some huge trucks. On occasion, you will find a Mexican vehicle doing ten miles per hour on the main highway, this is how some of them drive. The government has posted signs saying the road "was not built for high speed driving, it was built for economic development". Avoid high speeds and you will have a rewarding and trouble-free trip. There are very few traffic cops in Baja - it's up to you.

The Mexican government tourism department, as part of its program to make visitors welcome, has provided a fleet of specially-equipped green trucks to assist you if you have a problem while on the road. Called *Angeles Verdes* or Green Angels, they patrol the highway everyday. They can provide you with a small amount of emergency gas, oil or water, do minor repairs at no charge and supply some small parts at cost. There are generally 2 men in each truck and one of them speaks some English. These vehicles only patrol the paved part of the road. Don't expect to find them around if you are away from the highway. Your vehicle should be in top shape if you plan to venture off road. Should you break down on the highway, wait for the Green Angels don't leave your vehicle unattended.

There are no permits required to take your vehicle into Baja. Mexican insurance is required. If you are towing anything it must be on the policy too. If you are going to take one of the ferries to the mainland side of México you will need to have a vehicle importation permit. If the vehicle you are taking into México does not belong to you, you should have with you a notarized letter from the registered owner granting you permission to take this vehicle into México.

RV TRAVEL TIPS...

Full service RV Parks are popping up all over Baja. This is a large step forward and has made Baja very comfortable for the RV traveler. Most of the parks are very reasonably priced, kept very clean and offer almost all of the amenities you might find in the states. The locations of most of the parks with full hookups are noted in the Roadlog. A map showing where the RV parks are located and instructions on how to access the parks are located at the back of this book.

If you plan on taking your RV to Baja, it is your first trip and you are not going with a caravan perhaps some of the following information will assist you.

Fresh water for motorhomes to fill their tanks can be purchased. The water available at the parks is sometimes a bit brackish (as almost all water is in Baja) and certainly not what you will want to make coffee with. *Guácala!* (that's Spanish for yuk). The places where you can buy good water usually have a sign out front that says "*Agua Purificado*" (purified water). There is one in every town. Here you can fill your tanks with your own garden hose (take a long one - at least 75 feet long). Some of them actually have their own hoses used only for this purpose. This is where the water comes from that is bottled and delivered to the local residents on a daily basis. It is good sweet water that has been filtered and treated. If you can't find one of these places and you hear the water truck honking up and down the streets of the towns, stop the water truck and have him pour a few bottles in your tank. The charge will be quite reasonable; to fill a 25 gallon tank costs about $2.00 U.S. when they fill it using a hose and a little more if they pour the bottles into the tank. Don't forget to have a large funnel ready. (A large plastic soda or booze bottle with the bottom cut off makes a handy funnel.) A few RV parks have separate water available for drinking. Don't hesitate to ask about the water, the locals always know if it is salty (un poco de sal) and definitely know if it is safe to drink.

There are no <u>camper dump stations </u>in Baja. The only places you can dump your black water tanks are located in the RV parks. It is generally acceptable to dump grey water just about anywhere that seems sensible. We dump grey water into 5 gallon buckets and water the plants with it. (We do not put any chemicals in our grey water tank and use biodegradable soap.)

Electricity supplies in the RV parks are generally less consistent than we are used to and the voltage fluctuates. You probably will not be able to use your microwave and the air conditioner at the same time. Most of the parks will have signs warning you of any problems with power. If you don't see any signs, ask. Experienced Baja travelers carry their own voltmeters.

In those RV parks with washers and dryers you will find the machines only take U.S. quarters. Take plenty with you. They will sell you quarters but they typically charge you more in pesos than they are worth. Clothes dry fast on the line (if you remembered to bring a length of rope and a few clothespins). Washing soap is available in the stores.

Inverters are handy accessories in Baja. If the RV park should fill up and the power goes down, you can still run your VCR and television and recharge your electric toothbrush. Generators can be very bothersome to others. Please don't run them all night long; you'll get a lot of nasty looks if you do - and you might hear your neighbors leaning on their horns.

El Cardón Trailer Park
La Paz

PROPANE...

While it is possible to have portable propane tanks refilled at many locations by gravity feed, onboard propane tanks with automotive type fillers can only be filled at the large official propane stations. We refill our two five-gallon tanks at the large stations because they fill them fuller than is possible with gravity feed and they charge a lot less. Recently these propane stations have opened up in many locations in Baja. Most of the stations are located outside of the populated areas where an explosion would be less devastating. They are all open weekdays until 4:00 p.m., some are open Saturdays until noon; they do not close for siesta. They are all closed on Sundays and holidays. The locations of these stations are as follows:

ENSENADA: North of town on the east side of México 1.
ENSENADA: East of town on México 3, south side.
COLONIA GUERRERO: West side of México 1 at K172.
GUERRERO NEGRO: North of town on west side of México 1.
SANTA ROSALIA: Km 12 north of Santa Rosalía.
CONSTITUCION: Km 222 north of town
LA PAZ: Km 204 on México 1 south of town
LOS CABOS: Km 27 between San José del Cabo and Cabo San Lucas

RV CARAVANS TO BAJA...

Traveling in a motorhome is a very convenient way to enjoy Baja. Many isolated, beautiful campsites are accessible by motorhome and obviously there are no conveniences in these places so for many people the motorhome provides the necessary comforts needed. Many RV caravans tour Baja and I have listed a few of them in the Resource Guide. Information for the following article has been contributed by Kirk and Jan Brown of "Baja Winters" Caravans.

Caravanning with your RV.

For the first time RV traveler in Baja, caravanning is highly recommended. The leaders of the caravans can competently show you the way. They make sure your paperwork is all taken care of, offer you competitive insurance rates, assist you in case of a breakdown, show you the locations of the RV parks, markets and restaurants and offer companionship in your new venture. They can also assist you with basic things that are handled a little differently than they are back home, such as telephoning, banking, postal services, medical assistance, food and water.

Those who venture down Baja by road will notice that about every third rig they meet is a gringo or Canadian RV. Why not? There are no places stateside that can match the Baja winter combination of warm sunny days, cool nights, uncluttered beaches, and much, much more.

Caravan travel is very common in Baja. Some start up in Texas and Arizona, travel down the mainland, and arrive in southern Baja by ferry. Others depart from the San Diego area, making their way slowly, about 200 miles a day, stopping in the major tourist areas along the 1,070 or so miles to Los Cabos

Over a dozen caravan companies escort their groups into Baja during the winter season. These caravans are usually limited to about 20 vehicles. Prices vary, depending on the number of days, meals, side trips and overnight facilities that are included in the package. Prices range from a few hundred dollars for "escorted-only" formats where the RVer's pay their own expenses, to a few thousand dollars for deluxe formats that may include travel by ferry to or from the mainland, some with side trips to the famous

"Copper Canyon" east of Los Mochis, on the México mainland. At the higher prices, these caravans are structured for "full-time" entertainment activities. As the prices go down, so do the extras, until, at the low price range the format is "pay-as-you-go" with side trips and activities "your choice".

All the caravans, however, travel the same road, usually stay in the same parks, eat at the same restaurants, and make available a wide range of similar activities. A few caravans are tailor made for the snowbirds that want an extended stay or "the winter" in Baja. They escort their clients in the safety, comfort, and camaraderie found only in caravan travel to all the main tourist destination areas -- then let you stay where you like for as long as you like.

So many travelers are on the road south from Christmas to late February, it is wise to make reservations early as a limited number of RV parks fill to capacity. October and November caravaners have the peninsula pretty much to themselves and enjoy the warmer waters and the better fishing. Late spring, March and April, are also warmer and less crowded in the tourist areas, then, come May, most snowbirds head home to face their very own summer weather. Baja then warms up considerably and only the "hard-core" remain to face the summer, the rainy and the hurricane season.

The adage "there is safety in numbers" helps to allay any fears the first time RVer may have. Many gruesome stories are told about the terrible things that happened in México. Let's get one thing straight - Baja and México are different. Baja is a very peaceful place. The tourist is wanted, needed, catered to and protected in Baja. Baja's sparse population, remoteness and limited number of roads precludes most of the problems that have developed on the mainland side of México.

Many people return to Baja with a caravan every year. Some return by themselves, confident in what they learned from caravan travel. So, if Baja tweaks your interest, but you are a little apprehensive of foreign, third-world culture and travel, consider joining a caravan, and leave the planning and travel details to them.

Editor's Note: Kirk and Jan Brown, with many years of experience driving in Baja, take up to 7 caravans to Baja every year. Their brochure is available by calling Baja Winters at 1-800-383-6787.

ROAD CONDITIONS...

The Baja highway came about as the result of a campaign promise of President Echeverría. It was built rapidly and with very little asphalt. In some places one might think it was put down with a paint brush. They are constantly repairing the road. In the state of Baja Sur, south of Guerrero Negro, the road is generally in good shape with few potholes or bad spots. But in the state of Baja Norte from Guerrero Negro north to Cataviña it is a different story. Go slowly, between potholes enjoy the unusual desert scenery. Just in case, there is a welder (*soldadura*) in Cataviña and a few of them in Guerrero Negro. In México, when they are working on the road they put up a sign that says "*maquinas trabajando*" (machines working) in the U.S. we say "men working". Whatever gets the job done. Prior to this highway, the only road crew was a man with a pick, shovel and wheelbarrow and a sign that read "Donations for the road work."

After any rain the dirt on the sides of the road becomes very slick and slimy making traction almost impossible. Use caution if you must pull off. Water dissolves asphalt and after big rains the potholes can be numerous and big enough to swallow a Volkswagen, figuratively speaking. It takes a few days for road crews to get out and mark these places and sometimes they are so numerous they don't even bother. Truckers seem to know the road very well and they drive very cautiously. Try following one at a distance, when he slows down, you do too.

Cattle, horses and donkeys roam freely in all of Baja. Fences are inadequate or non-existent. These animals feed along the roadside and upon approaching them they sometimes become frightened and confused and will actually run *towards* your car. The law says that if you hit a cow, it is the farmer's fault. Try finding the farmer. My friend Chris Jensen, tells me that if you hit a cow you should cut off the part of the hide with the brand on it and the ear that has the tag on it. You then take these items to the local authorities and file a claim against the farmer. I think I would prefer to use my camera to record such evidence because I cannot picture myself standing in the middle of the road cutting up a dead cow.

In Baja, it seems road signs must take an act of Congress. For years many terrible turns were not marked. Today there seems to be an excessive amount of signs at these places. Road crews post "temporary" signs while working but don't remove them until they need them for the next job. They are constantly repairing the road and temporarily converting it to a one lane. Many times we've had fresh asphalt splattered on us. The layer of fine rock (grava suelta) they put on top of the fresh asphalt is slippery and dangerous.

GASOLINE...

There is only one brand of gasoline in Baja - Pemex. Regular gas is called Nova, unleaded is Magna Sin and diesel is diesel. Gasoline and diesel are available throughout Baja although sometimes stations run out of all fuels, especially on holidays. Octane ratings for regular and unleaded are lower than in the U.S. and gas additives are recommended. These are expensive in Baja, you might want to bring your own. It's also a good idea to have an extra gas filter with you, this is especially important for diesel rigs. There has been a problem with some gas station pumps not being correct and a slight overcharge being passed on to the buyer. There isn't much we can do about the accuracy of the pumps but there is another problem you can avoid by being alert to it. On occasion, the attendant will "forget" to clear the pump of previous charges prior to filling your tank. This occurs more in México than in Baja but has been known to happen here too. To prevent this from happening read the pump as you drive up and don't let the attendant start pumping gas until you have seen the meter read zero. A locking gas cap prevents this problem if you unlock the cap yourself and check the pump. Pre-pay, self-serve gas stations are starting to pop up in certain areas, which will circumvent this problem.

DISTANCES BETWEEN GAS STATIONS...

South of San Quintín the gasoline or "Pemex" stations are quite a distance from each other. On occasion, especially during peak holidays, one or more of these stations may be out of gas so it is a good idea to keep your tank as full as possible, top-off whenever you can and carry an extra five gallons. The following list is provided to give you the mileages between gas stations from San Quintín to La Paz. Diesel and Magna Sin are generally available at all stations listed here. South of La Paz stations are numerous. All references are from north to south.

San Quintín, large station on the left, all fuels
36 miles
El Rosario, 2 stations, usually no problem, 2nd one has diesel
76 miles
Cataviña, power off 3 to 5 p. m., no gas during this time. Diesel in the rear
65 miles
Parador Punta Prieta, frequently out of gas, no diesel
60 miles
Jesús María, sometimes out of gas, diesel stored above ground
20 miles
Guerrero Negro, frequently out on holidays, see note below
48 miles
Viscaíno, frequently has long lines, all fuels
43 miles
San Ignacio, watch pumps, all fuels
45 Miles
Santa Rosalía, pumps are inaccurate, watch closely, diesel
38 miles
Mulegé, station is south of town on México 1, all fuels
84 miles
Loreto, diesel in the rear
75
Insurgentes, station on left just before town, prepay
14 miles
Constitución, use large new station north of town, all fuels
72 miles
El Cien, station on right, diesel
62 miles
La Paz
2 main stations - both have all fuels
Intersections of Jalisco & Forjadores; 5 of Febrero & Abasolo.

In Guerrero Negro the station on the right at the curve in the road has had problems with water in all fuels. A better choice is to continue around the turn to the left one-half block to the station on left. There has not been a problem with the fuel here but they do not have diesel fuel.

Diesel fuel is available in San Felipe at the docks south of town where all the big storage tanks are located. It is in front of the Marina, at the water's edge and is marked on the city map of San Felipe in this book.

SPARE PARTS...

Your vehicle should be in top shape when you cross the border going south. There are mechanics in Baja ...but. There are spare parts available in Baja ...but. It is no fun waiting for repairs or parts to be found so do everything necessary before you leave. The road is rough and things do happen. Here is a short list of things you can digest while deciding what you might really need.

    A good spare tire, jack and lug wrench
    Canned tire inflator
    Electrical circuit tester, (amp meter) in case of a short
    Spare belts, have them changed and take the old ones
    Spare hoses and clamps
    A fully equipped tool box, check it out, your spouse borrowed something
    WD-40 and/or Silicone spray
    Emergency cones to set out and red vest to wear
    Spare parts for things you've had chronic problems with in the past
    Oil, gas additive and a grease gun with grease
    Extra fuel filters, especially for diesel rigs
    Oolie, (long cut-up strips of bicycle tire inner tubes), fixes anything
    Duct tape and wire

<u>Warning and disclaimer:</u> This list was created by a female. Imagine what you're really supposed to have.

JUST IN CASE - WORDS TO KNOW...

The following list of car parts is provided "just in case" you have to help someone who is having trouble. If you don't know how to pronounce the word point to the word and pray his mechanic knows how to read. The word for mechanic is *mecánico.* The word for his shop is *taller* and is pronounced *tah-yér.* Most of the words in the following list are not in your average dictionary - I learned them from first hand experience (usually the hard way).

Air - aire
Alternator - alternador
axle - eje or ejes
Battery - bateria
Bolt - tornillo
Brake lining - alineamiento de frenos
Brakes - frenos
Broken down - se descompuso
Cable - cable
Cylinder - cilindro
Disc brakes - frenos de disco
Distributor -distribuidor
Drive shaft - la flecha
Electrical tester - probador electrico
Engine - motor
Exhaust pipe - pipa de mofle
Fan - abanico
Fan belt - la banda del abanico
Flat tire - llanta baja
Four wheel drive - doble tracción
Fuse - fusible
Gasket - empaque
Gears - los cambios
Generator - generador
Gauge - amperimetros
Hammer - martillo
Head light - luces delanteras
Hoses - mangeras
Ignition - el encendido
Inner tube - cámara de la llanta
It doesn't work - no sirve
Jumper cables - cables
Key - llave

Leaks - está goteando
Muffler - mofle
Nut - tuerca
Oil - aceite
Pedal - pedal
Piston - piston
Pliers - las pinzas
Power steering - volante hydraulico
Power steering fluid -aceite hydraulico
Radiator - radiador
Rebuilt one - Renovado
Rim - rin
Runs rough - anda muy malo
Screw - tornillo
Shock absorbers - amortiguadores
Socket - dado
Spark plugs - bujías
Starter - arrancador
Switch -switche
Tire - llanta
Tire pressure - presión de la llanta
Tow truck - grua
Turn if off - apagalo
Turn it on - enciéndelo
U-joint - union or universal
Valve - válvula
Welder - soldadura
Wheel - rueda
Wind shield wiper - parabrisas
Wiring - alambrado
Won't start - no arrenca
Wrench - llave

This part is left blank for you to fill in new terms as you learn them.

BOAT PERMITS - ARRIVING BY SEA...

Recently the Hacienda (equivalent to the American IRS) has confiscated many boats that were left in Mexican waters without the proper paperwork. The fine to retreive these boats is one half of the value of the boat. The procedure for obtaining the proper paperwork for your boat is described below. Do not leave your boat in Mexican waters without the proper paperwork. If you are going to leave your boat it is best to have a Marina do all of the paperwork for you.

Arriving by sea at a port of entry in Baja you will be required to have your passport or birth certificate and a visa. (If you did not obtain the visa prior to leaving your home port you can obtain one from the Port Captain.) You will also be required to obtain a temporary importation permit for your boat. The procedure for obtaining this follows. Upon your arrival you will be required to fill out a "Rol de Tripulantes". The required documents for getting this form completed are: American registration document of the boat, (if the owner is not making the trip, it will be necessary for the owner to provide the captain of his ship with a notarized authorization letter). Passports or birth certificates and visas are required of all passengers. Once the "Rol de Tripulantes" is filled out (they suggest making five copies) you will need an immigration officer to stamp it and validate visas of all passengers. This "Rol de Tripulantes" and your visas are the temporary importation permit for the boat. These forms expire at the same time. Now you must take this paperwork to customs to be stamped. Next the Port Captain must stamp the papers. Finally, the papers must be stamped by Puertos Mexicanos. Here you will be charged a fee based on the weight of your boat plus 10% IVA tax. If you are asked for any other money by any of the other people, take note of who asked for it and report them to the Department of Tourism.

If you want to avoid all of this hassle, a tourist marina, for a fee, will handle all of the paperwork for you. It can also be handled by a Navy Agent but is quite expensive.

If you want to leave your boat in Mexican waters the boat must be registered in a bonded tourist marina. The marina will issue a Deposit Contract and the marina becomes responsible for the legal stay of your boat. Your boat can stay in México forever and your only responsibility is to come in once a year to renew the contract.

These are the rules today. Rules change in México, and even more changes can be expected as NAFTA proceeds. Check everything out thoroughly ahead of time to avoid any problems. Current information can be obtained from the Anacapa Isle Marina in Oxnard, California, 805-985-6035.

BOAT PERMITS - ENTERING BY LAND...

Boat permits are required for all boats taken into Baja, this includes inflatables, car-top, dingys and any additional boats aboard a large vessel. The charge in 1995 was, up to 23' - $18.60, 23" to 29'11" - $37.20, 30' and over - $55.80. These rates fluctuate frequently. Permits can be obtained from the Mexican Department of Fisheries, 2550 5th Ave., San Diego, CA 92101, phone 619-233-6956, or from the travel clubs.

BAJA BY BUS...

Passenger busses run the peninsula every day. It takes about 26 hours to go from Tijuana to La Paz and, at last check, was about $60.00 U.S. Greyhound has bus service between San Diego and the Tijuana bus terminal. From there service is available to all of Baja and to México. Newer, more luxurious, air conditioned buses are beginning to be used on the México mainland and they are now showing up in Baja. These *Plus buses*, as they are called, have movies - mostly in English with Spanish subtitles - and there are bathrooms on board.

Chapter 3

SURVIVAL TIPS

THE LAW IS NOT THE SAME...

In México you are guilty until proven innocent. However, you have the same constitutional rights as a Mexican citizen. If you feel you are really in trouble, ask for a lawyer *(abogado)* and they will appoint one. If there is a language problem, they will appoint an interpreter.

Realistically, you should not have any problems while in Baja. If you get stopped for a traffic violation do not pay the officer directly. Bribery (mordida)is a crime in México both for the one who offers and the one who receives. Insist that you pay your fine at the station. If you pay a fine, get a receipt. If you feel you have been wrongly cited go to the Department of Tourism and file a complaint. They have offices in all of the large cities. To process a complaint regarding police conduct or citations, note the following: Officer's name and badge number, Department of affiliation, patrol unit number and any other information you feel might be pertinent. The people at the Department of Tourism know your value as a tourist in Baja, and they are there to make sure your stay is a pleasant one. The economy of Baja hinges on the tourist and his money.

If you get a traffic ticket the police will take your driver's license to the station. If you get a parking ticket and they cannot find you, they might take your license plate to the station. Either can be retrieved at the station when you pay your fine.

ENTERING MEXICO - WHAT YOU'RE ALLOWED TO TAKE...

With NAFTA many changes are occurring. New rules have recently been posted at the border as to what you may take into México without duties being applied. The list of permitted items reads:

Shoes and clothing for personal use
Photo equipment and video camera for personal use.
Sports equipment for personal use.
The luggage that contains the above items.
3 liters of wine or liquor per person over 18 years of age
20 packages of cigarettes or 20 cigars
$50.00 of diverse merchandise per person
$300.00 in groceries per family (save your receipts)
Prescription drugs with prescriptions
1 computer and 5 programs
1 bicycle or motorcycle per person
GUNS ARE ILLEGAL IN MEXICO

If you are over the allowable amount and have to pay duty, the current amount is 20.8% for American and Canadian citizens and 30.8% for others. Duties will decrease a little each year as a result of NAFTA. Imported liquors are very expensive in México if you drink Scotch, bring it. As you pass through the border into México you will see a green or red light telling you whether or not you can pass. This light is set to select vehicles at random for further inspection. Very seldom, even with a red light, do they thoroughly inspect campers and motorhomes but on occasion they will do a thorough inside inspection.

RETURNING TO THE U.S. - WHAT YOU CAN BRING BACK...

When getting in line at the border coming back, avoid the two left lanes (these are diamond lanes for 4 or more passengers per vehicle) and try to get into one of the lanes closest to the stalls as they seem to go faster. You can be fined for taking a diamond lane with less than 4 passengers.

Upon your arrival back at the U.S. border, you will probably be asked what your citizenship is, where you have been and for how long. If they ask you what you're bringing back from Baja, you might want to have a list ready to read to them. We have avoided secondary inspection this way a few times; however, the majority of the time we usually get pulled into secondary anyway. What else should they do? Our camper is laden with Baja dust, overloaded with sea-shells and beach junque, fishing gear is strewn about, the coolers are loaded with fish and creatures from the sea and we are tired and dirty. With us, they are not looking for drugs or flagrant violations; they want to see what's inside the refrigerator: bacon, eggs, forbidden fruits, that kind of stuff. Here is how we solve the problem. Just prior to crossing the border we find some little lady along the roadside and give her all our leftovers. She is pleasantly surprised, and I don't have to put that food away when I get home. The agent at the border looks in the refrigerator, finds nothing, and sends us on our way.

It's great fun shopping in Baja. Many beautiful and interesting things are to be found. The folk-art is very colorful, unique and reasonable priced. U.S. residents receive a duty and federal tax exemption on the first $400.00 of personal and household goods purchased south of the border. These items must be for personal use and not for resale. This exemption may not be claimed more than once in a 30 day period. The next $1000 in items is dutiable at a flat 10 percent rate.

Prohibited Items:
Agricultural items, if they can carry plant pests or animal diseases.
Plants and seeds.
No cactus.
All forms of pork even if purchased in the U.S.
All poultry except thoroughly cooked poultry.
Game - check in advance.
Other meats are limited to 50 pounds per person.
No clams, mussels or oysters.
Eggs and potatoes are prohibited. (Make potato salad before crossing.)
Live birds or wildlife of any kind.
Whale bones, products of protected or endangered species.
Mangoes.
Fireworks.
Narcotics and dangerous drugs including medicine containing same.
Martial arts items, switchblade knives.
Wheat straw, seeds, animal feed, and all articles made from this material.

Permitted items:
Liquor: One liter (33.8 fluid ounces) of liquor per adult.
Mexican cigarettes, one carton. 100 cigars, not Cuban.
Cut flowers. Packaged, cleaned sugar cane, no stalks.
Bakery items and all cured cheeses.
Bananas, blackberries, cactus fruits, dates, dewberries, grapes, lycheés,
melons, papayas, pineapples, Mexican limes and lemons and most vegetables (not any potatoes except cooked ones). Nuts are generally okay. Coconut - meat only. Tamarind beans are now legal.
Lobster: 7 per person from first Wednesday in October to the first Wednesday after the 15th of March. They must be whole and in the shell and the shell must measure at least 3 1/4" from between the eyes to the where the tail joins the body.
Fish. There is not a set limit on the amount of fish you can bring back but if it is so much that it appears you may sell it commercially they will stop you.

You must register with U.S. Customs if you are taking out of the country or bringing into the country more than $10,000.00 in cash or monetary instruments.
Prescriptions drugs. If you are going to fill your prescriptions in México and intend to bring them back to the U.S. the following applies: Get a prescription from your U.S. doctor, (it cannot be for more than a 3 month supply), make sure the drug is approved by the FDA, keep your prescription after you have it filled (this is possible in México), show your prescription and the drugs to the customs agent upon your return to the U.S. The prescription must be in the name of the person importing the drug.
In summary, the rules do change, new pests, conditions and diseases occur and subsequently some items must be temporarily prohibited. You are not allowed to take back the bacon even though you bought it in California and this is the law. We have found that if you cooperate with the inspection people they can be very nice and will get you on your way in a hurry.

AGRICULTURAL INSPECTIONS...

There are 2 agricultural inspection stations in Baja. One is about 2 miles north of Guerrero Negro and the other is a few miles west of La Paz. Inspectors are looking for citrus, mangoes, potatoes and guayaba in an attempt to control pests and disease. They will probably want to look inside your refrigerator so be prepared. If you are going south, the inspection stations should not be a problem, but if they have confiscated some of your goodies you can replenish these items in the nearby towns. Just south of the Guerrero Negro inspection station you can replenish your fruits and vegetables at Mercado La Ballena in the town of Guerrero Negro. If they have taken anything at the station north of La Paz everything is available in La Paz at the CCC, a giant supermarket with everything.

GROCERY SHOPPING IN BAJA...

There are large supermarkets in Ensenada and La Paz where you can buy just about anything you want and pay for it with your credit card, dollars or pesos. Between these two bustling cities you will find many small grocery stores but they won't always have everything you need at one place. It can be a real adventure and quite a challenge to go into town with a grocery list to fill. You will more than likely meet a lot of nice people and have to go to a lot of interesting little stores. The bakeries (*panaderías*) turn out fresh *bolillos* daily. These small football-shaped rolls are delicious as dinner rolls or sliced for open-faced sandwiches the next day. Most communities have tortilla factories (*tortillerias*). Seafood is sometimes found at a small house back off the main street. Ask around as to who sells fresh seafood (Quién vende mariscos frescos?). You'll find a small selection of canned goods in every little *tienda de abarrotes*. Vegetables are usually only fresh at one or two places in town. Don't buy them if they are not fresh; keep looking for the main vegetable store. Wash all root vegetables very thoroughly before preparing. For meats you may have to find the *Carnicería* or meat market. They cut their steaks very thin in Baja and you may not recognize the different cuts you are used to. They do not always age their beef and it is sometimes pretty tough. We have bought delicious chicken in many parts of Baja but we've only been able to find legs and thighs. When buying cheese it is the custom to ask for a taste first. The many fresh ranch cheeses are delicious and abundant throughout Baja. Ice is available almost everywhere and is usually made from purified water. Eggs are generally sold in bulk flats so you might want to keep your own egg carton handy.

Staple items are expensive; fruits and vegetables are very reasonable and found all over the peninsula (except in the remotest of areas). Take enough paper goods and staples with you to last the trip. Paper towels and rolls of toilet paper put in with things that rattle will stop the rattling.

If you drink a lot of sodas it is a good idea to buy a case of bottles. You will have to pay a deposit on the carrying case and the bottles. Find the local soda distribution point or *"Deposito"* or nail a Coke or Pepsi Truck. When you need more, simply exchange the empties for full bottles. It is much cheaper this way. This also applies to beer. The liter sized bottles, called *Caguamas* or *Ballenas*, are the most economical way to purchase beer.

Hot Bolillos

31

Drinking water is available in all of Baja. Bottled water is available in almost all grocery stores, liquor stores, gift shops, etc. The water trucks that supply the homes with five gallon bottles go honking up and down the streets of the towns daily. Stop one and buy water from them if you need this amount. Purified water for motorhomes is covered in this book under the section on RV travel tips. If you are eating out in a restaurant by the side of the road I suggest that, to be on the safe side, you drink sodas or beer, not that the water is contaminated but it will be different from the water you are accustomed to. The *Vida* apple soda is delicious, it's called *mansana*.

CLOTHING...

Going to Baja is like going to 2 places at once. Depending on the time of year, the Pacific side can be very cold and windy and the Gulf side can be so hot it melts your toothpaste. Casual wear is accepted everywhere. You're probably going to buy a couple of T-shirts as momentos and resort clothing is available at quite reasonable prices in the cities, so, go light. In the winter time the nights are cool even in Cabo San Lucas but the days are generally warm and comfortable. An extra pair of old tennis shoes comes in handy to wear in the water in places where there are a lot of rocks or possibly stingrays. You should take enough personal care items to last your trip. Most things are available but the supply is inconsistent. One time recently, the only shaving razors we could find in Loreto were at the hardware store.

YOUR CAMERA...

You're allowed to take your camera and/or video camera to Baja along with 12 rolls of unexposed film and/or cassettes. You cannot take professional photographic equipment without a special permit. (They tend to think you are a professional if you have a tripod.) Film processing locations, called *revellados*, are sprouting up all over Baja - most of them with very quick service and they also sell film. Remember to keep your camera and film out of the heat and salt air as much as possible. We carry canned air to blow off the little bits of sand that jump onto our camera every time we take it out. It's available at your camera store.

YOUR PETS...

We take our dogs on many of our trips, especially if we are going to spend the majority of our time camping on one of Baja's beautiful beaches. The dogs love to run in the surf and have learned to ride on the backs of our ATCs when we go fishing "down the beach". We enjoy watching them have a good time too. The saltwater makes their coats beautiful.

You must have a current rabies vaccination certificate for your dog or cat when you return to the U.S. A certificate of good health, obtained from your stateside vet, is required by the Mexican government. We have never been asked for this paper-work but it is the law.

No dogs are allowed at the larger hotels in Baja, but they are allowed in the RV parks. A word of caution. There is no 'animal control' as we know it, in Baja. When they have a problem with too many dogs in town, they put out poisoned meat and get rid of all the dogs that are allowed to run free. This is usually done a few hours before the trash pick up and the dead animals are disposed of with the trash. Don't let your dog roam! If there are cattle near your campsite your dog might get ticks. Fleas are just as abundant in Baja as they are in Southern California. There has been no reported incidence of Lyme disease in Baja. Dog and cat food should be brought from home as the selection in the stores is generally nil or very basic. There are lots of veterinarians in most of the towns in Baja if your animal becomes ill or hurt.

TRAVEL CLUBS...

There are some very efficient travel clubs serving the Baja area. These unique clubs offer current Baja information, good savings on vehicle insurance and other attractive benefits, some of which are: restaurant, hotel and RV park discounts; assistance with getting all of your permits; current road information; monthly newsletters; group travel expeditions; and fishing tournaments.

Club Vagabundos del Mar covers more than just Baja. They also have group trips to Alaska, the western states, México and other places. They provide all of the benefits listed above plus a few unique benefits all their own. 800-474-2252.

Discover Baja Travel Club is specifically Baja oriented. If you want to know anything about Baja, call them and ask; they know the answers. Recently they have been doing trips into mainland México, broadening their scope. They provide all of the benefits mentioned above. 800-727-2252.

There are other clubs covering more specific interests such as boating, hunting and fishing, I have listed their names and numbers in the Resource guide.

TIPPING...

Tipping is quite conservative in Baja. The average laborers wage is about $8.00 U.S. a day. Don't over tip and make your vacation an expensive one. Here are some tips on tipping that you might use as a guideline.

If you find yourself in need of a taxi always ask the price of the trip before entering the cab. If the amount seems fair pay him exactly this amount, no tip is expected.

At the market you generally cannot take your grocery cart all the way out to your car. At the check stand the groceries are placed in special carts and pushed outside by industrious little boys. Here the equivalent of a U.S. quarter is an adequate tip. It is not considered rude to carry small amounts of groceries yourself.

At the airports or in the hotels, if you allow the bell man or sky cap to carry your luggage, the tip should be equivalent to one U.S. dollar for your total luggage unless you have an exorbitant amount, then, of course it would be more.

In restaurants the tip is 10%. Deduct the 10% IVA tax from the bill before figuring the tip amount. In restaurants you may be approached by traveling mariachis; ask the price before you ask for a song. $3.00 U.S. for one song is about average but they sometimes figure a dollar per musician and if there are seven musicians it can get quite expensive, very fast.

In Baja you will find some of the most aggressive window washers in the world. In gas stations or when you're stopped for a signal, all of a sudden someone is washing your windshield. What irks me about this is, first, they didn't ask if I wanted it cleaned and, second, just two hours before I crawled up on the hood and polished the windows clean myself. I try to be alert to these enterprising young men and if I see one coming I shake my index finger at them and they go away. (This little finger action also works to get rid of street peddlers and anyone else you don't want bothering you - I think their mothers taught them this means NO.) The window washer is expecting a tip for his efforts. Do not pay him if he did not ask first. If you agreed to have the job done beforehand, an appropriate amount would be about the equivalent of twenty-five cents U.S.

Chapter 4

UNDERSTANDING BAJA

GEOLOGY...

Baja's geology is truly remarkable. The mountains are raw and rugged; the deserts are surprisingly different than one would expect; the seacoasts are pristine and beautiful. Seeing all of this stirs up one's interest as to how it all occurred.

One of the best-selling books on Baja, The Baja Highway by John Minch and Thomas Leslie is written on the geology and biology of the peninsula. It's a great book to have along for a passenger to read aloud and everyone to enjoy. Much of the information in the following section has been supplied by John Minch.

Formation of the Peninsula:

Baja saw its beginnings during the Mesozoic era, 65 to 225 million years ago. It was during this time that the North American continent started shifting westward into the Pacific Ocean crust. The pressure of these two masses, or plates, pushing against each other lasted for a hundred million years. The land rippled and folded forming the bases for the mountain ranges of the land that would, in the distant future be Baja. Volcanoes spewed out molten lava. Volcanic islands were formed. During this time, erosion carried much of its debris westward forming a large sedimentary basin offshore. Today the edge of this basin is visible in areas of the northern coast of Baja and exists under the majority of southern Baja.

About 38 to 65 million years ago, in the early Cenozoic era, the Peninsula was a relatively quiet place. Erosion had created a gently rolling surface that stretched eastward into Arizona and Sonora. Major rivers flowed from Arizona and Sonora to the Pacific Ocean. Coastal California and Baja California began to slide northward along faults like the famous San Andreas Fault.

Baja first began to separate from México during the middle Cenozoic era, somewhere between 7 and 38 million years ago. The parting of these two lands took millions of years. Great sheets of lava and other volcanics were spread over large areas of Baja during this time. In lower coastal areas, shallow seas formed. The peninsula tilted westward as it split off from México creating the currently existing mountain ranges.

The shape of Baja as we know it today was finally developed when the mouth of the Gulf opened up between about 5 to 10 million years ago. Today, Baja is moving northward relative to North America at the rate of about two inches a year.

Baja is very "young" geologically speaking. There are only a few rocks which are older than Mesozoic (230 million years). When you compare this to areas such as the "Canadian Shield" where the rocks are 2,300 million years old or the oldest rocks in Greenland at 3,890 million years old Baja is still a baby. Baja has many earthquake faults which have a potential to be seismically active. Two very active faults, the San Jacinto and the Elsinore, enter Baja in the Mexicali valley area and pass into the Gulf of California. The Aqua Blanca Fault is also very active and has a potential for a 6.5 earthquake similar to the 1994 Northridge earthquake. The Aqua Blanca starts in San Matías Pass and runs northwest to Ensenada and then off-shore at Punta Banda. Southern Californians now living in Loreto, veterans of many earthquakes, frequently feel small earthquakes and a fairly large one hit there in 1995 creating an ominous rumbling, large dust cloud, landslides and some minor damage in the city. In July of 1995 a 6.4 earthquake hit just a few miles north of La Paz.

Ancient Life of Baja:

In the area around El Rosario, fossil remains of dinosaurs have been found. The dinosaurs that lived in Baja were of those that lived at the end of the dinosaur era. The age of the rocks in which they are found is approximately 83 to 77 million years before present. Worldwide, dinosaurs disappeared about 65 million years ago after 165 millions of years of evolution.

The Baja dinosaurs were an aquatic dinosaur called hadrosaurs. They lived in shallow water and remotely resembled a streamlined crocodile. They probably chased and ate fish.

In the late 1960's, geology students from the University of Southern California, under an agreement with the Mexican government, were allowed to dig for fossils in the El Rosario valley. Their campsite, located near the ocean, consisted of a number of huge army tents filled with tables of fossils all classified and numbered, and tented living quarters. The students, all studying for their masters in geology, invited my husband and me to their camp one evening. We were shown the almost complete remains of an ancient baby mammoth, pieces of a very large ancient petrified snake and many other interesting fossils. Under the agreement, the Mexican government allowed these fossils to be taken to the United States. Today, it is illegal for anyone to dig and/or remove these fossils without a special permit from the Mexican government.

It is difficult to say what the terrestrial flora of Baja was during the time of the dinosaurs because this information is poorly documented. In adjacent Southern California, we find evidence of palms, avocados, the Norfork Island Pine and other tropical to semi-tropical land plants. Much of the state of Baja California, southwest, was almost entirely covered by the ocean with only the northeast corner and the cape region existing as islands.

Hadrosaur

During the Paleocene era, 65 to 55 million years ago, there is evidence that Baja was tropical and green. During this period there were soils developing similar to those developing today in the tropics.

Ammonites, ancient giant petrified snails, have been found in El Rosario and near Santa Catarina. The ammonites at Santa Catarina lived with and in the same sea as the dinosaurs of El Rosario. Older ammonites, around 130 million years old, are found in an unpopulated area not far to the south of Santa Catarina.

There are many other interesting fossils in a large number of places in Baja. Some of the fresh water lake deposits contain fossils of turtles and crocodiles. Marine sediments in the cape region contain giant 5 inch sharks teeth along with fossils of whales and other marine mammals. The Occidental Buttes area contains remains of horses, camels and other grazing mammals which probably lived on a savanna.

Baja's Natural Resources:

Over many areas of Baja are extremely straight dirt "roads" that lead to nowhere. These are "roads" that were created by huge machines brought in to search for oil. These machines systematically dropped a huge heavy plate on the ground and devices recorded the "echo" which in turn created a map of the underground layers that showed where possible oil deposits might exist. Whether or not there is oil, probably only Pemex knows for sure. There are currently no producing wells in Baja. Baja Sur is underlain by a large sedimentary basin which is identical to the basin which underlies the Great Valley of California. The Great Valley of California is a very prolific oil production area; thus, we expect Baja Sur to also be very oil rich.

Baja is, of course, largely a desert. Water is scarce and precious. The higher ranges in the north and south receive significant amounts of rainfall. The northern cities receive water from the Colorado River via an aqueduct. Much of the rest of the Peninsula draws it's water from ground water aquifers. Rich farming areas such as the Vizcaíno and the Magdalena plains have tapped the aquifers and currently have closely watched monitoring programs to prevent over usage of the water. They are rapidly moving towards a dam building program to tap the winter rainfall which now runs off.

Gold, silver, copper, sulfur and many other minerals have all been successfully mined in Baja. Today, a few small mining operations still exist. The Mexican government owns the rights to anything that comes from the ground so not much mining goes on today. Someday, when the processing of minerals becomes more economically reasonable, agreements will be made with the government and quite likely mining will become more prominent.

The Baja Highway is available direct from John Minch and Associates, Inc., 26461 Crown Valley Parkway, Mission Viejo, CA 92691. $19.95

Cataviña

PLANTS...

Baja has many rare and unusual plants. A drive down México 1 will probably awaken your curiosity and make you want to know and understand more about these plants. Out of his love for Baja, Norman Roberts wrote the <u>Baja California Plant Field Guide</u>. He has been traveling in Baja since he was a young boy. His book stands alone in accuracy and completeness. It is filled with color photographs of Baja's rare and unusual plants and includes the botanical, English, and Spanish names of all the plants described. This book has all of the botanical information necessary to complete such a work appropriately and at the same time is interesting to both the tourist and the serious student.

Most of the plants of Baja California originated in neighboring regions of California and northwestern México. There are probably over 2700 species of plants occurring in Baja California but the number of endemic species (those not occurring elsewhere) is probably less than 700. This may be attributed to the fact that the separation of the peninsula from mainland México was relatively recent (in geologic terms). The lack of high mountains over two-thirds of the peninsula has also undoubtedly been a factor. Mountains, because of their elevation, act to create isolation.

Endemism in Baja California is particularly noticeable when the cactus family is examined. Of the more than 110 species of cacti found on or in the peninsula and the adjacent islands, 80 are endemic.

Traveling south down México 1, the traveler will notice a steady, gradual change in vegetation. The familiar plants of southern California are succeeded by unfamiliar central desert plants. Much further south the equally strange species of the cape Region appear. Coastal wetlands afford a fourth and totally different group of plants. Many of the plants can be seen growing near the paved transpeninsular highway or one of its laterals.

Two-thirds of Baja, including the islands, may be classified as desert; receiving less than 10 inches of precipitation annually, much of it less than half of that. Altitudes vary from over 10,000 feet to sea level and annual rainfall from 0 to 30 inches

The California region extends from the international border 200 miles south. Plant communities of the California region encompass coniferous forest, juniper-piñon woodland, chaparral, coastal sage scrub, and riparian areas including coastal wetlands.

The desert region makes up the majority of the peninsula. The desert is subdivided into subregions. San Felipe desert, south gulf coast desert, Vizcaíno desert, and Magdalena plain.

The cape region includes the Sierras de la Laguna and de la Giganta and their drainage's, and the regions south of La Paz. Plant communities of the cape region include oak-piñon woodland and arid tropical forest.

The coastal wetlands and dunes region includes parts of both the Pacific and Gulf coasts. The plant communities are considerably different from those of the surrounding deserts, especially in the mangrove forests of the southern coastal areas. Wetlands are populated by species distinct from the immediate adjacent vegetation, and dependent on wetter conditions than are provided by precipitation. Many of the wetlands in the peninsula are estuaries and exist on both coasts. In the southern half of the peninsula they are occupied mostly by mangroves.

Descriptions of some of the more prominent and unusual plants follows:

PITAYA AGRIA. *Machairocereus (Stenocereus) gummosus*. Sour Pitaya. Pitaya Agria. Pitahaya. Pitaya Agria is a formidable appearing, sprawling, many-branched, scrambling cactus. Stem tips resting on the ground take root, often forming impenetrable thickets 10 meters or more across. The heavy, dark green-gray stems may be up to 3 meters in length and have ribs with stout, flattened, dagger-shaped spines. The central spines are even larger. The large, fragrant, white flowers up to 8 cm wide have long, slender, purplish tubes. The bright red, fleshy, golfball-to-tennisball sized fruit is very popular with the natives. It is not as sweet as the fruit of the Pitaya Dulce but has a very pleasant taste. Pitaya Agria grows abundantly from Ensenada south to the Cape in many desert areas of Baja. A near-endemic, it occurs on almost all the major Gulf islands

Pitaya Agria

and also Punta Sargento in Sonora. Early Spanish sailors used the fruit to prevent scurvy. Branches were crushed and thrown in the water by the natives to stupefy fish.

During the late summer - early fall months, a few days after a rain, the fruits are swollen with juicy sweetness. In the area around El Triunfo south of La Paz the locals gather the fruit of both pitaya agria and pitaya agria and sell it by the bucket. One bucket - about 30 fruit - goes for about $5.00 U.S. Well worth the price when one considers how difficult they are to pick. They make excellent daiquiris.

PITAYA DULCE. *Lemaireocereus (Stenocereus) thurberi*. Organ Pipe Cactus. This much-branched, erect cactus has no main trunk in its northern range. In the southern half of the peninsula it often has a short trunk before branching into 5 or more columns of up to 8 meters in height.. The flowers are cream colored. Pitaya Dulce occurs sparingly from mid-peninsula to the Cape Region. It is absent from some of the drier regions of the Vizcaíno and Magdalena Plains. Pitaya Dulce has a sweet, watermelon-colored, globular, spiny fruit about the size of a golf ball. They ripen in late summer and are prized by man and animal because of the flavor, which is somewhat like watermelon. Missionaries' records indicate the natives were generally hungry except during Pitaya season. Then they gorged on this wild harvest, spending the entire season in a state of euphoria. Aborigines followed the harvest from south to north, leaving behind some very upset Missionaries.

Note: Other species of cacti on the mainland have yellow or white fruit and are also called pitaya.

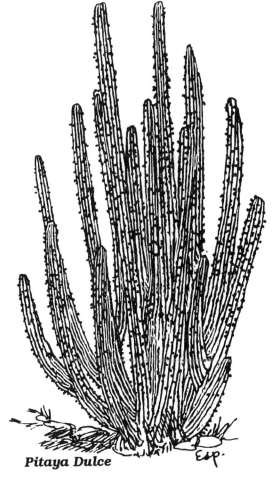
Pitaya Dulce

OCOTILLO. *Fouquieria splendens.* Ocotillo has no main trunk but many slender, 3-4 meter long, whip like, thorny, stiff branches which spread fan like from the base. Within 72 hours after a rain clusters of tiny green leaves emerge. On plants over 2 meters tall bright red tubular flowers soon appear. Ocotillo is found abundantly on desert slopes and plains as far south as Guerrero Negro. The flowers are eaten by animals. Cuttings will take root when stuck into the ground, giving residents a living fence for yards and patios. Branches make good fences and ramadas.

In the L.A. Bay area ocotillo becomes conspecific with Palo Adan, which it closely resembles.

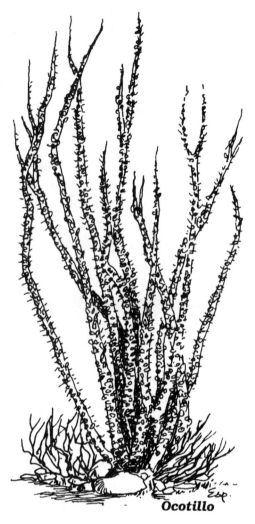
Ocotillo

CARDON. *Pachycereus pringlei.* Cardón Pelón. The cardón dominates many of the deserts of Baja; some are believed to be over 200 years old and to weigh 10 tons. The spongy pulp readily absorbs and stores water, allowing an accordion-like action of the ribs with intake and loss of water. Spacing between the ribs depends on the water available and decreases as water becomes scarce. Once the spines are destroyed they do not return, a fact not lost on the aborigines who often found it necessary to climb the trunk in order to reach the fruit. This effort was aided by using a long pole consisting of a Cardón rib with a hook formed by tying a short branch to one end.

The flowers of the cardón open at night and are pollinated by bats.

Traveling south on Highway 1, the first real *cardonal* (Cardón forest) is found in Arroyo El Rosario 16 km east of the town. The cardón is often mistaken for the smaller Saguaro of Sonora and Arizona, but the Saguaro does not grow in Baja.

Mission documents report that aborigines used the prickly Cardón fruit as a staple food and ate them after grinding into a *pinole* or poured water through the ground fruit and drank the juice.

Cardón

40

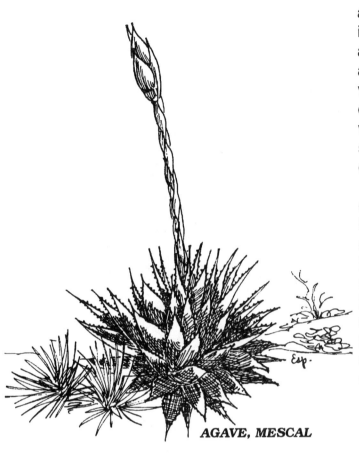

AGAVE. Century Plant. Mescal. Maguey. In most species of agave, the plant dies after flowering. Agaves have played an important role in both the Mexican and aboriginal economies since ancient times as a source of food, drink and fiber. Agaves provide food at different growth stages: early inhabitants often survived for months with no other food. The agave remains a staple for subsistence ranchers, especially during dry periods.

The agave was pit roasted by the aborigines. A wood fire in a pit was used to heat stones. The agave, or Mescal as they called it, heads were trimmed of their thick leaves, thrown onto the hot stones, then covered with the trimmed leaves and fibers. A layer of dirt followed, on which another fire was built. After three days of roasting, the Mescal was removed and eaten. The stems also were and are still eaten during the asparagus stage after roasting in the same fashion.

Tequila is made from the agave.

AGAVE, MESCAL

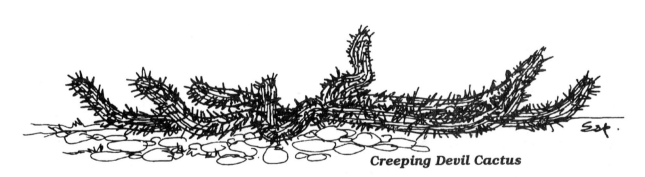

Creeping Devil Cactus

CREEPING DEVIL CACTUS. *Machairocereus (Stenocereus) eruca.* Chirinola. Creeping devil cactus has heavy thick stems that seem to crawl along the ground possibly because of their weight. The stem tips ascend to 1-2 meters. Stems often root where they touch the ground. As the stems grow forward, the oldest part dies.

Creeping Devil is endemic to Baja and grows in alluvial soil of the Llano de Magdalena near the west coast. It is visible from the highways in this area. It may be in danger of extinction because of its narrow range and the fact that much of this range is coming under cultivation.

"The Plant Field Guide to Baja California" is available from Natural History Publishing Co., P.O. Box 962, La Jolla, CA 92037.

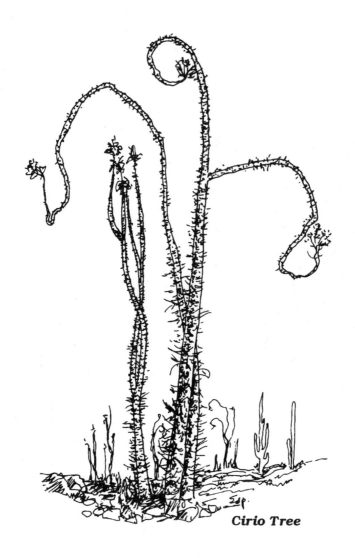

Cirio Tree

CIRIO. *Idria Columnaris*. Boojum Tree. Cirio is the most unusual plant of the peninsula. Young trees most closely resemble an inverted carrot in shape. The pole-like adult tree has a stout, tapering, columnar trunk up to 2 feet in diameter at the base, reaching a height of over 80'. The cirio is much less massive than the cardón but may exceed it in height. Cirio may branch into several stems at the top. New growth may take place within 72 hours after a rain. During a dry spell the leaves quickly turn yellow and fall. Cirio grows from the southern end of the Sierra de San Pedro Martír to the Sierra Tres Vírgenes and on Isla Angel de la Guarda, forming forests in the Vizcaíno region and often occurring with yucca, ocotillo, cardón and many other plants. Heading south on the west side of the peninsula, cirio can first be seen on the hills inland from a few miles south of El Rosario. Cirio is a near-endemic. A small colony grows in Sonora near Libertad on the Mexican mainland.

The Spanish name, Cirio, denotes a resemblance to the tall wax candles used by the early missionaries. A mature branching Cirio makes an excellent nesting site for several species of hawks.

Elephant Tree

ELEPHANT TREE. *Pachycormus Discolor*. Torote. Copalquín. Endemic to Baja California there are several different species of these weirdly shaped trees. The trunk is covered with smooth, grayish-white to yellowish bark that repeatedly peels off in papery layers, revealing a blue-green, waxy-smooth, spongy inner bark. The trunk is very thick in proportion to the size of the tree. Blooms are pink. The bark is used by the locals for tanning and dyeing. A tea from the twigs is used for stomach trouble. The gum is popular as a medicine for various ailments.

MISSIONS...

The 1500's, "the century of discovery," was also a period when Catholic missionaries fanned out into the New World, putting forth zealous efforts to convert its inhabitants to what they perceived as superior European ways. During this time, Spaniards acquired most of the land and provided the majority of church delegates sent to pacify and train native Americans in an expanding system of religio-cultural centers that came to be called "missions."

Church activities on mainland México kept missionaries busy well into the 17th century, although their eyes were on the California peninsula as it was prospected now and then by pearlers and other seekers of wealth. From 1683 to 1685, a major military-religious expedition did attempt to establish a beachhead on the peninsula, but it resulted in a costly failure. Finally, in 1696, a party led by Jesuit Padre Juan María de Salvatierra made landfall near the mouth of a palm-lined arroyo at 26 degrees north latitude. Thus began the arduous task of the building of Misión Nuestra Señora de Loreto, mother of the California missions. The Jesuits had an exclusive mandate to convert the natives. They were allowed to hire and direct their own army and such civilian helpers as were needed. All California peoples were considered to be under the rule of the Spanish government, but the Jesuits were the crown's only representatives and therefore had remarkably free hand to further the agenda of their order. When the Jesuits were expelled from the Spanish world in 1767, the Franciscans (in 1768) and the Dominicans (in 1773) took up the missionary chores in California. The work of all these orders, despite its religious and cultural inspiration, proved disastrous to the inhabitants. Previously nomadic people were concentrated in relatively large groups with poor sanitation and at the same time they were exposed to Old World diseases against which they had few natural defenses.

The major groups of peninsular Indians, Kumihay, Pai Pai, and Cócopah in the north, Cochimí in the central portion, and Guaycura and Pericú in the south, totaled an estimated 24,000 when the Jesuits established their first mission in Baja California. Today, many people on the peninsula carry some fraction of Cochimí, Guaycura, or Pericú heritage, but these cultures disappeared completely by the mid-nineteenth century. Only the groups of the northern peninsula are represented by descendants who speak the languages and preserve some of the ancestral lore.

Despite its difficulties, the mission system was the key to the European development of the Baja California peninsula. To quote Dr. W. Michael Mathis, who has spent much of his life studying the missions of Baja California. "Each mission is a monument to the struggle of man against adversity".

Following is a brief history of each mission. The numbers in parenthesis refer to the *Roadlog* pages in this book where access to the mission sites can be found. Enjoy your visit but leave the site exactly as you find it.

Misión El Descanso. Established by the Dominicans in 1817 and abandoned in 1834 for lack of personnel. Located two miles from the Pacific Ocean about 8 miles north of Misión San Miguel Arcángel de la Frontera and about one-third of the way between Tijuana and Ensenada. Only the site is known, no visible ruins exist. There is currently a greenhouse operation on the site.(RL4)

Misión San Miguel Arcángel de la Frontera. Founded by Father Luis Sales in 1787, this was the second site for this mission, the previous site having been abandoned for lack of water. The remains of the mission's adobe walls are located on the north side of the old Tijuana - Ensenada road, adjacent to a primary school, 3.5 miles after turning under the toll road at La Misión. (RL4)

Misión Nuestra Señora de Guadalupe del Norte. This mission was established in 1834 by Dominican Father Félix Caballero in the fertile Guadalupe Valley between Ensenada and Tecate. Agricultural products consisted mainly of pears, apricots and grapes. Of note was the size of the cattle herd, in 1840 it had 4915 head, the largest herd in the Dominican mission field. Raids by hostile rancherías from the northeast burned the mission to the ground and it was abandoned in 1840. There are no remains, however, a church marks the approximate site. (RL8)

Misión Santa Catalina Vírgen y Mártir. Founded by the Dominican Father José Loriente in 1797. The mission population grew rapidly until it is said to have had one of the highest populations of the northern missions. Hostile Indians from the east continually raided the mission until it was destroyed and ultimately abandoned in 1840. The whereabouts of the actual mission site is known but there are no visible ruins. (RL16)

Misión San Pedro Mártir de Verona. Founded by the Dominican Father José Loriente in 1794. It was built in a remote mile-high mountain valley deep in the Sierra San Pedro Mártir. Pine forests and mountain meadows didn't lend themselves to cultivation but cattle were raised fairly successfully on the meadows. Because of its isolation, the cold climate, and a low population the mission was abandoned in 1824. Some ruins of foundations remain. (Not accessible from the highway)

Misión Santo Domingo de la Frontera. Established in 1775 on the east side of the arroyo of the same name to the east of what is now Colonia Vicente Guerrero. In 1798 the water supply dwindled and the mission was moved upstream three kilometers. From 1810 to 1828 the mission supplemented its income with the sale of sea otter pelts and salt from nearly salt pans at San Quintín. Salt was distributed to all of the northern missions from here. European diseases wiped out the population forcing the closure in 1839. (RL22)

Misión Nuestra Señora del Rosario de Viñadarco. Established in 1774 on the edge of the broad Arroyo del Rosario this was the first mission built by the Dominicans. The arroyo floods frequently and the mission was moved because of this. The second site, established in 1802, is located 2 miles southwest of the village and is only ruins today. The first site, abandoned in 1817, is about three-fourths mile south-east of town on the north side of México 1 before reaching Rancho Moret. In the 1980's, Doña Anita Espinosa, through donations from her friends, had a replica of the old mission built next to the highway in the town. She has filled this new "mission" with artifacts from the surrounding area and it has become a fine museum. (RL22)

Misión San Fernando Rey de España de Velicatá. This is the only mission built by the Franciscans during their short time in Baja California. Established in 1769 by Fray Junípero Serra before he moved on to San Diego in Alta California, it became an important way station on *el camino real* leading to the new California being developed in the north. San Fernando originally ministered to about 1500 Indians but a major epidemic during the years of 1777-80 caused great demographic losses and the mission had wasted away by 1818. The remains of it's structures and fields are in an arroyo about three miles west of El Progreso. (RL30)

Misión Santa María de los Angeles. Founded by the Spanish Jesuit Victoriano Arnes in 1767, only a few months before the expulsion of the Jesuits from Baja California it was the last and most northernmost of the Jesuit's missions. Franciscans occupied the mission for a few months but it was vacated for the sight at San Fernando Velicatá. Water was plentiful and good at Santa María but the terrain is not conducive to agriculture. Today the adobe structures are in ruins. It is located about 12 miles east of Rancho Santa Inés and Cataviña. It is not accessible by road as a large landslide has occurred in the path. (RL30)

Visita de Calamajué. Founded in 1766 by Jesuits Victoriano Arnés and Juan José Díez who discovered, after completion of a church edifice, that the water was so highly mineralized their crops would not grow. They left after only a few months, transferring their mission to become that of Santa María discussed above. Faint remnants of foundations are still evident near the dirt road that traverses the beautiful Arroyo de Calamajué. (RL38)

Misión San Francisco de Borja Adac. If the name "Borgia" or "Borja" (Spanish spelling) sounds familiar and conjures up impressions of poisonings and intrigue, you may be surprised to know that a member of the Borja family supplied the money to build this mission and also those at Calamajué and Santa María. María, Duchess of Borja, left a sizable amount of her estate to the Jesuit Pious Fund. The mission was named for St. Francis Borja, her ancestor, who was an early Jesuit Saint. Within a few years after its founding by Bohemian Jesuit Padre Wenceslao Linck in 1762, San Borja served nearly 3000 converted Indians living around the mission, but marginal growing conditions forced missionaries to bring in food from other missions. As elsewhere, rampant "white man's" diseases ravaged the population. Less than 100 Indians remained when the Dominicans left in 1818. Poor 21 mile dirt roads come to San Borja from both El Rosarito and the pavement leading to Bahía de Los Angeles. In 1801, work was halted on the present stone church and it was never quite finished although it did replace a previous adobe structure and is one of the best preserved of the Baja California missions. (RL46)

Misión Santa Gertrudis la Magna de Cadacamán. A mission long planned by the Croation Jesuit Fernando Consag who carried on extensive explorations for its site and converted many people north of San Ignacio to be its initial constituency. However, when it was finally founded by German Jesuit Jorge Retz in 1752, its endowment was moved north from Misión San José del Cabo, recently closed, and the name Santa Gertrudis was bestowed according to the wishes of the original donor, the Marqués de Villapuente. Missions called Dolores del Norte and Santa María Magdalena never were founded in California; misreadings of this history have contributed to beliefs in "lost missions." A view of Santa Gertrudis today makes one wonder how this location could have served as the spiritual center for over 3000 neophytes to Christianity. Flash floods have removed most of the tillable land, a small stone church and some founda-

Bell Tower at Santa Gertrudis

tions are all that remain of this once extensive mission. There are a few families who still use a portion of the two-century-old irrigation ditches and tend the few old grape vines, olive trees and date palms, along with their own crops. (RL56)

Misión San Ignacio de Kadakaaman. Dedicated in 1728 by Juan Bautista de Luyando who was also the donor of its endowment. The Jesuits introduced date palms to the region, and dates are still the primary crop. Blessed with a good water supply from an underground river, San Ignacio proved to be one of the more successful of the Jesuit missions. Serving about 3500 Indians in its heyday, disease reduced the number to 120 by the end of the 18th century. The church here was begun by Mexican Jesuit José Mariano Rotea about 1763 and completed by Spanish Dominican Fray Juan Crisóstomo Gómez in 1789. It is one of the best preserved in Baja California due to its massive construction from quarried volcanic rock and to the continuous occupation of the site. (RL66)

Misión Nuestra Señora de Guadalupe de Huasinapí. Founded in 1720 by a German Jesuit Everardo Helen in a mountain arroyo about 25 miles west of Mulegé. Guadalupe was abandoned in 1795 because its neophyte population had diminished to the point that it could not work the fields nor tend the herds. Today, only a few vestiges of the mission works can be seen at the site, reached on rugged dirt roads from Mulegé on the gulf, or San Juánico on the Pacific. (RL74)

Misión Santa Rosalía de Mulegé. Founded by Spanish (Basque) Jesuit Juan Manuel Basaldúa in 1705 and, in its early years, ministering to about 2000 Cochimí converts. As with other missions, the population was soon reduced by diseases and, in 1770, a flood leveled most buildings. The church was rebuilt on a low bluff from which it overlooks the town some four hundred yards downstream. The tropical ambiance of Mulegé makes it one of the most beautiful mission settings in Baja California and has proven to be a favorite with visitors since it was restored in the 1970's. (RL74)

Misión Santa Rosalía de Mulegé

Misión La Purísima Concepción de Cadegomó. By 1730, eleven years after its beginning, its founder, Spanish Jesuit Nicolás Tamaral had baptized 2000 Indians and produced surpluses of grains, cattle and fruits. The mission workers' skills at road building were also widely admired throughout the adjoining missions. Inexorably, local converts were decimated by epidemic diseases and the mission dwindled to nothing by 1822. People in the picturesque little town of La Purísima point to a pile of stones as the only remains of the once thriving religious community, although extensive ruins of the real mission site are about one-half mile north on the road to San Isidro. (RL80)

Misión San José de Comondú. Founded by Spanish Jesuit Julián de Mayorga in 1708, some 20 miles north of its present location, to which it was moved in 1737. Because of San José's favorable climate and reliable water supply, a non-Indian village began to grow up around the mission in the late 18th century even as the native population disappeared. The church one sees today is not a restoration, but rather a partially new structure built largely from the cut stones that remained from the original Jesuit church, a unique design for California in which the nave was composed of three parallel barrel vaults. Two miles down the arroyo is the sister village of San Miguel de Comondú, once the site of a visiting chapel of the San Javier mission but never a full-fledged mission. Here was a small church building in which visiting padres conducted services. Juan de Ugarte, the father of California agriculture, founded San Miguel in 1714 and directed the construction of important agricultural terraces and irrigation works. Both of the Comondú communities were important producers of sugarcane, grapes and fruit as long as the peninsular economy was isolated and people had to depend on local produce. (RL80)

Misión Nuestra Señora de Loreto Conchó. The site for this mission was chosen by Italian Jesuit Juan María de Salvatierra in 1697 with the intent that it serve as the seat of the entire mission system to be built in the Californias. It was the first of the 17 missions started by the Jesuits during their 70 years of control. Loreto's continued operation never resulted from success in local agriculture but rather from the Jesuits' strong ties to the far more prosperous missions of their fellow Jesuits across the gulf on the Yaqui and Mayo rivers. In 1829, a massive *chubasco*, or summer storm, almost destroyed the town which has had to be rebuilt several times following floods and an earthquake. The mission church at Loreto, finished in 1744, has been remodeled and an excellent small museum opened under the Mexican government's mission rehabilitation project. By about 1750, Loreto had inherited a visiting station once operated by San José de Comondú at Londó, some 20 miles north of Loreto. The remains of a barrel-vaulted stone chapel can be seen a few hundred yards from the paved road. Near the gulf shore, some six miles east of Londó, is the site of San Bruno, the site occupied as a fort and proto-mission by the 1683-1685 expedition headed by Admiral Isidro de Atondo and Padre Eusebio Francisco Kino. (RL82)

Misión San Francisco Javier de Biaundó. In 1699, the Italian Jesuit, Francisco María Piccolo, of the Loreto mission decided to follow up on reports of numbers of Indians living in a lush valley in a mountainous region called Viggé west of Loreto. After a rugged journey, Piccolo arrived, realized the area's potential, and asked permission to build a mission. Shortly after, the ground was dedicated and construction began. Several years later Padre Juan de Ugarte came to the site, found it wanting and located a better one five miles to the south. About 1710, the mission was moved. Padre Miguel del Barco, an important Jesuit historian, became the local missionary in 1738 and, between 1744 and 1758, supervised the building of the elegant stone church that graces the deep arroyo setting to this day. Many consider a visit to San Javier to be the most rewarding offered by the peninsular missions; its beauty remains little diminished by its nearly two and a half centuries of existence and its romance much enhanced. (RL82)

Misión San Luis Gonzaga Chiriyaqui. Founded in 1737 by German Jesuit Lamberto Hostell at a site 25 miles east-south-east of present-day Ciudad Constitución, this mission was open only about thirty years (1737 - 1768) before epidemics eliminated all but three hundred of its converts who were moved to Todos Santos. The still-existing stone church was built by Padre Juan Jacobo Baegert in the1750's and required only a little restoration under the Mexican government's mission restoration program. A few families live near the church and raise dates, figs, oranges and mangos. (RL78)

Misión Nuestra Señora de los Dolores Apaté. Originally sited in 1721 by its founder, Mexican Jesuit Clemente Guillén, at a place a bit inland from the shore opposite the north end of Isla San José. It was later moved inland a few miles to a place called Tañuetía and then over the hills to an arroyo called Chillá where the mission became known as La Pasión. The mission was closed in 1768 due to its declining population. Today the original site is part of Rancho los Dolores, a favored stopping place for yachts. (RL86)

Misión Nuestra Señora del Pilar de La Paz Airapí. Even though the La Paz area was the first (1535) to be visited by the Spanish, it was nearly two centuries later that they returned to establish a permanent settlement. In 1720, the official founder, Spanish Jesuit Jaime Bravo, with the help of brother Jesuits Clemente Guillén and Juan de Ugarte supervised the building of a fort and church, preparatory to baptizing the residents. Diseases took such a toll of the local Indians by 1749 that the mission was moved to its visiting station on the Pacific shore, Todos Santos (see below). No evidence remains as to the exact location of fort or church, but they are believed to have been near Av. Dieciseís de Septiembre and Av. Revolución. (RL92)

Todos Santos. The Jesuits recorded no indigenous name; the site began its Spanish era and received its name in 1724 as a visiting station of Misión de La Paz. Here, in 1733, Italian Jesuit Sigismundo Taraval dedicated Misión de Santa Rosa. In 1749, Santa Rosa was closed and the mission at La Paz moved to Todos Santos where it acquired the latter name. Misión de Todos Santos lasted a considerable time because the inhabitants were augmented by Indians from other missions as they were phased out. As elsewhere, epidemics assured a rapid decline of native people despite fertile land and excellent water. The 120 year mission presence ended in 1854 when the last Dominicans left the peninsula and the mission churches were taken from the Dominican order and were secularized. The village of Todos Santos continued to grow with a mestizo population and today is one of the most charming communities on the peninsula. Nothing remains of mission period buildings, but the present church, built in 1840, is near the original site. (RL94)

Misión Santiago el Apóstol Aiñiní. Established by Italian Jesuit Ignacio María Nápoli near the site of present-day Santiago in 1724 after an abortive attempt to locate near present-day Buena Vista in 1721. A major revolt of Pericú and Guaycura people began in 1734 when rebellious neophytes killed Santiago's minister, Padre Lorenzo Carranco. The uprising spread throughout the southern missions and by the time the missionaries regained control several years later, a few of the Spanish forces and a number of Indians had been killed. During and after the revolt, a series of epidemics practically eliminated the population of the Santiago mission; numbers plunged from a reported 110 to 40 before the mission was closed in 1795. (RL98

Misión San José del Cabo Añuití. Founded in 1730 by Spanish Jesuit Nicolás Tamaral, this most southerly of the missions served as a supply and tentative rest stop for Manila galleons. In less than 20 years disease took all but 100 of the original population and the mission was converted to a visiting station of Misión Santiago in 1748. During the 1760's, Bohemian Jesuit Ignacio Tirsch painted a graphic and detailed picture of the mission and its site - which can be identified as the hill near the beach and just southwest of the heart of the present town. (RL96)

A DIFFERENT CULTURE...

The customs and daily lives of the people of Baja have been greatly changed by the building of the paved highway in 1973. Over most of the peninsula there were very few people. Those who did not live in the cities had little money and lived off of the land and the sea. Most of the people had no refrigerators; meat and seafood were salted and dried; vegetables were eaten fresh from their gardens and sodas and beer (if they had any) were kept in a cool place. Social functions were limited or non-existent. Travel was limited to about 10 miles per hour. Families with 10 children or more were not uncommon. Education was only available in the cities so many were uneducated.

With the highway came dramatic changes. Now they had refrigerators and the gas to run them, availability of fresh foods from far away, medical assistance, tools for farming, cattle and the means to get them to market, buses to get the children to school and a source of income from tourism.

Those communities that were by-passed by the highway soon realized the significance of these modern day advantages. People actually disassembled their houses and moved them closer to the road, totally abandoning the communities where they had lived. This is evidenced by older maps of Baja that show towns where nothing exists today.

Prior to these changes the people of Baja dressed differently. The women did not wear long pants. Men never wore shorts or tank tops. Tourists were shunned when they wore shorts or were scantily clad. Today, the dress codes have changed but they are still more conservative than ours. In the cities and towns you will hardly ever see a Mexican man without a shirt. The women also dress much more conservatively than most of the tourists.

When you go to Baja, if you go to places that are way off of the highway, you will see a lot of the old culture still in place. If you stop at a ranch house, it's nice to have candy or small toys to give to the children, and perhaps, something for the parents.

There is one thing you should be forewarned of, in the country it is not a good idea to walk right up to a house and knock on the door. Keep your distance until you are sure their "security system" of usual dogs is not going to eat you up. Sometimes a dog will approach you very aggressively. Don't run. I have found that if you raise your arm as if you're going to throw something at him he might back down. While riding a bicycle or ATC if the dogs chase me, I stop and yell at them. I carry a stick to use along with my yell; however, I have never struck a dog as they always turn tail when they see the stick.

If you should have an appointment to meet a Mexican you can expect him to be late. When he shows up be grateful that he did. He knew you would be on time. They are not as uptight and concerned with promptness as we are. This is mañana land which means if it doesn't happen today it will happen mañana and mañana doesn't always mean tomorrow; it just means "not today".

Learning the full name of a Mexican citizen can be confusing at first. In the name "María de Rosario Perez Sanchez de Cabrillo" we find: Sanchez is her mother's maiden name; Perez is her father's name; Cabrillo is her husband's name and she may be called María or Rosario according to her preference. Many women do not use their husband's name except in legal matters. In areas of Baja it is common for a person to have two last names that are the same. In the Loreto area the name Davis is quite common and I know of quite a few people who's last name is Davis Davis. This does not imply intermarriage, the name Davis has been here since the 1690's. They have large families and the families have chosen to stay in the same areas for a long time. In the very southern portion of Baja I know of a father and son whose last names are both Riva Palacio (here they have chosen to keep this famous name).

HOLIDAYS...

Mexican people are festive and love to celebrate. They are wrapped in tradition and glory in their religion. When they celebrate they go all out and everyone participates. Many times, during more important holidays, businesses will close so the owners can participate in the festivities. Birthdays are celebrated just as they are in the U.S. with the cake, candles and a wish. México has it's own holidays; try to plan a trip to watch the festivities. Some of the dates listed here are variable if a fiesta must be celebrated on a week-end.

January 1: New Year's Day, *Año Nuevo.* Carnivals.

January 6: *Día de Los Reyes*, the Day of the Kings. They celebrate the gifts the kings brought to Jesus. This is the traditional time for gift giving in México as Christmas is in the United States.

February 5: Proclamation of the Constitución. *Día de la Constitución.* Commemorates the Constitutions of 1857 and 1917, by which México is now governed.

February 24: Flag day.

There are festivals and carnivals on the Tuesday before Ash Wednesday.

Easter week: Called *Semana Santa* this is the big holiday for all families. You will find the beaches, hotels, parks and highways filled with festive people. In most towns they have a large parade down the main thoroughfare. Many businesses close down for the whole week.

March 21, Birthday of President Benito Juarez.

May 1: Labor day. *Día de Trabajo*, the day of work.

May 5: *Cinco de Mayo.* The anniversary of the battle of Puebla. Holiday to commemorate the Mexican victory over the French at Puebla in 1862.

September 15-16: Independence Day. At 11:00 p.m. on the night of the 15th, the cry of freedom, grito de Dolores, is re-enacted in the town square, commemorating the opening of the Revolution for Independence.

October 12: Columbus' discovery of America

November 1: All Saints Day. *Día de Todos Santos.*

November 2: All souls day. Day of the Dead. *Día de Los Muertos.* On this day and the day before, all of México celebrates their dead. It is a festive time and teaches all that death is part of life. The cemeteries are decorated with flowers, offerings are made of fruits and candles set to burn. Special offerings are sometimes made of the favorite foods of the departed.

November 20: Anniversary of the Revolución of 1910.

December 12: Day of Guadalupe, México's patron saint,

December 16 to 24. The nine days of Christmas or *Posadas* - celebrated everywhere.

December 25: Christmas, *Navidad*, many government and some private places are closed until after New Years.

51

FAMOUS COMIDA...

When you get down south (and if you've gotten this far in the book surely you'll make it now) you will see why recipes are important - especially seafood recipes. Almost everything you will eat will come from the sea. It will be so fresh and sweet, so abundant, and so reasonably priced - maybe free if you retrieved it yourself - that you'll want to learn how to prepare it. You're probably going to miss our stateside bread so there is also a recipe for my dad's campfire bread that always tastes delicious.

Baja has many fine restaurants; included here are some famous recipes of the more well-known gourmet chefs of Baja.

SOPA DE MARISCOS MALARRIMO

This recipe is contributed by Enrique Achoy, owner of the famous Malarrimo Restaurant in Guerrero Negro. Enrique is an excellent gourmet cook and he prides himself on having only the freshest seafood. The recipes he serves in his restaurant were procured through years of study and travel to attain only the finest methods of preparing his dishes. In the following recipe for seafood soup, Enrique suggests you not use halibut or shark meat as they tend to curl and become tough. This recipe serves 4 persons.

PREPARE: 1 cup cooked octopus, diced
8 small shrimps, shelled and deveined
4 chocolate clams in the half shell (cleaned)
1 cup "Catarina" scallops (bay scallops)
2 cups diced or chunks of white sea bass, pargo, dorado, etc.
3 chopped tomatoes, seeded and peeled.
1 tablespoon flour
1/2 white onion, sliced
1 clove garlic, mashed
2 bay leaves
1 pinch of rosemary
1 pinch of fresh oregano
1/2 cup chopped cilantro, stems discarded
1/2 sliced bell pepper
1 quart of water
Salt and pepper

Have all of the seafood ready. Heat the oil and fry the mashed garlic in it. When the garlic turns light brown remove it and discard. Sauté the onions and bell pepper 2 or 3 minutes. Add the tomatoes and sauté with the onions and pepper about 5 more minutes. Add water and the bay leaves and bring to a boil. Dust all the seafood except the clams with salt and pepper and flour and add to the boiling stock along with the chopped cilantro. When it comes back to a boil add the clams, oregano and rosemary. Let boil for about 7 minutes, do not overcook. Correct the salt and pepper and serve immediately. Suggestions: Add 1/2 cup of Santo Tomás, San Emilión red wine and lightly stir. Serve with hot corn tortillas or pan bolillo. Serve with a wedge of lemon or Mexican lime and salsa *Huichol* (available in Mexican markets).

ROCK CRAB CIELITO LINDO

Seven miles south of San Quintín, out on the beach, there is a motel and restaurant called Cielito Lindo. The owner, an American named Juanita Cortés, has a source for fresh rock crab claws. Her recipe, a favorite with many old Baja travelers, goes into print right here for the very first time.

Ingredients: 1 kilo fresh raw stone crab claws. 4 tablespoons ground paprika,
black pepper, 1/4 pound margarine or butter.

Crack the crab claws lightly with a hammer, do not remove the shells, this is only to make it easier to remove the shells when eating and to let the flavors blend as you cook. In a large iron skillet melt 2 or 3 tablespoons butter or margarine. Heat until very hot but not so hot it burns the butter. Add the crab, stirring and turning until the crab turns bright reddish orange, add another tablespoon of butter during this time. Lower the flame and sprinkle lightly with black pepper. Do not salt. Completely cover with paprika stirring and turning constantly for 30 seconds more. Be careful as the paprika burns easily. Place on plates and pour drippings over crab. Serves 2 persons.

DONA ANITA'S LOBSTER TACOS

In El Rosario lives a legend in the history of Baja. Doña Anita Espinosa. She has spent her lifetime helping the poor, aiding the sick children and over-seeing the welfare of her community. She was a key person in the formation of the Flying Samaritan Program, a group of American medical people who fly down and treat the people of Baja. For many years she had a restaurant at the side of the road and the specialty of the house was lobster tacos. When I asked her for permission to print her recipe she graciously agreed and was honored at my request.

MUST HAVE; Cooked, preferable boiled, lobster. When cool shred the lobster into quarter inch strips - by hand in the Mexican way.

MIX   5 cups finely shredded, boiled lobster
1 cup finely chopped spanish onion
1 cup Best Foods mayonnaise
1 cup sour cream
4 garlic cloves, smashed very fine
Juice of 6 or 8 Mexican limes

STUFF   Flour tortillas by placing 3 or 4 tablespoons on the side of each
one and rolling the tortilla up in a roll around the lobster.

Cook   In large iron skillet that is very lightly oiled. Roll the tacos around until they are lightly browned on all sides and heated through. Serve with the salsa recipe that follows. Serves 8 - 10.

ALFREDO'S B.B.Q. FISH MARINADE

Alfredo's Restaurant Embarcadero is on the Malecón in Loreto. He loves to fish and to cook. His famous recipe was given to me as follows, it is for 30 people.

MIX   1 cup soy sauce
       1 cup lime juice (preferably the small yellow Mexican limes)
       1 cup oil and 1 cup vinegar
       2 teaspoons each of salt and pepper
       1 teaspoon garlic powder
       1 teaspoon Lawry's season salt
       2 teaspoons powdered achiote (available in Mexican markets)
       1/4 cup sesame seeds
       1 clove fresh minced garlic

DIP   Fish filets, each side, set aside in cool place and marinate for 1 hour.

**Mike's Rock Oven
at Puerto Escondido**

MIKE'S BAJA BREAD

This recipe takes 2 people, one to make the bread and one to make the coals. The easiest way is to bake the bread in a large dutch oven, preferably the three legged kind with a lid, placing coals on all sides. My dad created this recipe and I remember having fresh baked bread on Malarrimo beach! The illustration above shows one of our campsite ovens that we made to bake this wonderful bread in.

WARM   Large pan, bucket, or bowl and put 3 cups very warm water in it
ADD   4 heaping tablespoons sugar
            2 packages dry yeast
MIX   Thoroughly for 3 minutes
ADD   1 level tablespoon of salt
            9 cups of flour, gradually worked in
MIX   By hand for at least 10 minutes, (kneed, punch, work it out).
            Coat the outside with salad oil and cover with damp cloth.
            Now put the dough in a warm spot ,with no draft, for 1 hour until
            doubled in size. (the inside of the cab of your truck, windows up, is
            ideal in Baja, if it's cold start the engine and turn the heater on.
PUNCH   it down for 3 minutes. Make into 2 loaves and then let it rest and
            place in large dutch oven (greased slightly). Cover and let rise in
            warm place for 45 minutes.
BAKE   Put dutch oven on coals, with more coals on top and some around
            the sides. About 35 minutes.

Savor the flavor. The recipe does not call for oil or shortening. This permits you to use lots of butter while enjoying the bread.

LOBSTER TOMATAL STYLE

If you lived in a fishcamp and had nothing to eat but lobster day in and day out you'd come up with the best way in the world to cook lobster. The lobster fishermen at El Tomatal, where our place is, taught me this recipe.

MUST HAVE; Small, fresh live lobster that kicks hard when you pick it up.

HEAT Large skillet, containing butter and lots of chopped garlic.

CUT Live lobster, lay it on a board shell side up, spread out flat, cut it in half from between the eyes, down the middle of the back, through the middle of the tail. This takes a *big* very sharp knife. Clean out the white intestine and the black line going through the back of the meat. The yellowish colored part of the intestine is considered a delicacy and imparts a delicious flavor to the meat while cooking. Break off the legs and feelers and discard. (You can throw the legs in a pot of boiling water for a few minutes and eat the meat inside for nibbles later on.)

PLACE Lobster, still in the shell, hopefully still twitching, meat side down in skillet and cook for 4 to 8 minutes depending on size, turn it over, spoon some butter and chopped garlic from the bottom of the pan on the meat, cover and cook 4 more minutes.

SERVE With mayonnaise and Mexican limes.

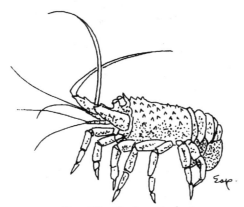

Pacific Spiny Lobster

FISH TACOS

Almost every town in Baja has a good "Tacos de Pescado" stand. We've tried lots of them. Pilar's in Todos Santos rates among the best because they always use very fresh Dorado (Mahi Mahi). Recipes vary from one place to another as nobody measures exact ingredients but this one works.

FILET Your dorado, cabrillo or other sweet meat fish, then slice each filet down to finger size pieces. Place in a very cold place.

MIX 1 cup flour
1 teaspoon baking powder
1 teaspoon salt
2 eggs, slightly beaten
1 teaspoon sugar
Enough milk to make a slightly runny batter

DIP fish fingers into mixture

FRY In hot oil, deep enough to cover

SERVE In fresh warm corn or flour tortillas topped with finely shredded cabbage, mayonnaise, yogurt or sour cream, José's salsa, marinated onions and guacamole (recipes follow) and a squeeze of Mexican lime.

JOSE'S SALSA

Jose doesn't come from Baja. He comes from Obregón over on mainland México. He has lived with us for eighteen years and is like a son to us. He loves to cook and we find his salsa superb.

CHOP	4 or 5 ripe tomatoes
	1 large spanish onion (white with yellow covering)
	1/2 cup cilantro leaves, discard stems
	3 to 6 serrano chills, you decide
MIX	all of the above together
ADD	1 teaspoon of salt (José adds more)
SERVE	On just about any kind of seafood, eggs, or whatever.

MARINATED ONIONS

SLICE	Six large white onions, separate rings and place in bowl
ADD	2 cups vinegar, salt and pepper to taste and
	marinate in refrigerator for 2 days, turning occasionally

GUACAMOLE

CHOP	2 serrano chilis, 1 large spanish onion & 1 large tomato
MASH	3 ripe avocados
MIX	all of the above, add salt and pepper and a squeeze of lime

MARGARITAS

Everybody makes what they call Margaritas in Baja. The difference between a good Margarita and a bad one is the quality of the Tequila and the relative ambiance that surrounds you when you drink it. This recipe comes from the bar of the Oasis Hotel in Loreto. Nicki has been stirring up these concoctions for many years, and the hotel supplies all the ambiance one requires.

MIX	4 parts Cuervo Especial Gold Tequila
	2 parts Controy
	1 part lime juice or more to taste, use Mexican sweet limes.
	Lots of ice, preferably crushed
STIR	until very cold, shake in shaker or mix in blender
POUR	Into glasses that have been moistened on the rim with lime and
	dipped into salt.

A perfect toast might be: *Salud, Amor y Pesetas y tiempo para disfruitarlas.* Health, Love and Money and the time to enjoy them.

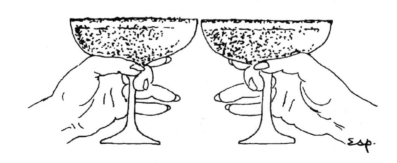

Chapter 5

CITY MAPS

In this section I have created a brief overview of each of the larger cities. My maps were derived from property tax maps shared with me by the Delegados (roughly equivalent to our Mayors) of the different districts. I drove the streets of many of the towns to double check the accuracy of the maps and discovered that if someone had purchased more than one city block and made it into one site they blocked off the street in doing so and this does not always show on the map. As I did not drive all of the streets of all of the towns there may still be some error.

Very few of the towns actually have street signs; however, the streets do have names and signs are beginning to appear in the larger cities. If you are looking for a certain place it is still best to count the blocks in case the signs are lacking.

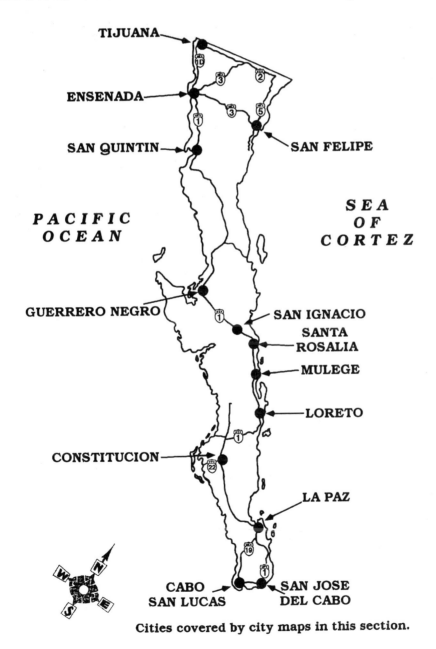

Cities covered by city maps in this section.

TIJUANA...

Tijuana is the main gateway to Baja California and the busiest border crossing in the world. It is a bustling, fast paced, crowded city of over 1,300,000 people. In 1830, only a ranch existed here; seventy years later there were just 240 residents. It was in the 1920's when prohibition was going on in the U.S. that Tijuana came to life. Overnight the town grew by leaps and bounds and by 1929 they had opened up a gambling casino and a race track along with lots of tawdry bars and whorehouses. Tourists came in droves. Tijuana was wild and wicked and the world knew it. In 1935, the government closed down the gambling casino and efforts were made to clean up the town. For many years afterward the town suffered economically.

In the 1980's, a major clean up was undertaken. Sales taxes were imposed and the money was used wisely. The shops on Avenida Revolución, the main tourist street, were painted and cleaned up. The street was redone with attractive stones and planters and new street lights were installed. At the same time reliable trash pick-up was initiated throughout the city, and the people were educated in the importance of cleanliness in all phases of their lives.

Today, hundreds of curio shops are crowded into a six block stretch of Avenida Revolución attracting tourists from all over the world. You can buy, among other things, custom hand-carved furniture and doors, wrought iron in any shape or design you desire, leather goods, beautifully designed silver jewelry from Taxco in central México, embroidered ethnic clothing, pottery dishes and pots for plants, hand-woven blankets and wall hangings and a myriad of folk-art items. Bargaining has been the accepted way to purchase - don't be afraid to try.

Today Tijuana has Agua Caliente race track, dog races, Jai Alai games at Fronton Palace, bull fights, many nice hotels and restaurants and has become a nice place to visit. You can park your car on the U.S. side and take a cab, bus or walk to Avenida Revolución, or you can drive over and park at one of the many supervised parking lots. If you take your car over, the return through U.S. customs goes much faster now since they expanded the number of gates and opened up the Otay Mesa border crossing. The average wait is about one-half hour.

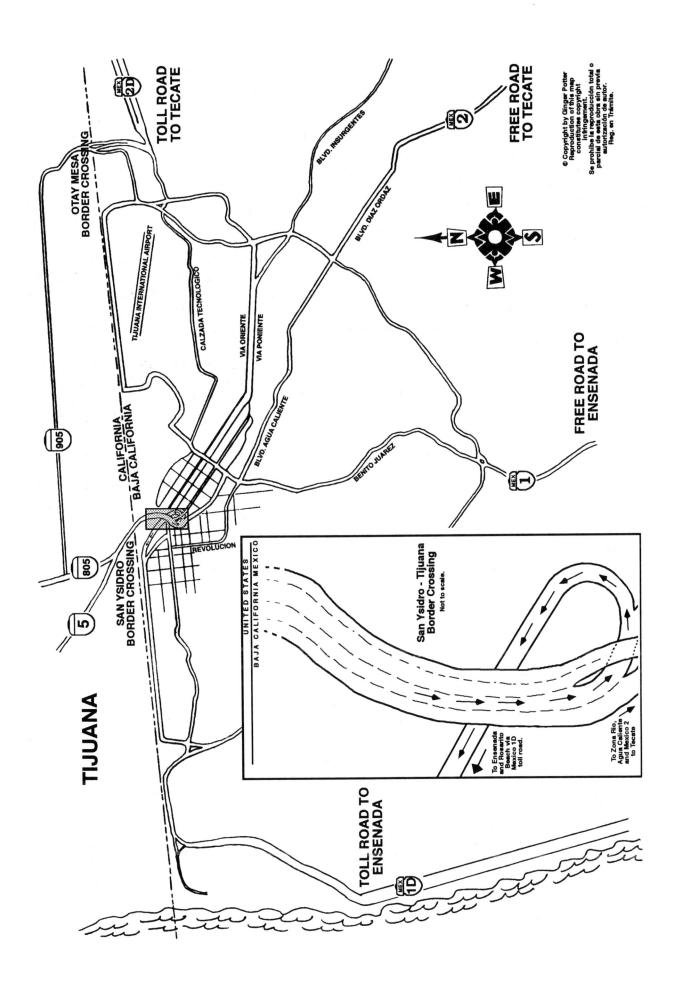

TIJUANA

OTAY MESA
BORDER CROSSING

TOLL ROAD
TO TECATE

FREE ROAD
TO TECATE

BLVD. INSURGENTES

BLVD. DIAZ ORDAZ

TIJUANA INTERNATIONAL AIRPORT

CALZADA TECNOLOGICO

VIA ORIENTE

VIA PONIENTE

BLVD. AGUA CALIENTE

BENITO JUAREZ

CALIFORNIA
BAJA CALIFORNIA

SAN YSIDRO
BORDER CROSSING

REVOLUCION

FREE ROAD TO
ENSENADA

905

805

5

TOLL ROAD TO
ENSENADA

MEX 2D

MEX 2

MEX 1

MEX 1D

N E S W

UNITED STATES
BAJA CALIFORNIA MEXICO

San Ysidro - Tijuana
Border Crossing

Not to scale.

To Ensenada
and Rosarito
Beach via
Mexico 1D
toll road.

To Zona Rio,
Agua Caliente
and Mexico 2
to Tecate

ENSENADA...

The development of Ensenada began in 1877, when, as a by-product of the gold mines in the interior, it became an official port of entry. In the mid-1880's it became the headquarters for several land and colonization companies. By 1921, the population was 2,178. In 1971, the population had grown to over 70,000. Today it is over 230,000. It is a lively little city and yet somehow retains a sleepy atmosphere.

Seafood processing, commercial fishing, tourism and shipping are the major economic resources of Ensenada. It is Baja California's busiest seaport, with facilities to repair and dock large vessels. Cruise ships visit almost daily and passengers flock to the sidewalk cafes and curio shops.

Street signs are lacking on the back streets. New signs are going up as of this writing. Hopefully they will do all of the streets.

The many large hotels, RV parks and restaurants accommodate tourists from all over the world. Sportfishing for tuna, marlin, yellowtail and rockfish is quite close by. A winery invites tours and free wine tasting. A trip to nearby La Bufadora (a blowhole on Punta Banda, the southern hook of the bay), makes an interesting day's excursion. South of town about 6 miles is the large complex of "Estero Beach Resort". This hotel and RV park, located on the edge of the bay has many nice, relaxing rooms, an outdoor waterfront restaurant, two shops, one with some exquisite items, a small-boat launch ramp and a small, but quite noteworthy, pre-Columbian museum. Tennis courts and water sports equipment are available for guests.

Some 30 miles south of town in picturesque Santo Tomás valley is the resort of El Palomar. During the summer this makes a good day trip. They have a large swimming pool, water slide, tennis courts and not far from their hotel and restaurant, you can walk over and view the ruins of a mission. They also have an RV park with full hookups.

60

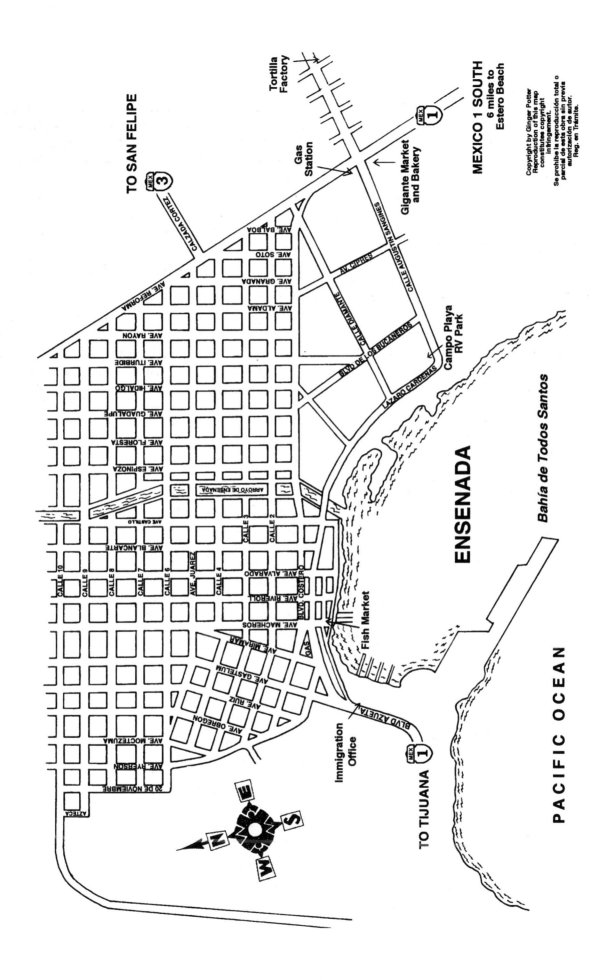

TO SAN FELIPE

MEXICO 1 SOUTH
6 miles to
Estero Beach

Tortilla
Factory

Gas
Station

Gigante Market
and Bakery

AVE. BALBOA
AVE. SOTO
AVE. GRANADA
AVE. ALDAMA
AVE. RAYON
AVE. ITURBIDE
AVE. HIDALGO
AVE. GUADALUPE
AVE. FLORESTA
AVE. ESPINOZA
AVE. BLANCARTE
AVE. CASTILLO

AVE. REFORMA

CALZADA CORTEZ

AV. CIPRES

CALLE DIAMANTE

BLVD DE LOS BUCANEROS

CALLE AUGUSTIN SANGINES

LAZARO CARDENAS

Campo Playa
RV Park

ARROYO DE ENSENADA

CALLE 3
CALLE 2

CALLE 10
CALLE 9
CALLE 8
CALLE 7
CALLE 6
CALLE 4

AVE. JUAREZ

AVE. ALVARADO
BLVD. COSTERO
AVE. RIVEROLL
AVE. MACHEROS
AVE MIRAMAR
AVE GASTELUM
AVE RUIZ
AVE OBREGON
AVE. MOCTEZUMA
AVE. RYERSON
20 DE NOVIEMBRE
AZTECA

ENSENADA

Bahía de Todos Santos

Fish Market

GAS

Immigration
Office

BLVD AZUETA

TO TIJUANA

PACIFIC OCEAN

SAN QUINTIN...

Long ago in the days of pirates and whalers this place was called the "Bay of Five Hills" and was frequented by American ships involved in contraband trade. The "five hills" are volcanic cinder cones located at the water's edge, west of town.

In the late 1800's, the area was chosen as the base for a colonization project, first by Americans and then by the English. Water was insufficient for dry farming and these efforts failed. These attempts to develop San Quintín produced a large flour mill, 20 miles of railroad headed for San Diego, a pier, and an interesting cemetery.

The town of San Quintín is located 6 miles east of the ocean. A natural bay opens to the southeast of the volcanoes. Because of sand bars, the bay is closed to nautical traffic of any significant draft. It says in the history, "In the early 1900's steamships anchored in front of the town." I don't believe it. In aboriginal times, it was one of the most densely populated areas of Baja. There are salt beds near the coast and in 1856 they produced enough salt to be noted in the National Treasury of México.

Today San Quintín is an agricultural giant. Hundreds of huge trucks carry tomatoes and other vegetables north to Ensenada and to the United States for shipment to far away places. (This stretch of the main highway is almost always in a state of disrepair from the constant heavy truck traffic.) Tomatoes are definitely the main crop; however, they do grow quite a lot of brussell sprouts. The local Mexicans were not familiar with brussell sprouts when they first began growing them here and one was heard to say, "Why do the Americans bother with such small cabbage?" Should you see fields of beautiful flowers, they are growing them for the seed. Many of the property owners in the valley rent their land to the giant "Los Piños" company for the planting of tomatoes. A large number of mestizo Indians have been brought here from mainland México to do the planting and picking.

At the site of the old flour mill, Al and Nolo Gaston have built the "Old Mill Motel, Restaurant and RV Park." Saving and using in a very unique and attractive manner, all that remained of the original mill, they have created a remarkably interesting and relaxing place offering sportfishing and drawing many U.S. anglers. Some of the best sport fishing is just outside the entrance to the bay. The new launch ramp was built to handle the largest of trailerable boats. Accommodations and fishing charters can be booked through the Baja Outfitter before you cross the border; see Resource Guide.

About 7 miles south of town is the La Pinta Hotel and Cielito Lindo Motel restaurant and campground. Both of these places can also arrange fishing trips. Cielito Lindo prepares a delicious fresh cracked-crab feed. Old Baja travelers frequently stop for this feast. Be early.

Old Cemetery in San Quintín

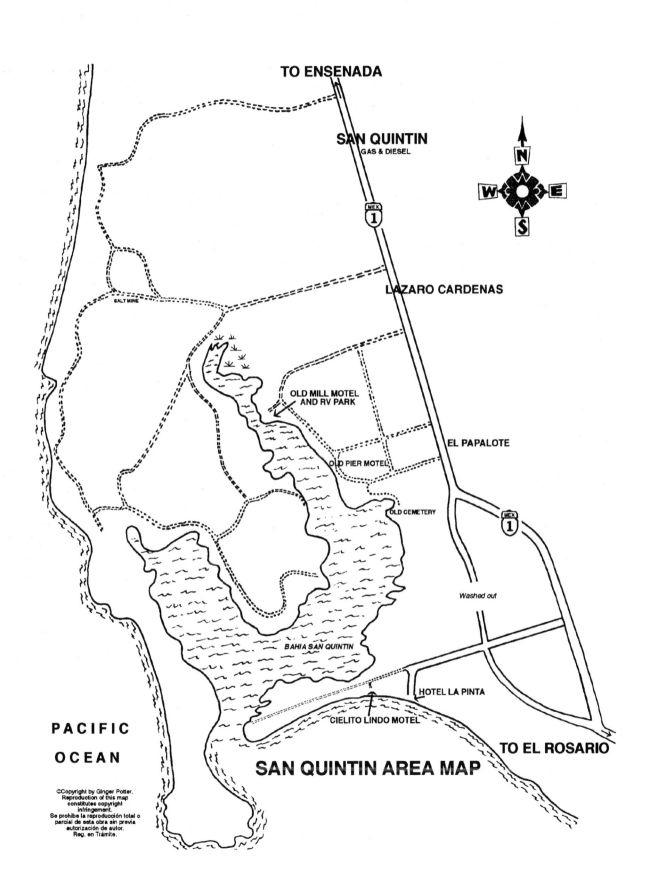

TO ENSENADA

SAN QUINTIN
GAS & DIESEL

MEX 1

LAZARO CARDENAS

SALT MINE

OLD MILL MOTEL
AND RV PARK

EL PAPALOTE

OLD PIER MOTEL

OLD CEMETERY

MEX 1

Washed out

BAHIA SAN QUINTIN

HOTEL LA PINTA

CIELITO LINDO MOTEL

TO EL ROSARIO

PACIFIC

OCEAN

SAN QUINTIN AREA MAP

GUERRERO NEGRO

Located on the north side of Scammon's Lagoon this windy and dusty little community is unique among the towns in Baja. Salt brought man to this place. Miles of natural salt flats line the shores of the neighboring Laguna Ojo de Liebre (Scammon's Lagoon). In the 1800's, many attempts were made to harvest the salt commercially and some were fairly successful - but none survived long. In 1957, the existing Exportadora de Sal, S. A., began operations here. They not only mine the existing salt but have built hundreds of salt evaporating pans to create more salt. Originally they were not allowed to sell this salt within México, it was only for export, hence the name, "Exporter of Salt." The original founder of the salt works, Daniel K. Ludwig, a wealthy shipping magnate from New York, sold the company to Mitsubishi in 1975. Following the sale, the Mexican government stepped in to enforce the law that says "all minerals in Mexico belong to Mexico." Today the Mexican government owns the controlling portion of the business and Mitsubishi owns the balance. They work closely together.

A large portion of the people in Guerrero Negro work for the salt works. Commercial fishing is also of economic importance. Enterprising individuals are recognizing a new potential and are going after the tourism market brought here by the annual migration of the grey whale. Existing restaurants, trailer parks, markets, motels and hotels are prospering and more are being built to cater to the eager whalewatchers.

The most well established motel, trailer park and restaurant in town is the Malarrimo, owned by Enrique Achoy. Enrique has permits to take you to play with the whales. The restaurant here is famous for it's seafood. He has modest rooms for rent, an enclosed RV Park (full hookups but no pull-throughs) and he speaks English.

Before the Mercado La Ballena opened, grocery shopping in Guerrero Negro meant going to five or six different places and then not always finding what you needed. Now a fairly good selection of food is available in one place. In the rear of the store the vegetable selection is good. Their meats are imported from other parts of Mexico where the quality is better.

There is also a large seafood house that sells frozen seafood (including lobster) and block ice. To get there, turn north on the street between the water tower and Las Dunas Motel (next to the Mercado La Ballena) and go to the end. It is in the two story white house across from the generating plant.

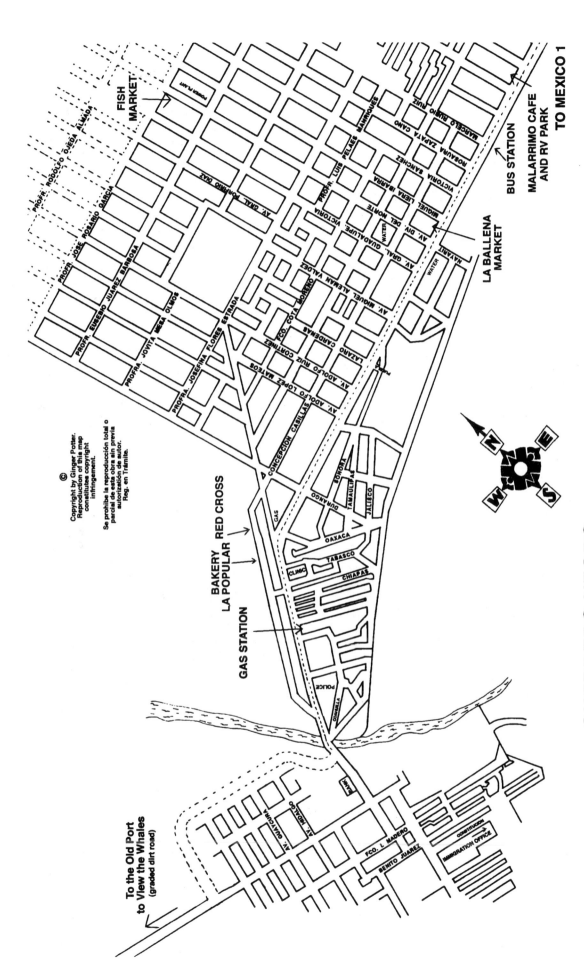

GUERRERO NEGRO

SAN IGNACIO...

It is a wonderful respite to pull off the hot desert into this beautiful desert oasis. The road from México 1 into town leads you through a grove of date palms and lush greenery over the river into one of the oldest towns in Baja. The mission here is one of the most beautiful of all the missions. The "zócolo," or town plaza, with its giant Indian laurel trees is worth visiting. It is across from the church.

El Padrino RV park (full hookups) is on the right side of the road into town just past the La Pinta Hotel. Just behind the trailer park you can take a cool dip in the river. Tourists are invited to visit the mission and photographs are allowed; however, they do not allow flash photography. Many people have tried capturing the beauty of the hand-hewn mission doors on film. The renaissance paintings inside the church are well preserved and beautiful.

Most services are available in San Ignacio; grocery stores, restaurants, a bank, and the hotels are all pretty easy to find. This is one of those small Baja towns where they don't need street signs or storefront signs because everybody knows where everything is. If you need something special, ask, they probably have it. A new museum featuring replicas of cave paintings has opened next to the mission. It is definitely worth a visit.

From San Ignacio you can make arrangements to see the cave paintings in the San Francisco mountains. The mountains are a few miles north of town and have many beautiful painted caves. These trips take you by mule to visit the different caves, the best time to go is in the fall. The trips last a few days and require planning and special gear.

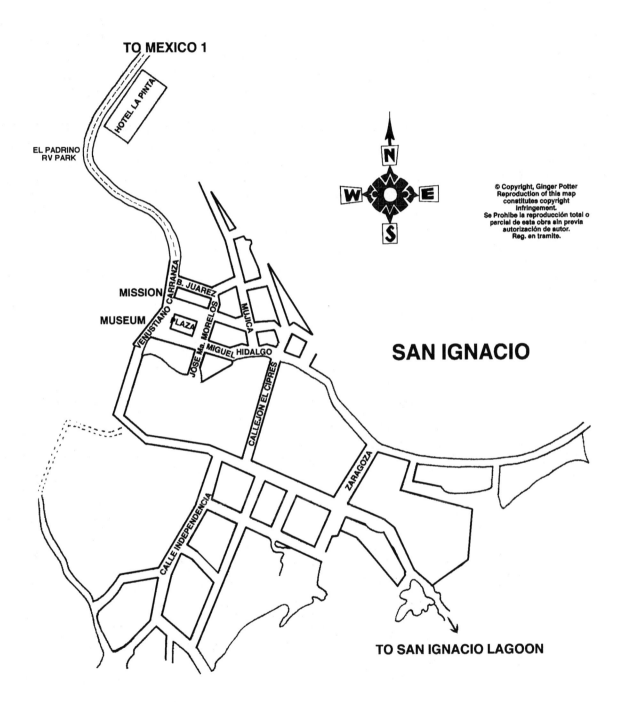

TO MEXICO 1

HOTEL LA PINTA

EL PADRINO
RV PARK

MISSION

MUSEUM

PLAZA

B. JUAREZ

VENUSTIANO CARRANZA

JOSE Ma. MORELOS

MIGUEL HIDALGO

MUJICA

CALLEJON EL CIPRES

ZARAGOZA

CALLE INDEPENDENCIA

SAN IGNACIO

TO SAN IGNACIO LAGOON

© Copyright, Ginger Potter
Reproduction of this map
constitutes copyright
infringement.
Se Prohibe la reproducción total o
parcial de esta obra sin previa
autorización de autor.
Reg. en tramite.

SANTA ROSALIA...

Santa Rosalía is an unbearably hot, dusty mining town with absolutely nothing for the tourist other than a bakery, an auto parts house and an interesting metal church. The gas station is a rip off, having been closed down twice by the government for jerry-rigging the pumps.

Copper was discovered here in the late 1800's. A French company, Boleo Mining Company mined the ore until 1953. A look around as you drive through town reveals all the remnants of the mining operation. Just north of town the accumulation of black rock, a side product of the mining operation, is now being hauled off for use in RV Parks and areas around homes where mud is a problem. Boy have they got a surprise coming - this stuff sticks to your shoes and grinds into everything.

During the 1920's there were a few old sailing vessels sitting abandoned in the "harbor." These vessels eventually sank here and might make a good diving adventure. Some parts of the ships have broken off and floated to shore in the area. A restaurant north of town displays some of these interesting artifacts.

The metal church was designed by Eiffel of Eiffel Tower fame. It is made of galvanized iron and was shipped here from Europe. French influence in the architecture is still obvious throughout the town. Monotonous mine-workers homes, all alike, line the streets south of the main street. The old Hotel Central, across the plaza from the church, for years was in a state of neglect but recent efforts to refurbish it have helped. The Hotel El Morro, located just south of town on a potentially beautiful site, has very poor service and questionable rooms, they would have a nice view if they would wash the windows once in awhile. The new Las Palmas RV Park has full hookups and is nice and clean. It is located south of town next to a lagoon.

Should you need auto parts this town has one of the biggest supplies in all of Baja. The owner speaks good English if you don't try to speak Spanish. On request he ships parts by bus to all of the surrounding towns.

Just off shore, fishing is supposed to be very good. On the left side of the entrance to town there is a small shop selling fishing tackle, the owners are very nice people and can probably assist you in hiring a boat.

For many years old Baja travelers have stopped at the bakery here for *bolillos*. They are superb. The bakery, El Boleo, is still going strong and the bread is just as good as ever.

Old Mining Train at Santa Rosalía

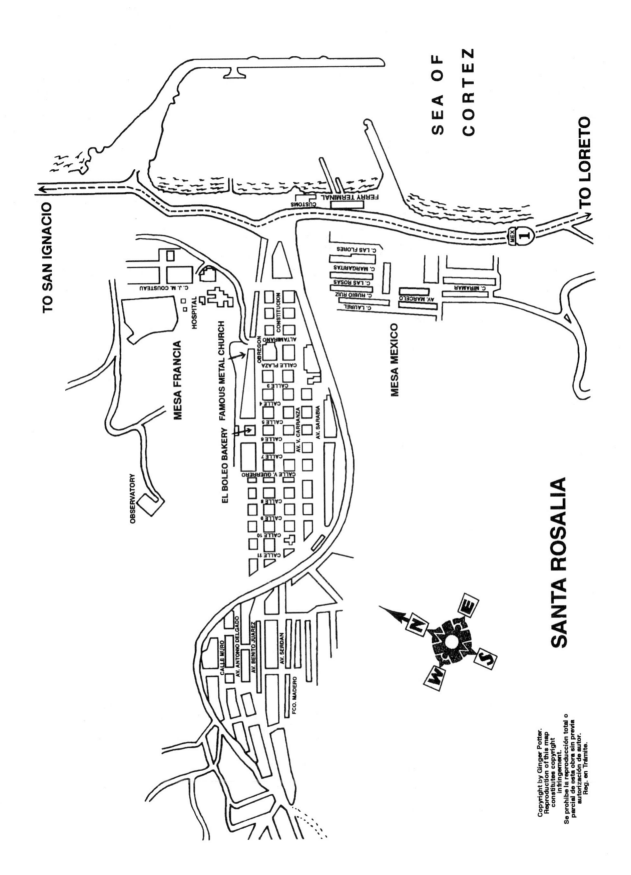

SANTA ROSALIA

SEA OF CORTEZ

TO SAN IGNACIO
TO LORETO

OBSERVATORY

MESA FRANCIA

C.J. M. COUSTEAU
HOSPITAL

EL BOLEO BAKERY   FAMOUS METAL CHURCH

CONSTITUCION
ALTAMIRANO
OBREGON
CALLE PLAZA
CALLE 3
CALLE 4
CALLE 5
CALLE 6
CALLE 7
CALLE 8
CALLE 9
CALLE 10
CALLE 11

AV. V. CARRANZA
CALLE V. GUERRERO
AV. SARABIA

CALLE MURO
AV. ANTONIO DELGADO
AV. BENITO JUAREZ
AV. SERDAN
FCO. MADERO

MESA MEXICO

C. LAUREL
C. RUBIO RUIZ
C. LAS ROSAS
C. MARGARITAS
C. LAS FLORES
AV. MACELO
C. MIRAMAR

FERRY TERMINAL
CUSTOMS

MEX 1

N E S W

MULEGE...

Nestled in a valley filled with palms at the mouth of the River Santa Rosalía de Mulegé is the village of Mulegé. This quaint little town with its crooked narrow streets and old Spanish architecture saw it's beginnings long before the building of the mission in 1705. Missionaries found a large population of Indians already established here when they found this sight and built the Misión Santa Rosalía de Mulegé. The river, originating from an underground source and only about 3 miles long, has always provided an abundant source of fresh water. In 1706, one of the first 'roads' built on the peninsula was built from here to Loreto.

It is easy to understand why Mulegé is home to so many Americans. Water, electricity, telephones and all the 'necessities' of life are provided at very reasonable cost. Many Americans have their own boats and enjoy endless hours of sportfishing. The village has numerous markets, restaurants, repair shops, hardware and dry goods stores.

For the visitor, Mulegé has comfortable services. The Las Casitas Hotel and Restaurant has a lovely outdoor patio where one can enjoy a leisurely lunch - if their parrot doesn't eat it all. Out on Sombrerito Point the La Almeja restaurant (right at the mouth of the river) serves delicious seafood at a very reasonable price. In town the Los Equipales restaurant has good American and Mexican food and is a little more up-scale. The Taco stand in the middle of town on the south side of the street, "Tacos Dany", is also a great place to stop for lunch. There are many guest houses, *Casas de huespedes*, a large modern laundromat, and fresh vegetables from nearby farms are available in the local markets.

One of the better dive shops in Baja, Mulegé Divers, is on the main street going into town. They have rentals and air for certified divers. For non-certified divers they offer a 'resort course' in which you receive basic instruction and then go diving with them under controlled conditions. Claudia and Miguel, the owners, know the waters in this area and can take you out to some beautiful diving spots.

Arrangements for sportfishing boats and guides can be made at the Serenidad Hotel south of town or the Orchard RV park. By boat it is only a few minutes to Bahía de Concepción where a multitude of different kinds of fish are found. North of Mulegé, out around the islands, tuna, marlin, dolphinfish and sailfish are caught from May through September. Around the mouth of the river a few large black snook are still lurking. They are a real challenge to bring to the boat.

Old Prison, Mulegé

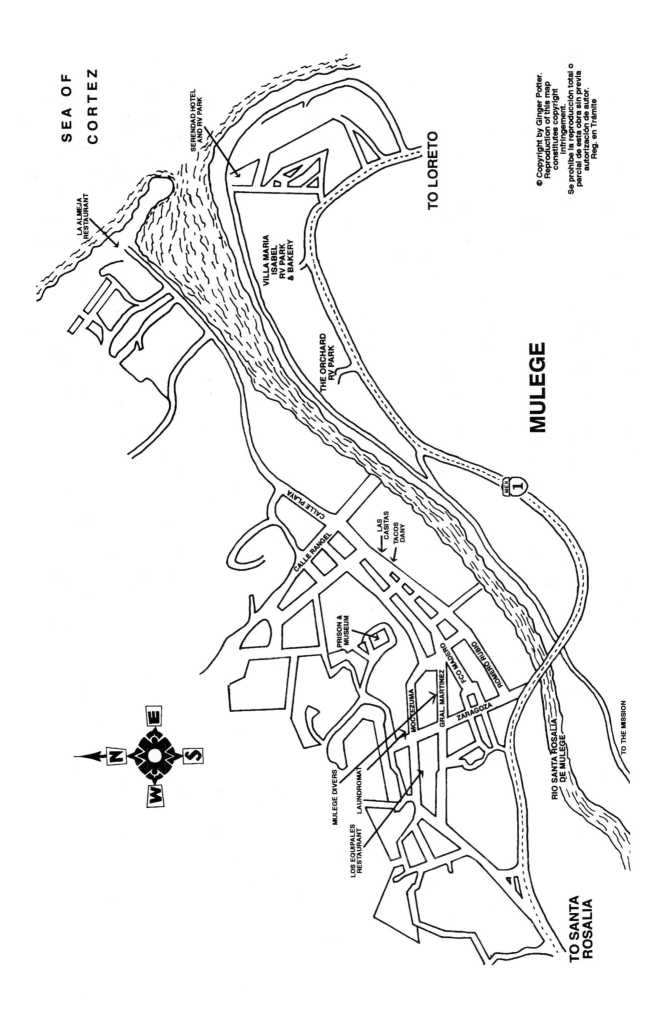

SEA OF CORTEZ

LA ALMEJA RESTAURANT

SERENDAD HOTEL AND RV PARK

VILLA MARIA ISABEL RV PARK & BAKERY

THE ORCHARD RV PARK

TO LORETO

MULEGE

CALLE PLAYA

CALLE RANGEL

LAS CASITAS

TACOS DANY

PRISON & MUSEUM

MOCTEZUMA

GRAL. MARTINEZ

FCO MADERO

ROMERO RUBIO

ZARAGOZA

MULEGE DIVERS

LAUNDROMAT

LOS EQUIPALES RESTAURANT

RIO SANTA ROSALIA DE MULEGE

TO THE MISSION

MEX 1

TO SANTA ROSALIA

N E S W

LORETO...

Almost 300 years ago, Loreto became the capital of the entire California territory (including Alta California). In 1828, a devastating hurricane wiped the whole town out. The following year they moved the capital to La Paz where it has remained since. The mission here, Misión Nuestra Señora de Loreto, is the mother of all the California missions. Construction on this mission started in 1697 and until just recently the ravages of time showed their toll. The Mexican government's mission rehabilitation project has restored this mission and a small museum has opened next to it.

México's Department of Tourism has spent millions to develop the Loreto area. The large resort complex south of town at Nopoló includes a challenging 18 hole golf course, paved palm lined streets, a few very nice homes, lots of lots for sale and infrastructure for a complete resort development. The golf course is beautiful but from the highway somehow appears out of place with its lush rolling greens, lakes and bridges against the stark desert background.

In town, Loreto has all of the amenities. Hotels, restaurants, curio shops, RV parks, a good market, and Alfredo's Sportfishing. His place is out on the malecón to the left of the main street. It's the place to make arrangements to go fishing - and there are usually lots of fish around here. For atmosphere and quiet relaxation, I highly recommend the El Oasis Hotel at the south end of the malecón. The Oasis has quiet waterfront rooms, good food and sportsfishing trips can be arranged at the front desk. The Hotel Misión de Loreto near the center of the malecón has a refreshing patio where good food is served but there is no view of the water. Pescador Market has good fresh beef and their homemade chorizo (Mexican sausage) is very tasty.

There are 3 nice RV parks in Loreto. Follow the signs; they are well advertised. Two are located south of town on the water's edge; however, you have no view of the water from where you will park. The other RV park is in town.

A trip into the hills east of town to the Misión San Javier is an interesting day's adventure. This mission is one of the most well preserved and beautiful of the old missions. It is a two hour (about 16 miles) drive on a dirt road. The turnoff is about a mile south of the entrance to Loreto from Mexico 1. Check road conditions before going.

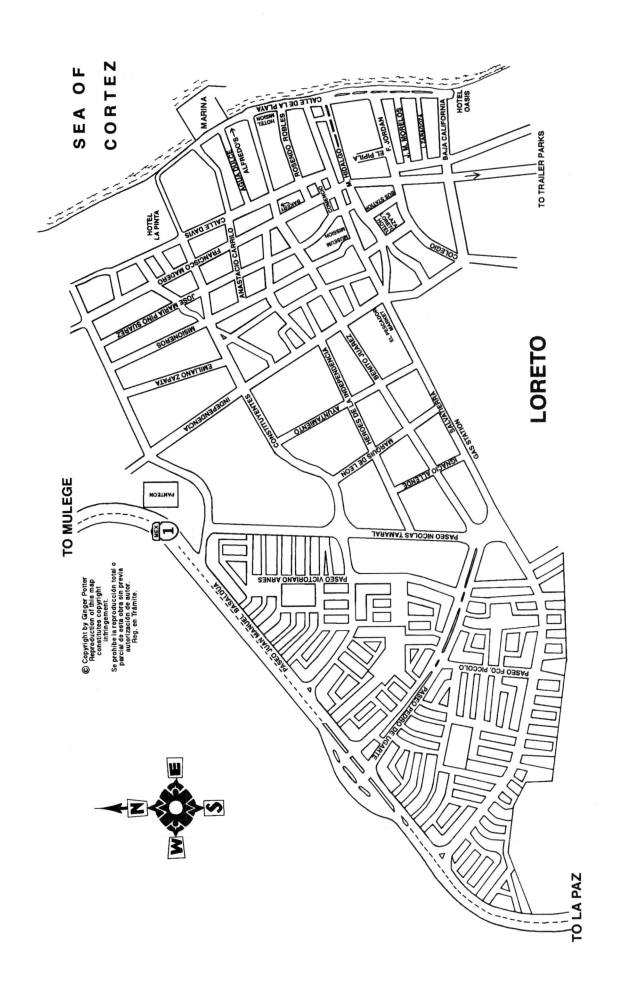

SEA OF CORTEZ

LORETO

TO MULEGE

TO LA PAZ

TO TRAILER PARKS

MARINA

CALLE DE LA PLAYA

HOTEL MISSION

ROSENDO ROBLES

M. HIDALGO

EL PIPILA

F. JORDAN

J. M. MORELOS

I. ZARAGOZA

BAJA CALIFORNIA

HOTEL OASIS

AGUA DULCE

ALFREDO'S

HOTEL LA PINTA

CALLE DAVIS

FRANCISCO MADERO

JOSE MARIA PINO SUAREZ

ANASTACIO CARRILLO

BAKERY

COMERCIO

MUSEUM MISSION

BUS STATION

HOTEL PLAZA LORETO

COLEGIO

MISIONEROS

EMILIANO ZAPATA

INDEPENDENCIA

CONSTITUYENTES

AYUNTAMIENTO

HEROES DE LA INDEPENDENCIA

BENITO JUAREZ

EL ESCADOR MARKET

MARQUIS DE LEON

SALVATIERRA

IGNACIO ALLENDE

GAS STATION

PANTEON

MEX 1

PASEO NICOLAS TAMARAL

PASEO VICTORIANO ARNES

PASEO JUAN MANUEL BASALDUA

PASEO PEDRO DE UGARTE

PASEO FCO. PICCOLO

N E S W

CONSTITUCION...

From the air this whole area appears to be a huge crossword puzzle. Farms spread from west of town to the base of the mountains. This area has been a rich agricultural area for many years. The road was paved from north of here at Santo Domingo to La Paz in the 1950's to provide easy transportation of agricultural products. Today, agriculture is still an important economic resource but the water supply is finite and while every effort to conserve the water has been made, the supply continually dwindles. New wells at the base of the mountains are now being planned.

Constitución is a very large community. All services are available here. There are some good mechanics and parts are readily available, a couple of small hotels, 2 trailer parks, many small restaurants, bakeries, etc. Most of the services are here for the locals and were not built with the tourist in mind. The central market is worthy of note; it is located at the corner of Rosauro Zapata and Nicolas Bravo and has fresh fish, meats, and vegetables that are abundant and reasonably priced.

I suggest you purchase gas north of town at the big new Pemex station on the west side of the street. It is north of the area covered by the map.

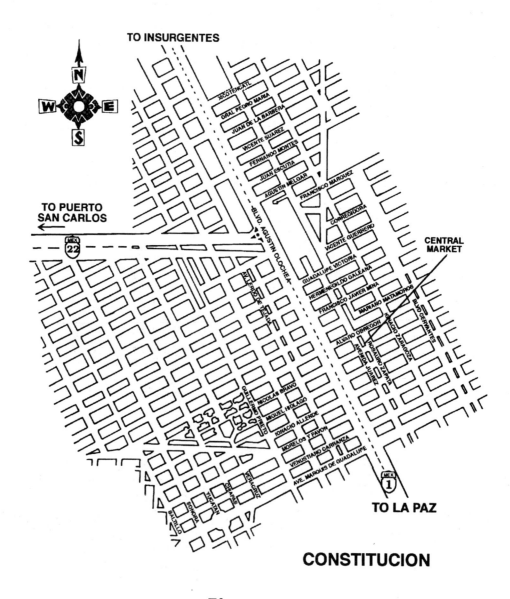

CONSTITUCION

74

LA PAZ...

La Paz has a tumultuous history. In 1533, a group of Spanish explorers landed here and most of them were killed by the Indians. In 1535, Hernán Cortés attempted to colonize the place but political problems on the mainland cut off his supplies and he had to retreat. In the 1600's another attempt was made, only to end when a fire destroyed most of the supplies and buildings. The year 1683 saw another colony fail when the Indians rebelled and murdered several of the colonists - at a banquet given in their honor by the Spaniards. Two more attempts in the 1700's also failed because of Indian rebellions and epidemics.

Finally in the early 1800's, La Paz became a permanent settlement and in 1829, became the capital of the Southern Territory of California. Rich beds of pearl oysters lay offshore and pearling supported a flourishing economy until the 1940s when a mysterious disease destroyed the oyster beds in all of the Sea of Cortez.

Tourism boomed here in the 1950's as word spread of the great numbers of billfish just outside of the bay. Sportsmen flew in from everywhere and La Paz quickly gained the reputation of being one of the billfishing centers of the world. Then Japanese longline fishing boats came and reaped tremendous harvests of billfish from the gulf, greatly reducing the population. The Japanese are no longer allowed to fish in the gulf.

Today the population of La Paz is over 175,000. Sportfishing and tourism are still important economic factors. However, with the development of Cabo San Lucas as a sportfishing center, this type of tourism has fallen off in La Paz. Diving, sea kayaking and camping on the offshore islands are now bringing tourists to La Paz.

La Paz has all services and, as a tourist, you will be well received. Try seeking out the back street restaurants and shops, enjoying the difference in culture. The Los Arcos Hotel, located in the center of town on the malecón (a sea-walk along the beach) is one of the nicest places to stay and the Cabanas Los Arcos next door to the hotel are attractive and reasonably priced. The open air restaurant in front of the Hotel La Perla on Obregón has good food and wonderful ambiance. La Paz has many hotels, motels and hostels and restaurants for every taste and budget. For dinner, I recommend the Bismarck II Restaurant at the corner of Degollado and Ignacio Altamirano. Try the restaurant at the Aquarios Hotel on Ignacio Ramirez and Degollado for an authentic Mexican breakfast at an unbelievably low price.

The Museum of Anthropology is located on the corner of Altamirano and 5 de Mayo. Just recently they have uncovered a few 2400 year old complete human skeletons on the edge of La Paz bay and they intend to move one of them to the museum.

Many of the street signs on the back streets are turned around - probably by vehicles turning too close to them - follow the map and count the blocks. Some of the one-way streets are not marked as such. Traffic cops earn their keep in La Paz - keep your eyes open. Double parking on the main street is very expensive, I can vouch for this.

Malecon
in La Paz

75

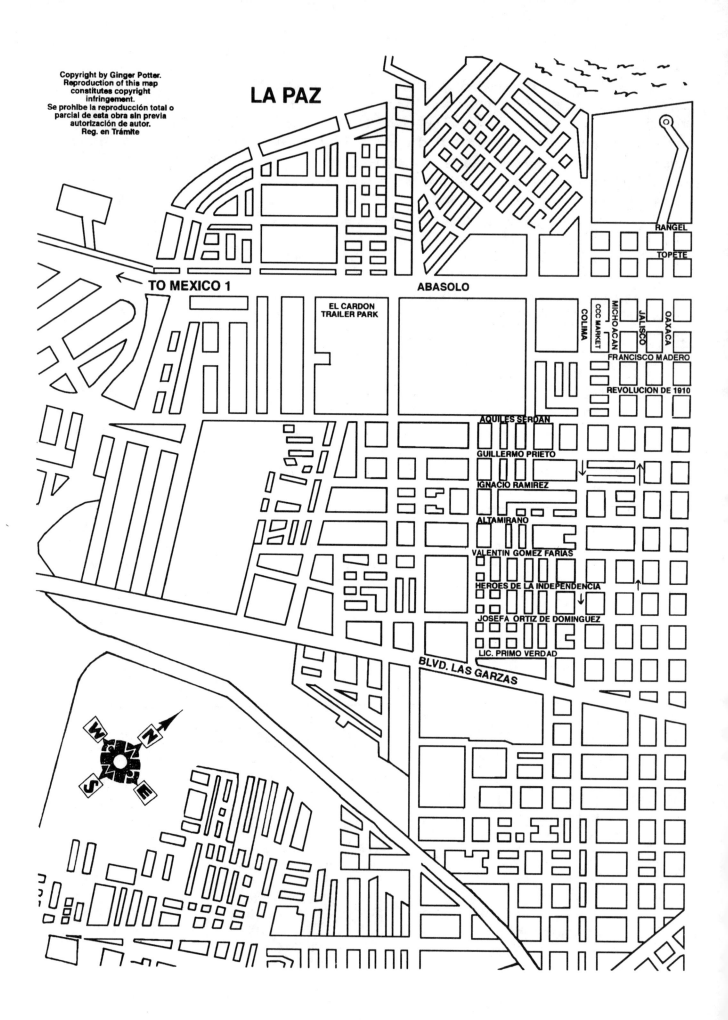

LA PAZ

RANGEL

TOPETE

TO MEXICO 1

ABASOLO

EL CARDON
TRAILER PARK

COLIMA

CCC MARKET

MICHOACAN

JALISCO

OAXACA

FRANCISCO MADERO

REVOLUCION DE 1910

AQUILES SERDAN

GUILLERMO PRIETO

IGNACIO RAMIREZ

ALTAMIRANO

VALENTIN GOMEZ FARIAS

HEROES DE LA INDEPENDENCIA

JOSEFA ORTIZ DE DOMINGUEZ

LIC. PRIMO VERDAD

BLVD. LAS GARZAS

W N S E

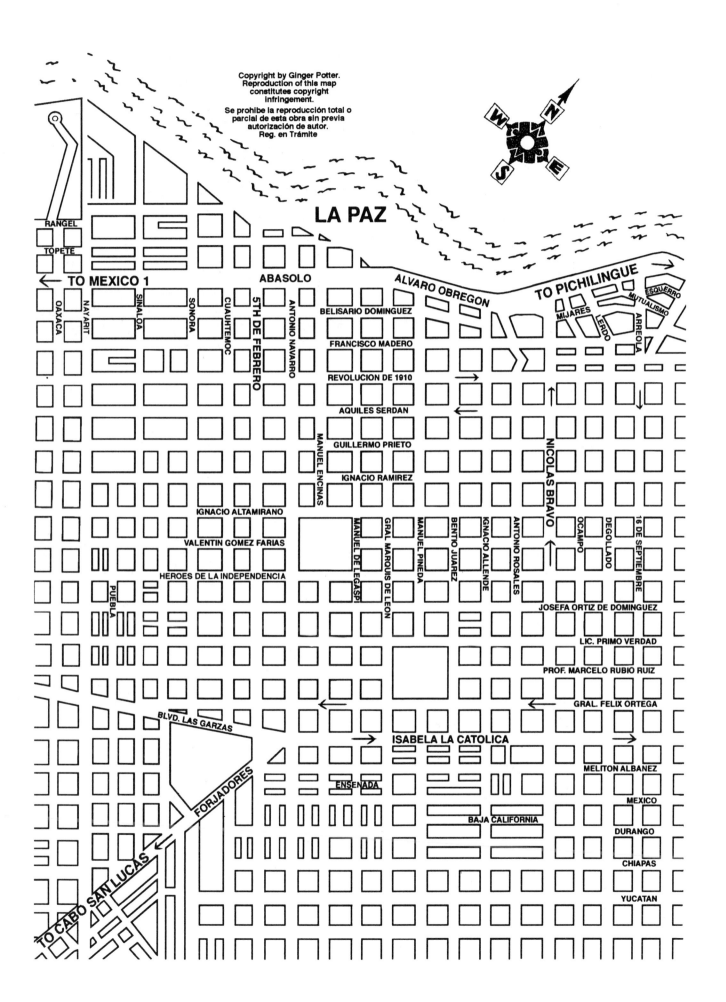

LA PAZ

RANGEL
TOPETE

← TO MEXICO 1

ABASOLO

ALVARO OBREGON

TO PICHILINGUE →

OAXACA
NAYARIT
SINALOA
SONORA
CUAUHTEMOC
5TH DE FEBRERO
ANTONIO NAVARRO

BELISARIO DOMINGUEZ

FRANCISCO MADERO

REVOLUCION DE 1910

AQUILES SERDAN

GUILLERMO PRIETO

IGNACIO RAMIREZ

MANUEL ENCINAS

IGNACIO ALTAMIRANO

VALENTIN GOMEZ FARIAS

HEROES DE LA INDEPENDENCIA

PUEBLA

MANUEL DE LEGASPI
GRAL MARQUS DE LEON
MANUEL PINEDA
BENITO JUAREZ
IGNACIO ALLENDE
ANTONIO ROSALES
NICOLAS BRAVO
OCAMPO
DEGOLLADO
16 DE SEPTIEMBRE

MIJARES
LERDO
ARREOLA
MUTUALISMO
ESQUERRO

JOSEFA ORTIZ DE DOMINGUEZ

LIC. PRIMO VERDAD

PROF. MARCELO RUBIO RUIZ

GRAL. FELIX ORTEGA

BLVD. LAS GARZAS

ISABELA LA CATOLICA

MELITON ALBANEZ

ENSENADA

MEXICO

BAJA CALIFORNIA

DURANGO

FORJADORES

CHIAPAS

YUCATAN

TO CABO SAN LUCAS

SAN JOSE DEL CABO...

One of the nicest little towns in Baja, San José still retains its old México atmosphere. New stores have opened up, but most of them are neatly tucked into the old buildings and the quiet old ambiance has been retained. Situated just a few miles below the Tropic of Cancer, the area is lush and tropical. Here papayas, mangoes, bananas and other fruits grow. At one time sugarcane was the principal crop.

San José has a good municipal market (on Castro at the west end). Within this market there are stalls with fresh ranch cheeses, three or four butcher shops and fresh fruit and vegetable stands stocked from nearby fields.

Damiana, a supposed aphrodisiac, grows wild in the hills and valleys in this area. The leaves of the Damiana plant are used to make a tea that is served after dinner in some Mexican homes. The English enjoy this tea and for years it was harvested here and shipped to England. You can still find little packages of damiana in the stores around town. The tea is steeped in very hot water with copious amounts of sugar added. The plants are not so easily found today because when they harvested them they tore them up - roots and all. A liqueur made from the damiana plant, (called Damiana,) is sold in most of the liquor stores in Baja. In the Los Cabos area, some places use it in their margaritas.

In 1993, a storm brought over fifty inches of rain in one night. Many of the houses along the highway were washed away. All of the back streets were flooded with water and then mud. The sewers were filled with mud. Plants, trees, cars, fences were swept away by the torrents of water. The then new four lane highway from here to Cabo San Lucas was totally washed out in three places. It took a year to repair the damage. The original highway was funded in part from an additional sales tax imposed on the area stores from San José del Cabo to Cabo San Lucas. Many of the merchants were very upset when the road washed out. They had believed that they had paid for a road that wouldn't wash out.

The town boasts some very nice gourmet restaurants, five star hotels at the water's edge, curio shops and all services one would require. North of town on the highway, there is a large supermarket filled with American goods. I've found their shrimp, octopus and squid quite fresh and reasonably priced. This market is located about 1 mile north of the area covered by the map, on México 1 on the east side of the highway. It is right next to the large Pemex station.

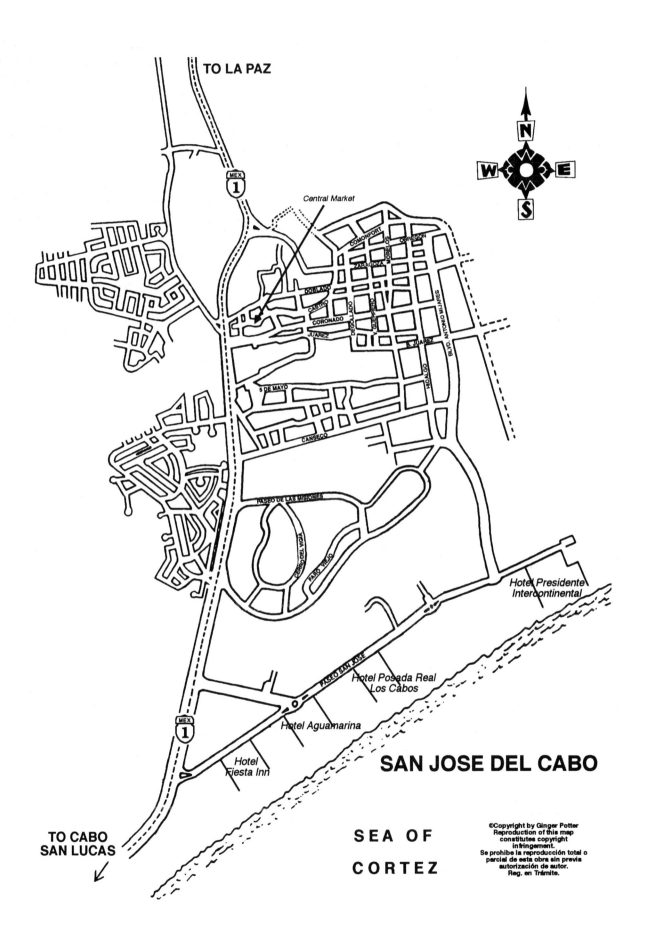

TO LA PAZ

MEX 1

Central Market

COMONFORT
ZARAGOZA
MORELOS
OBREGON
DOBLADO
CASTRO
CORONADO
DEGOLLADO
GUERRERO
JUAREZ
B. JUAREZ
BLVD. ANTONIO MIJARES
HIDALGO

5 DE MAYO

CANSECO

PASEO DE LAS MISIONES

CERRO DEL VIGIA
FARO VIEJO

Hotel Presidente
Intercontinental

PASEO SAN JOSE

Hotel Posada Real
Los Cabos

Hotel Aguamarina

MEX 1

Hotel
Fiesta Inn

SAN JOSE DEL CABO

N
W E
S

TO CABO
SAN LUCAS

SEA OF

CORTEZ

CABO SAN LUCAS...

This rapidly growing world class resort sits nestled at the base of a mountain at the very tip of Baja. A natural bay has been modified to create a secluded marina. Tourists come to "Cabo" from around the world to enjoy some of the finest sport-fishing known today. Billfishing tournaments with prizes in the six figure range occur regularly. The beautiful, warm, clear blue waters provide the utmost in diving, snorkeling, and swimming. Many five-star hotels in the area accommodate sun-seekers from around the world.

Jeff Klassen's Los Cabos Fishing Center has rental fishing tackle for both surf fishing and off shore fishing. He can arrange a charter boat or will personally give you surf fishing lessons. His store is located at #9 Madero just off of Blvd. Marina.

It was only relatively recently that Cabo became famous, in 1950 the population was 548. Today it is home to many Mexicans and foreigners alike. The large mountain on the west side of town, Pedregoso, suitably houses a few of the more elite with some of the homes in the million dollar range. Land to the north of town sells fast and condos and home-sites along the stretch from San José to Cabo are selling rapidly. This is land's end and it seems everybody is buying a piece of it.

Cabo is a wonderful little city. The streets are a little irregular as they are in most bayside cities. The markets are small, no superstores yet, and the many little sidewalk cafes are charming. Curio shops line the streets. Massive new hotels and condos seem to sprout up overnight. Cabo is a great town for young people with it's discos and taco stands. The "yachties" also love it here as evidenced by their magnificent ships in the harbor.

Not far from town are many beautiful sandy coves. Access to these little beaches has been marked by signs along the highway that say "Acceso a la playa". Many of these beaches have very strong currents and swimming is difficult or impossible even for the strongest swimmer. The beaches still offer clean white sand and privacy.

Sportfishing and wonderful warm winter days with cool nights attract the winter crowd. Rightfully so, this town has the best of both. Summers are hot and humid and tourism usually drops off a bit during this time.

West of town the magnificent Finisterra Hotel sits high on the hill overlooking the Pacific Ocean on one side and the Gulf waters on the other side. Below the Finisterra the Hotel Sol Mar and it's adjoining condos fill a small valley. Both of these hotels share a beautiful wide white sand beach where whales are frequently sighted offshore. In front of town to the east a short distance is the Hotel Hacienda Beach Resort situated right on a beautiful wide sandy beach. Right in the middle of town, blocking the view of the bay, the huge Plaza Las Glorias Hotel dominates the scene. Other hotels and condos are everywhere. Cruise ships visit the harbor daily bringing hundreds of tourists to shop and play.

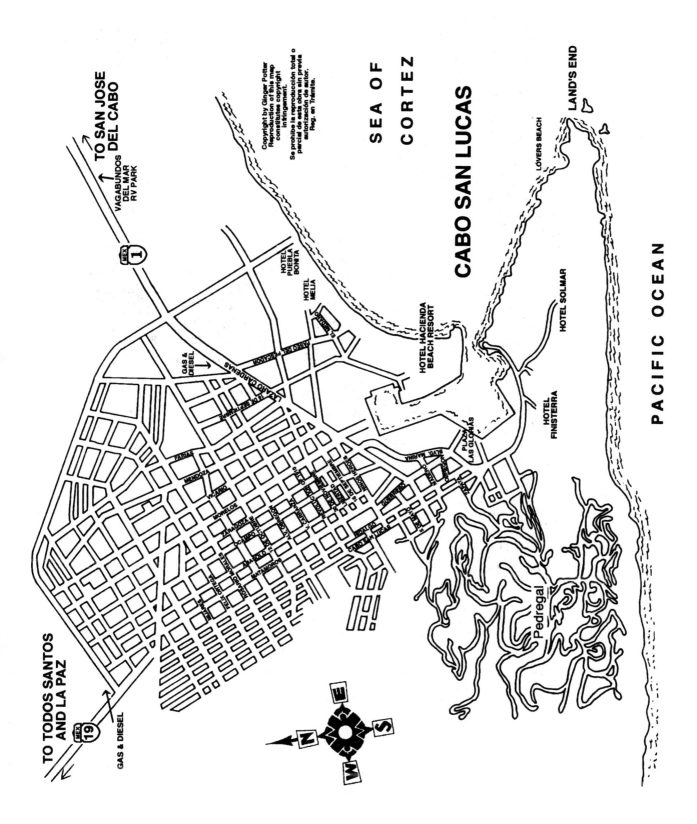

TO SAN JOSE DEL CABO

VAGABUNDOS DEL MAR RV PARK

MEX 1

TO TODOS SANTOS AND LA PAZ

MEX 19

GAS & DIESEL

HOTEL PUEBLA BONITA

HOTEL MELIA

GAS & DIESEL

LAZARO CARDENAS

16 DE SEPTIEMBRE

FARIAS

MENDOZA

VICARIO

MORELOS

ZARAGOZA

CAMPO

ZAPATA

GUERRERO

CABO SAN LUCAS

HOTEL HACIENDA BEACH RESORT

PLAZA LAS GLORIAS

HOTEL FINISTERRA

BLVD. MARINA

HOTEL SOLMAR

Pedregal

LOVERS BEACH

LAND'S END

SEA OF CORTEZ

CABO SAN LUCAS

PACIFIC OCEAN

Copyright by Ginger Potter. Reproduction of this map constitutes copyright infringement.

Se prohibe la reproducción total o parcial de esta obra sin previa autorización de autor. Reg. en Trámite.

N E S W

SAN FELIPE...

Located on the eastern side of the Sierra San Pedro Mártir on the upper Sea of Cortez, San Felipe enjoys a warm comfortable climate in all but the late summer when it becomes unbearably hot.

Totuava, that giant member of the white seabass-corbina family were prolific here twenty years ago. Today the species is endangered and protected by the Mexican Department of Fisheries. I remember one evening many years ago when my dad hooked up with a totuava while surf fishing thirteen miles south of town. The battle was on and he chased the fish up and down the beach for a long time. How long a time I don't remember, but my uncle fell asleep before my dad brought the fish to shore, believing the whole time that he never would. After beaching the monster they tied the live 125 pound fish by its tail to my uncle's arm and waited for *the response* as the fish flipped all over the sand.

Commercial fishing, shrimping in particular, has always been the economic mainstay of San Felipe. Recently the Mexican government put in effect a ban on commercial fishing of any kind in the whole upper gulf. Now the shrimp boats must go south. Along with the totuava, the shrimp boats had almost wiped out the vaquita porpoise. This small porpoise was unnecessarily killed by the hundreds in the nets of the shrimp boats. Recently, I saw a small pod of them just off shore north of Puertecitos. It was a beautiful sight. I like things like that.

To the north and the south of town the beaches are lined with Americans' homes. In some camps they appear in rows as tight as the houses of San Francisco. They all await water delivery, have questionable sources of power and know about the summer heat, yet this is what they are looking for. There is something special about the sunrise on the gulf and the sunset over the mountains, and they enjoy hanging their hats here. More power to them.

Tidal differences in the upper gulf are sometimes more than twenty feet. This makes for good clammin' and there are lots of clams along the beaches here. Many hot-springs dot the shoreline along this area. In more than one place the locals have permanently embedded bathtubs into the rocks for the wonderful pleasure of enjoying the soothing and softening fresh hot sulfur water.

All services are available in San Felipe, but again, as in most of Baja, you will have to search around town to find everything you might need.

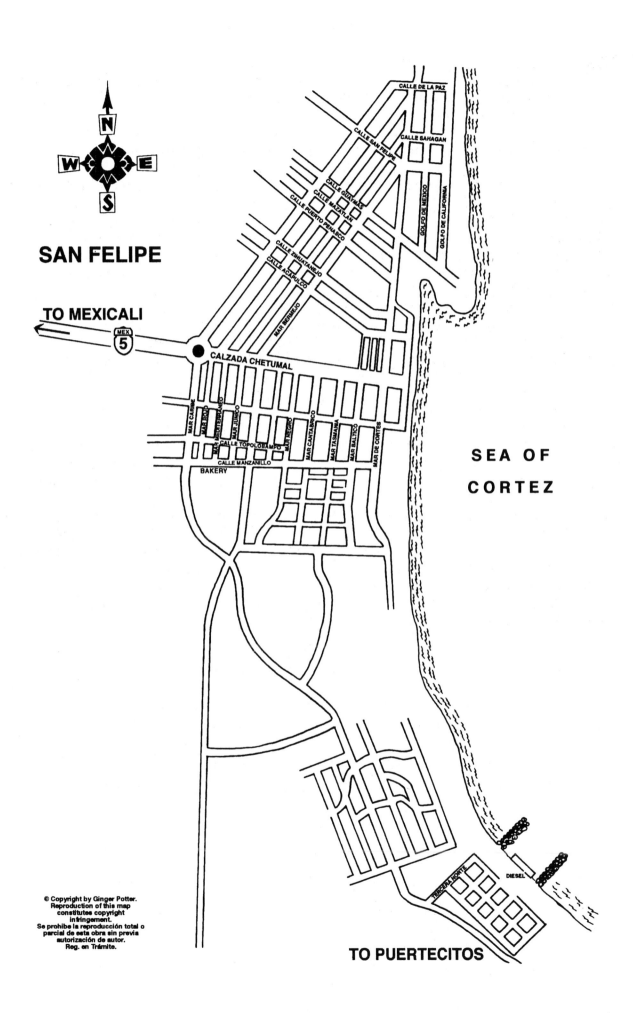

SAN FELIPE

TO MEXICALI

SEA OF

CORTEZ

TO PUERTECITOS

Roadlog quick reference guide.

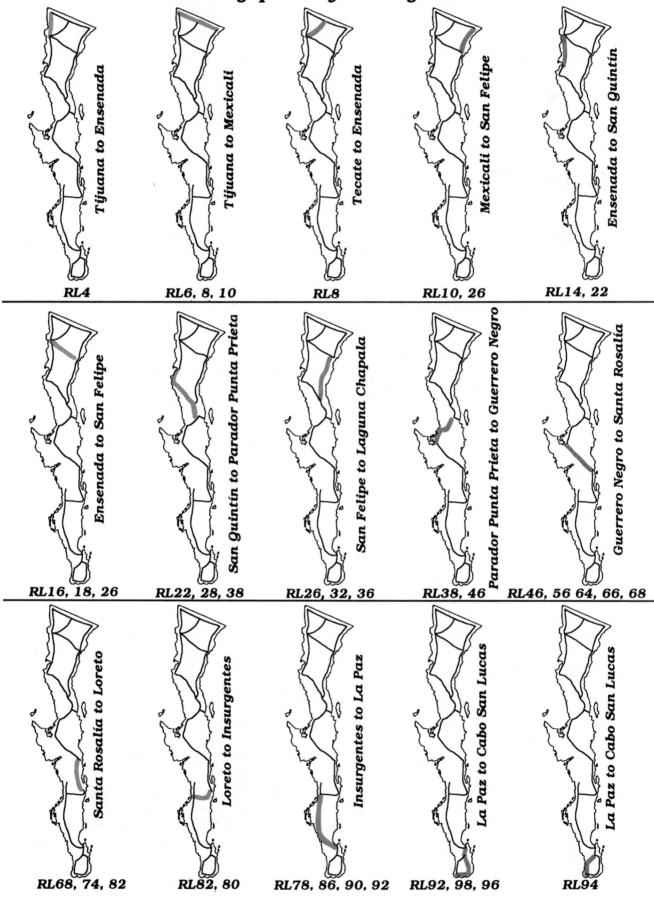

Tijuana to Ensenada
RL4

Tijuana to Mexicali
RL6, 8, 10

Tecate to Ensenada
RL8

Mexicali to San Felipe
RL10, 26

Ensenada to San Quintín
RL14, 22

Ensenada to San Felipe
RL16, 18, 26

San Quintín to Parador Punta Prieta
RL22, 28, 38

San Felipe to Laguna Chapala
RL26, 32, 36

Parador Punta Prieta to Guerrero Negro
RL38, 46

Guerrero Negro to Santa Rosalía
RL46, 56 64, 66, 68

Santa Rosalía to Loreto
RL68, 74, 82

Loreto to Insurgentes
RL82, 80

Insurgentes to La Paz
RL78, 86, 90, 92

La Paz to Cabo San Lucas
RL92, 98, 96

La Paz to Cabo San Lucas
RL94

Chapter 6

ROADLOG

SECTIONS AND SIDE TRIPS

TIJUANA - ENSENADA --- RL4
TIJUANA - MEXICALI --- RL6, 8, 10
TECATE - ENSENADA -- RL8
MEXICALI - SAN FELIPE -- RL10, 26
ENSENADA - SAN QUINTIN --- RL14, 22
ENSENADA - SAN FELIPE -- RL16, 18, 26
SAN QUINTIN - PARADOR PUNTA PRIETA ----------------- RL22, 28, 38
SAN FELIPE - MEXICO 1 AT CHAPALA --------------------- RL26, 32, 36
PARADOR PUNTA PRIETA - GUERRERO NEGRO -------- RL38, 46
GUERRERO NEGRO - SANTA ROSALIA ------------------- RL46, 56, 64, 66, 68
SANTA ROSALIA - LORETO ----------------------------------- RL68, 74, 82
LORETO - INSURGENTES ------------------------------------- RL82, 80
INSURGENTES - LA PAZ -------------------------------------- RL78, 86, 90, 92
LA PAZ - CABO SAN LUCAS via Mex 1 --------------------- RL92, 98, 96
LA PAZ - CABO SAN LUCAS via Mex 19 ------------------- RL94
SIDE TRIPS:
PUNTA CANOAS - SANTA ROSALILLITA SIDE TRIP --- RL34
MALARRIMO BEACH SIDE TRIP------------------------------ RL52
BAHIA ASUNCION SIDE TRIP ------------------------------- RL52
BAHIA TORTUGAS SIDE TRIP ------------------------------- RL52
INSURGENTES - LA PURISIMA SIDE TRIP --------------- RL70
CIUDAD CONSTITUCION - SAN CARLOS SIDE TRIP --- RL76
INSURGENTES - LOPEZ MATEOS SIDE TRIP ------------ RL78

How to Use the Baja Spacemaps and Roadlogs...

To efficiently use the Roadlog with its accompanying space maps first find the page that includes the area you want information about. This can be done by using the page guide. The page guide precedes the Roadlog and, for your convenience, is repeated at the very back of this book.

Each page of Roadlog matches its facing page with the space-map printed on it. Mileages are in kilometers and follow the kilometer markers along the highway. In the more remote areas where there are no kilometer markers or many of them are missing we have reverted to miles.

All of the city names printed in **bold print** in the Roadlog are described in detail in the section "Cities, Towns and Maps" on pages 58 through 82.

All Roadlog maps are shown in the same relation to magnetic north - as indicated by the compass arrows in the bottom right corner - so that your view of the countryside will remain consistent. The small maps of Baja are marked to show your general position in the peninsula. Page numbers of connecting maps are given in the margins of every Baja spacemap.

ABOUT THE ROADLOG...

In this edition of the Baja Book the Roadlog has it's own page numbers. Each Roadlog page number is preceded by **ROADLOG** OR **RL** to distinguish it from the rest of the book. All of the maps have been updated and the corresponding roadlogs are new.

To accommodate the roadlogs it is necessary to repeat three maps (pages 3 & 5, 35 & 37, 93 & 95). Note that several times the roadlogs direct you to turn back a page. This is because of the east west path of the highway (Loreto to Ciudad Constitución, pages 81 to 79, San José del Cabo to Cabo San Lucas, pages 97 to 95 and in a few other places).

Each spacemap covers about 70 air miles of Baja at a scale of one inch equals 7.8 miles or 12.6 kilometers.

Most of the roads in Baja do not have names. This is still a fairly primitive country. There is only one paved road that extends the length of the peninsula and this is México 1- also known as the "Baja highway". In the north the alternate toll-road for México 1 is México 1D and this only extends from Tijuana to Ensenada. México 2 and its toll-road alternative, México 2D, run west to east just south of the border and extend from Tijuana to Mexicali. México 3, an upper peninsula inland route, runs from Tecate to Ensenada to San Felipe. Mexico 5 runs from Mexicali to San Felipe in the north eastern portion of the peninsula. There are 2 or 3 short paved side roads in the southern portion of the peninsula.

Paved highway ▬▬▬	🏃 **Beachcombing**	♟ **Missions**
Unpaved road ■ ■ ■ ■ ■	◿ **Diving**	♠ **Resorts**
	🐟 **Fishing**	⌐ **Surfing**
Minor road, not for standard cars • • • • • • • • • • •	★ **Gas stations**	◣ **Windsurfing**
⚓ **Anchorages**	⌐ **Hunting**	🚐 **RV parks, camping**
⊂ **Clamming**	⊏⊐ **Landing fields**	

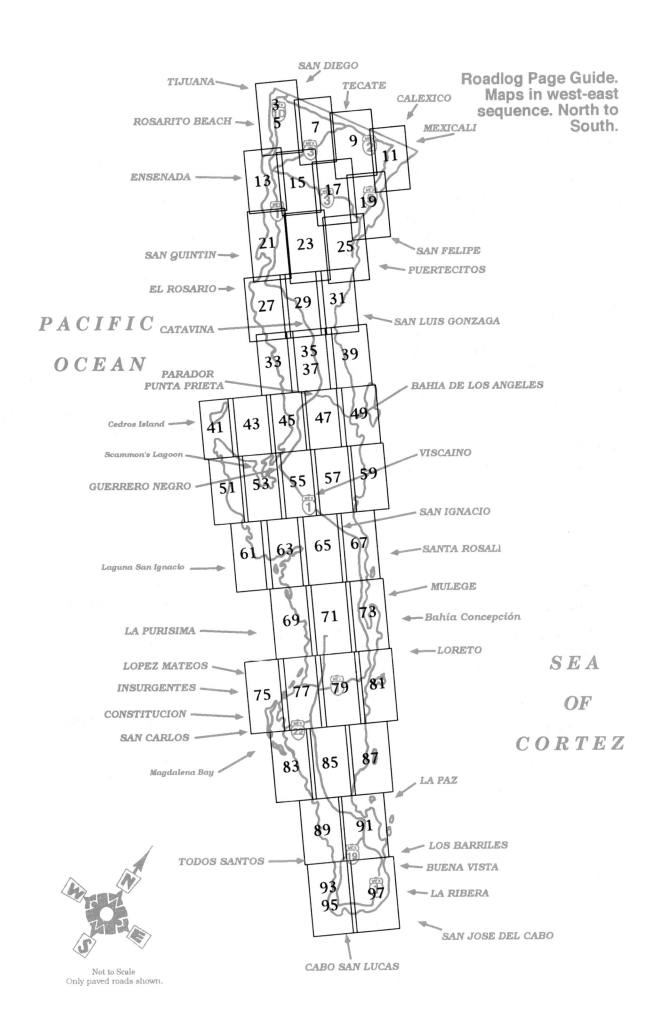

PACIFIC

OCEAN

SEA

OF

CORTEZ

SAN DIEGO

TIJUANA

ROSARITO BEACH

TECATE

CALEXICO

MEXICALI

ENSENADA

SAN FELIPE

SAN QUINTIN

PUERTECITOS

EL ROSARIO

CATAVINA

SAN LUIS GONZAGA

PARADOR
PUNTA PRIETA

BAHIA DE LOS ANGELES

Cedros Island

Scammon's Lagoon

VISCAINO

GUERRERO NEGRO

SAN IGNACIO

SANTA ROSALI

Laguna San Ignacio

MULEGE

Bahía Concepción

LA PURISIMA

LORETO

LOPEZ MATEOS

INSURGENTES

CONSTITUCION

SAN CARLOS

Magdalena Bay

LA PAZ

LOS BARRILES

TODOS SANTOS

BUENA VISTA

LA RIBERA

SAN JOSE DEL CABO

CABO SAN LUCAS

Roadlog Page Guide.
Maps in west-east
sequence. North to
South.

Not to Scale
Only paved roads shown.

BAJA BOOK IV

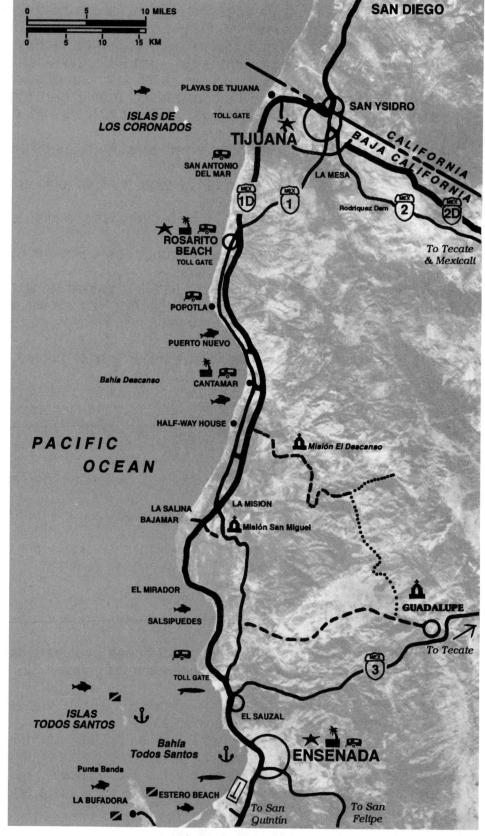

SAN DIEGO

PLAYAS DE TIJUANA

ISLAS DE
LOS CORONADOS

TOLL GATE

SAN YSIDRO

TIJUANA

CALIFORNIA
BAJA CALIFORNIA

SAN ANTONIO
DEL MAR

LA MESA

MEX 1D

MEX 1

Rodriquez Dam

MEX 2

MEX 2D

To Tecate
& Mexicali

ROSARITO
BEACH
TOLL GATE

POPOTLA

PUERTO NUEVO

Bahía Descanso

CANTAMAR

HALF-WAY HOUSE

PACIFIC
OCEAN

Misión El Descanso

LA SALINA
BAJAMAR

LA MISION

Misión San Miguel

EL MIRADOR

SALSIPUEDES

GUADALUPE

MEX 3

To Tecate

TOLL GATE

ISLAS
TODOS SANTOS

EL SAUZAL

Bahía
Todos Santos

ENSENADA

Punta Banda

ESTERO BEACH

LA BUFADORA

To San
Quintín

To San
Felipe

SEE RL 7

SEE RL 13 & RL 15

ROADLOG 3

TIJUANA-ENSENADA...70 miles, 112 kilometers.

The inset map of the Tijuana city map in this book describes how to get on the correct road after crossing the border, I suggest you look at it as road signs are inadequate and many people get lost. My directions lead you to the toll road, México 1D.

K0   As you cross the border into Tijuana pass under the arch and look for the "Ensenada Cuota" sign. Keep in the lane next to the right-hand lane but bear left as the "Ensenada Cuota" road curves left and you will come out heading west on a divided road next to the border fence. After 2 miles the road turns left (just after the crest of a steep hill), get into right lane, take Playas - Ensenada cuota turn-off.

K9   México 1D curves left, (south) at intersection with Playas de Tijuana road. Do not take Playas de Tijuana road, stay to left.

K10   Toll gate. 3 tolls between here and Ensenada. No tolls south of Ensenada.

K19+   Real del Mar. Golf course and homes.

K22   San Antonio del Mar resort development and Baja Malibu are on right. El Oasis RV Parkust ahead on right.

K29+   Rosarito Beach, road to right passes through town. Road coming in from left (north) is old, non-toll road from Tijuana.

K34+   Road right to the non-toll free road that parallels divided México 1D for next 20 miles. Free road is generally in poor condition but allows easy access to numerous resorts, trailer parks and restaurants. We stay on toll-road, México 1D. Second toll gate ahead.

K49   Puerto Nuevo turn-off. Good, reasonably priced lobster dinners.

K53   Cantamar. Small town with some services.

K65+   La Misión turn-off. Trailer park Alisitos, La Fonda and La Misión restaurants. Free (libre) road continues south under toll road, turning inland past ruins of Misión San Miguel; (ruins) and rejoins México 1D north of Ensenada.

K72   Outdoor Resorts RV park and just beyond is the La Salina turn off to several beaches with camping.

K77+   Jatay and Bajamar, new development of American homes around golf courses.

K83+   El Mirador turn-off. Restaurant, bar, gift shop, restrooms, wonderful view, during the winter months you'll see whales on their migrations north and south. Drive carefully as you continue south, there are some really **big dips** ahead caused from the land settling down into the ocean.

K87   Salsipuedes. Camping and fishing.

K94   Playa Saldamando. Camping. More big dips ahead.

K99   Toll gate. This is the last one. Just ahead is San Miguel village and libre road from La Misión (see above).

K100   Ensenada libre road rejoins highway. Proceed past various factories and warehouses. Large Pemex gas station on left with Magna Sin (unleaded) and diesel.

K102   Side road to left is México 3 from Tecate. El Sauzal. Numerous RV Parks along here. **Propane** station ahead on left.

K109+   Follow road right at fork to Ensenada Centro. After third speed bump is "Delegación de Servicios Migratórios" (Immigration Office) on the right where you can pick up your visas - needed if you are going south.

K112   Enter downtown **Ensenada** Intersection of Blvd. Azueta and Blvd. Lázaro Cárdenas.

End of Log...

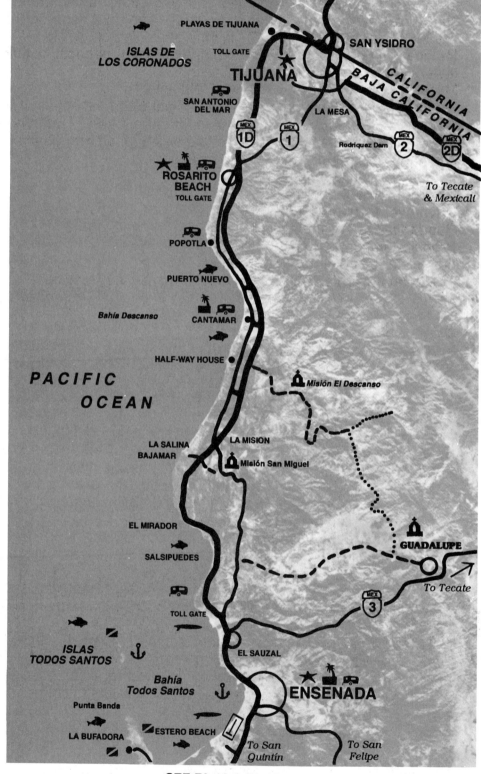

SAN DIEGO

0   5   10 MILES

0   5   10   15   KM

PLAYAS DE TIJUANA

TOLL GATE

SAN YSIDRO

ISLAS DE
LOS CORONADOS

TIJUANA

CALIFORNIA

BAJA CALIFORNIA

SAN ANTONIO
DEL MAR

LA MESA

MEX
1D

MEX
1

Rodriquez Dam

MEX
2

MEX
2D

ROSARITO
BEACH

TOLL GATE

*To Tecate
& Mexicali*

POPOTLA

PUERTO NUEVO

Bahía Descanso

CANTAMAR

HALF-WAY HOUSE

**PACIFIC
OCEAN**

Misión El Descanso

LA SALINA
BAJAMAR

LA MISION

Misión San Miguel

EL MIRADOR

SALSIPUEDES

GUADALUPE

To Tecate

TOLL GATE

MEX
3

ISLAS
TODOS SANTOS

EL SAUZAL

*Bahía
Todos Santos*

ENSENADA

Punta Banda

ESTERO BEACH

LA BUFADORA

*To San
Quintín*

*To San
Felipe*

SEE RL 7

SEE RL 13 & RL 15

ROADLOG 5

TIJUANA-MEXICALI...105 miles, 169 kilometers.

This log takes you via the old road. A new toll road (almost finished at this writing) begins in Otay Mesa and parallels the old road much of the way.

From the Tijuana Border crossing stay in the right hand lane and continue on the Rio Tijuana/Zona Rio road. This puts you on Paseo de Los Heroes. Continue along this divided road until you come to the traffic circle with the statue of a man on a horse in the center. Turn right here, go 2 signals to Blvd Agua Caliente and turn left. This is the beginning of the old road to Tecate and Mexicali. If you are lost, look for the two tall identical buildings, the "twin towers", they are on Blvd. Agua Caliente.

M 0.0   Mileage at beginning of Blvd. Agua Caliente.

For the next 6 miles you will pass by Tijuana's finest hotels, the famous Agua Caliente race track, lots of businesses and markets. Traffic is generally very heavy on this street. After 7 miles you can turn left and go over and catch the toll road if you prefer - we continue straight.

M 6.9   Large Pemex station on right.
M 7.6   Road narrows to 2 lanes.
M 8.6   Drive over Rodriquez Dam.
M 10.5   Road to left to Tijuana Airport.
M 14.7   Propane station.
M 21.5   La Quinta, cattle farms everywhere.
M24.7   Prison on left. This is one of the harshest prisons in México.

(continued on RL 8)

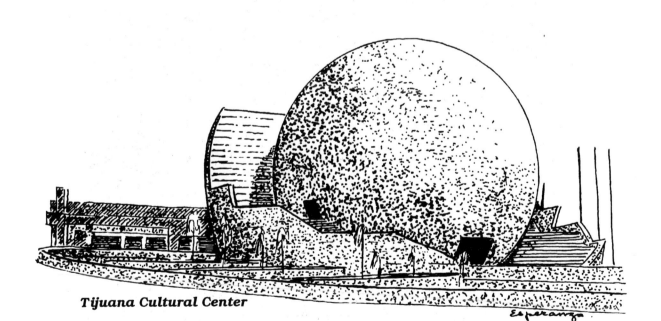

Tijuana Cultural Center

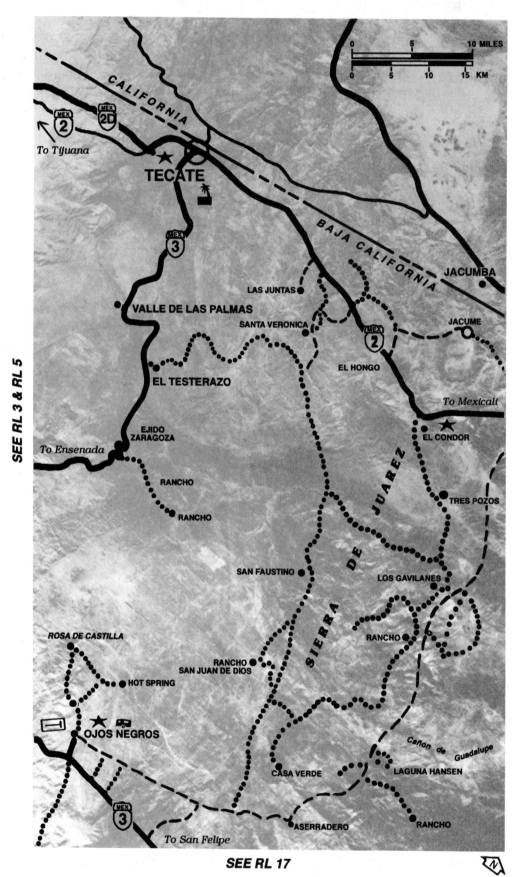

SEE RL 3 & RL 5

SEE RL 9

CALIFORNIA

To Tijuana

TECATE

BAJA CALIFORNIA

JACUMBA

LAS JUNTAS

VALLE DE LAS PALMAS

SANTA VERONICA

JACUME

EL HONGO

EL TESTERAZO

To Mexicali

EL CONDOR

EJIDO
ZARAGOZA

To Ensenada

RANCHO

TRES POZOS

RANCHO

SAN FAUSTINO

LOS GAVILANES

SIERRA   DE   JUAREZ

RANCHO

ROSA DE CASTILLA

RANCHO
SAN JUAN DE DIOS

HOT SPRING

Cañon   de   Guadalupe

OJOS NEGROS

CASA VERDE

LAGUNA HANSEN

ASERRADERO

RANCHO

To San Felipe

SEE RL 17

N

TECATE-ENSENADA...67 miles, 119 kilometers.

Entering through the Tecate border station (open 6:00 AM to Midnight) continue straight four blocks to Avenida Benito Juarez and turn left. Go left one block and turn right on Calle Ortiz Rubio, this is México highway 3. Continue straight south. This trip leads you through some of the valleys where famous Tecate pottery is made. The earth here is good red clay. You'll also pass through the vineyards of L.A. Cetto and Domecq. It is pleasant drive, the road is 2 lane and wider than México 1.

K3	Pass over the Tijuana - Mexicali toll road.
K16.5	Rancho Los Carlos with signs of pottery being made here.
K31	Valle de Las Palmas. A large broad agricultural valley where olives, grapes, and grains are grown. Gas and diesel are available here.
K 40	Altitude 660 meters, with a view forever.
K 73	Domecq winery and vineyards. Free tours and wine tasting.
K 77	Valle of Guadalupe. There is an interesting community museum here. Turn right, 3 miles for Ejido Francisco Zarco.
K 81	Vineyards of L. A. Cetto Winery.
K 86	Rancho María Teresa off to the right. Camping, full hook-ups for RVs.
K 95	San Antonio de Las Minas. Small community, no services.
K105	Go over bridge and go left for Ensenada, 10 Km.

(End of log)

Road Runner

TIJUANA-MEXICALI...*(continued from RL6)*

M25.4	A toll road on-ramp. Toll is based on number of axles on your vehicle. Free road continues to left under the toll road. We take toll road. After getting on toll road we realized the free road was definitely more picturesque - winding through the valleys and towns.
M 30.3	Ensenada turn-off on your right via México 3.
M30.4	Tecate turn-off.
M 33.6	Freeway ends here (June 1995); however, construction is going on and appears near finished in many areas between here and Mexicali.
M 42.3	Rancho Banchetti.
M 42.7	Rancho Ojai.
M 46.8	El Hongo. Ojos Negros. This graded dirt road connects to the road between Ensenada and San Felipe after approximately 55 miles or 90 Kms.
M 48.5	Ejido Chula Vista.
M 61.4	Large Pemex station, Magna Sin and diesel.
M 67.6	Entering La Rumorosa, all services here. Check out the bakery.
M 71.4	Toll Road on-ramp.

(continued on RL10)

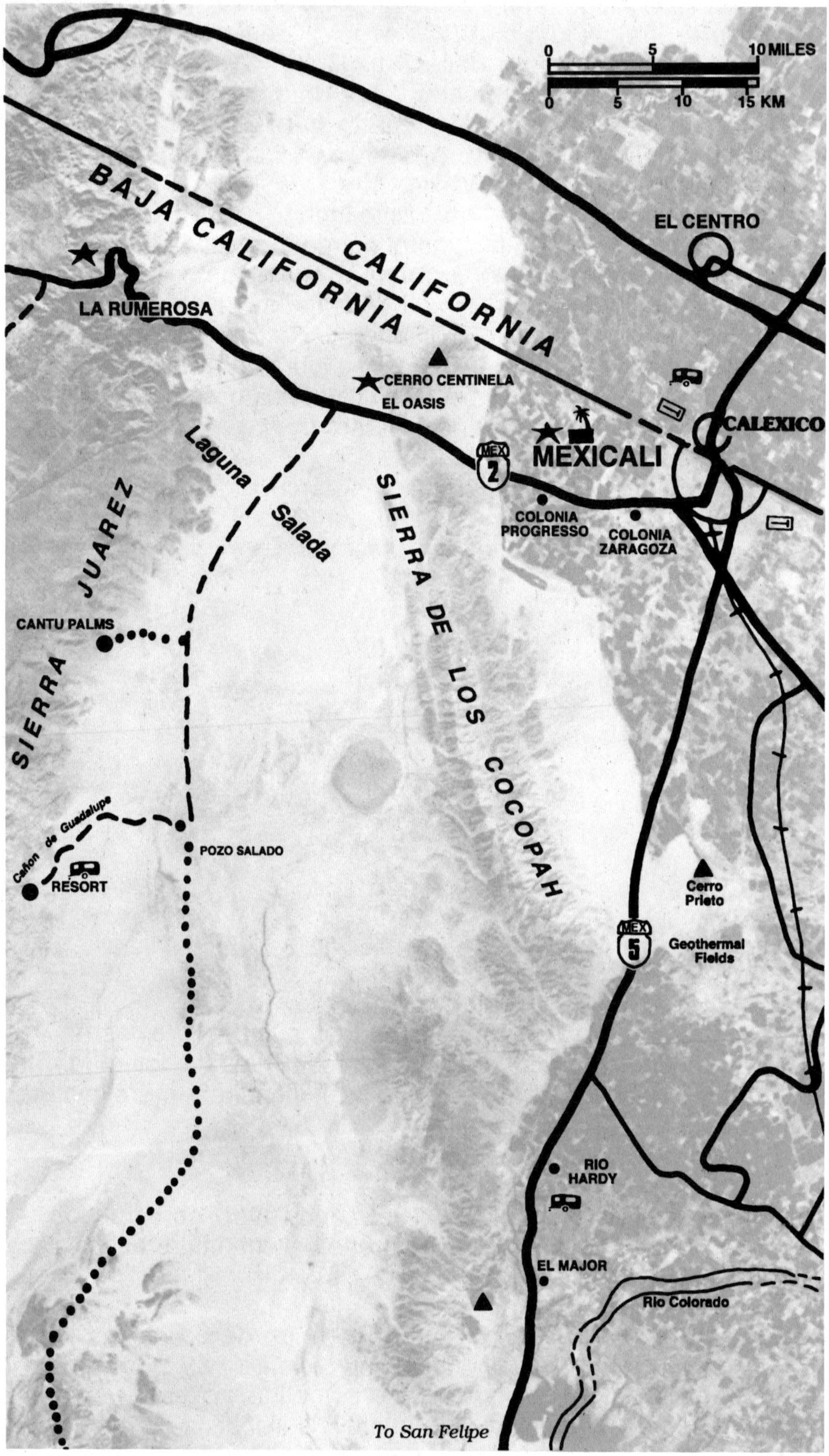

BAJA BOOK IV

10 MILES
15 KM

CALIFORNIA

EL CENTRO

BAJA CALIFORNIA

LA RUMEROSA

CERRO CENTINELA
EL OASIS

CALEXICO

MEX 2

MEXICALI

SEE RL 7

Laguna Salada

COLONIA PROGRESSO
COLONIA ZARAGOZA

SIERRA JUAREZ

SIERRA DE LOS COCOPAH

CANTU PALMS

SEE RL 11

Cañon de Guadalupe
RESORT

POZO SALADO

Cerro Prieto

MEX 5

Geothermal Fields

RIO HARDY

EL MAJOR

Rio Colorado

To San Felipe

SEE RL 19

N

ROADLOG 9

TIJUANA-MEXICALI... *(continued from RL8)*

M 72.4 Imposing granite mountains with Manzanita trees growing out of the cracks between the boulders. Now we begin our ascent down the Cantú grade. Twelve miles - all down hill. Lots of turn-outs and places to get water for the radiator. The view down into the Imperial Valley with the Salton Sea in the distance is awesome.

M 86.2 Bottom of the grade.

M96.0 Guadalupe Canyon Resort turn-off to the right. The resort is located 34 miles from here over washboard and rougher road. (After 27 miles turn right for another 7 miles). The canyon has private campsites with mineral baths. One-hundred twenty-five degree mineral water flows from the earth at the rate of 120,000 gallons per day. Within the palm oasis there is also a cold water stream that flows all year. Tours to nearby rock art sites can be arranged at the camp.

M 108.9 A traffic light - you are on the outskirts of Mexicali. Follow signs to *garita internacional* to return to the United States.

End of log...

Adobe Oven

MEXICALI-SAN FELIPE...116 miles, 187 kilometers.

From the border crossing at Calexico continue south along Calzada Lopez Mateos to México 5 south to San Felipe. Miles start at zero at the border.

M 8.5 Bear right on México 5.

M 32.2 Rio Hardy. Water sports on the waters of the Colorado river. At one time this area was great for duck hunters. Every year my dad and my husband came here for limits on duck, quail and sometimes geese. Now the area is built up and the birds fly on by. Some hunting is still done on the delta but the Mexican government has made it a paperwork and permit affair. Not only that, now you must have an approved guide with you.

M 88.0 Intersection of México 3 from Ensenada.

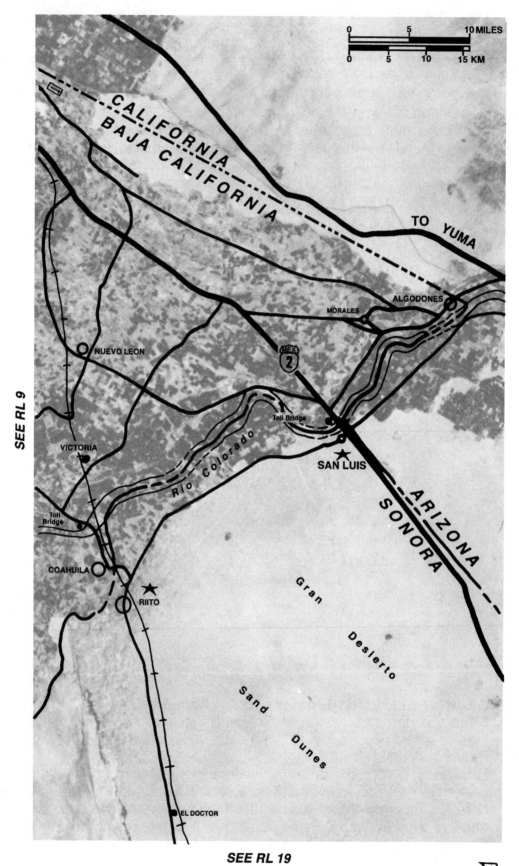

SEE RL 9

10 MILES

15 KM

CALIFORNIA

BAJA CALIFORNIA

TO YUMA

ALGODONES

MORALES

MEX 2

NUEVO LEON

Toll Bridge

VICTORIA

Rio Colorado

Toll Bridge

SAN LUIS

ARIZONA

SONORA

Toll
Bridge

COAHUILA

RIITO

Gran

Desierto

Sand

Dunes

EL DOCTOR

SEE RL 19

N

ROADLOG 11

ANIMALITOS...

Baja, though mostly a desert, has lots of animals and bugs. Lynx, raccoons, red-tailed foxes, bighorn sheep, deer, mountain goats, antelope, jack rabbits, cotton-tailed rabbits, wild pigs, burros, mountain lions (puma), cougars, coyotes, shrews, kangaroo rats, white footed mice are some of the animals. Bird-watchers can have a field day, Scammon's Lagoon and San Quintín bay are prolific with birds, eagles, hawks, falcons, migratory game birds, quail, dove, geese, black brant and many kinds of shorebirds.

Baja has its share of creepy crawlers too. Some of these are described here.

Centipedes: Centipedes hide under damp wood and seem to prefer sandy soil. They do sting and, like the scorpion, have a poison similar to a bee-sting. The darker the color, the more poisonous the bite. They range in color from pale yellow to black and are found all over Baja.

Mata venado spiders: A very large spider, about 4 inches across with long legs and fuzz on the body, runs very fast. White or brown color depending on area where it lives. It is said they can kill a deer, in humans their bite causes paralysis and amnesia. Not common in Baja but some do exist in the south.

Wingless wasp: Looks like a large fuzzy white or brownish ant. Stings like a wasp. Common in the southern portion of Baja.

Diamond back rattlesnake: Common all over Baja. Poisonous.

Yellow-bellied sea snake: Black on top with brightly colored yellow on the bottom. Avoid at all costs; highly venomous. Although not common in the waters off of Baja there have been a few seen both on the Pacific side and in the Sea of Cortez. Sometimes found washed up on shore - still alive.

Scorpions:
Scorpions come out at night to feed. During the day- time they live beneath the soil. They do sting and should be avoided. Should you get stung, the poison is similar to that of a bee- sting and antihistamines will relieve the itching and irritation. The darker the color of the scorpion the more potent the poison. Their colors range from pale yellow to red to black. They are found all over Baja.

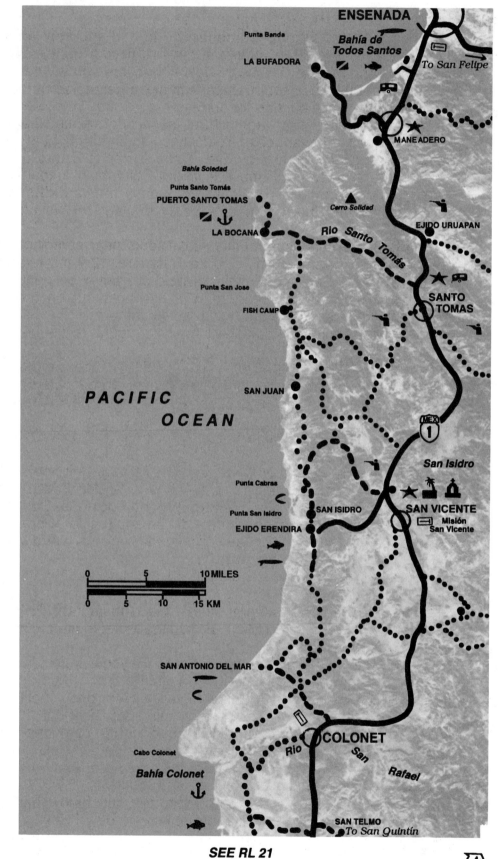

B A J A   B O O K   I V

ENSENADA

Punta Banda

Bahía de Todos Santos

LA BUFADORA

To San Felipe

MANEADERO

Bahía Soledad

Punta Santo Tomás

PUERTO SANTO TOMAS

Cerro Solidad

LA BOCANA

EJIDO URUAPAN

Rio Santo Tomás

Punta San Jose

SANTO TOMAS

FISH CAMP

PACIFIC OCEAN

SAN JUAN

MEX 1

San Isidro

Punta Cabras

SAN VICENTE

Punta San Isidro

SAN ISIDRO

Misión San Vicente

EJIDO ERENDIRA

0   5   10 MILES

0   5   10   15 KM

SAN ANTONIO DEL MAR

Cabo Colonet

COLONET

Rio   San

Bahía Colonet

Rafael

SAN TELMO
To San Quintín

SEE RL 15

SEE RL 21

N

ROADLOG 13

ENSENADA-SAN QUINTIN...121 miles, 195 kilometers.

K0 Turn right on Blvd. Lázaro Cárdenas, go to end and turn left, going uphill to Ave. Reforma. The large shopping center on your right includes a Gigante superstore and market. This is the last superstore you will see until you reach La Paz, over 800 miles south. Ensenada has other stores of the same type but this one has a large parking lot and is on our road. Stock up now. (300 miles south of here there is an agricultural inspection station; they will confiscate citrus, potatoes and mangoes.) To continue south turn right at this intersection.

K15 Paved road right leads through Ejido Chapultepec to Estero Beach Resort and 3 RV parks. There is an impressive pre-Columbian museum at the Estero Beach Resort. Caution. There are five poorly marked **killer speed bumps** ahead (They call them "topes" - oddly enough this is also the word for gophers).

K21 Maneadero. Farming community. Road forks near center of town, right fork goes to Punta Banda, 8 mi, and La Bufadora, 12.9 mi, left fork up a slight grade is Mex 1. Gas and diesel available at Pemex on right, diesel is in the rear of the station. La Bufadora is a blowhole out on the point. It is an interesting side trip. There are restaurants out there.

K41+ Ejido Uruapan to left. An oak-shaded picnic ground is just below north side of road.

K45 Begin descent down into Santo Tomás Valley. Steep and sharp turns. The original vineyards of the Santo Tomás Winery were located here but frequent storms washed them out and now they planted a new vineyard a few miles south of here.

K48 Dirt road right is to La Bocana and Puerto Santo Tomás, 18 mi, a beautiful section of Baja coastline.

K51 Santo Tomás. El Palomar RV park and restaurant (full hook-ups). It's a short walk from the park to the sparse remains of Misión Santo Tomás. There is also a campground just south of town with no hook-ups. Continue south 5 mi. then begin climbing up long winding hill on south side of arroyo. This hill can be quite dangerous during heavy rains - falling rocks and wet, slimy adobe mud running across the highway.

K78 Paved road right to Ejido Eréndira, 12 mi., and seacoast. Surfing, fishing, shelling and camping.

K89 San Vicente. Gasoline, several stores. Good restaurant, Estrella del Sur, on left past Pemex, English spoken. El Camino Motel (quite basic) is on the south side of town on the left.

K96 Rancho Santa Marta orphanage on right. Beyond is rich, rolling Valle Llano Colorado and many grapes, olives and other crops.

K124 Panadería Carmen on right above highway. Very good "bolillos", these are a crusty french-type roll somewhat football shaped about 8" long. They are baked in brick ovens heated with hardwood in the centuries-old manner. You can find them in most all of the better bakeries here in Baja, however, they sell fast and you might have to ask what time they are ready and come back the next day at that time.

K126+ Cross bridge and enter Colonet. Dirt road right just before bridge goes west to San Antonio del Mar, 7.1 mi. Good clamming and surf fishing.

(continued on RL22)

RL14

B A J A   B O O K   IV

SEE RL 13

SEE RL 17

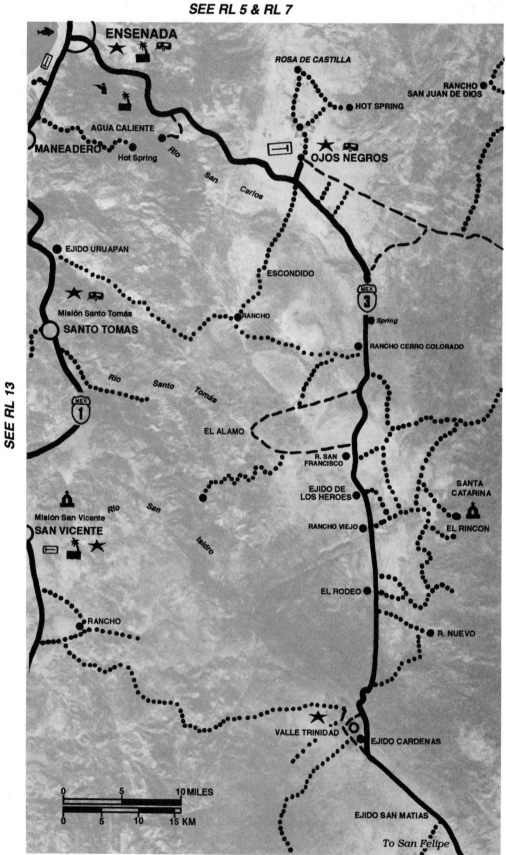

ENSENADA

ROSA DE CASTILLA

RANCHO
SAN JUAN DE DIOS

HOT SPRING

AGUA CALIENTE

MANEADERO

Hot Spring

Rio

San

Carlos

OJOS NEGROS

EJIDO URUAPAN

ESCONDIDO

Misión Santo Tomás

SANTO TOMAS

RANCHO

MEX
3

Spring

RANCHO CERRO COLORADO

Rio   Santo   Tomás

MEX
1

EL ALAMO

R. SAN
FRANCISCO

SANTA
CATARINA

Misión San Vicente

SAN VICENTE

Rio   San

Isidro

EJIDO DE
LOS HEROES

RANCHO VIEJO

EL RINCON

RANCHO

EL RODEO

R. NUEVO

VALLE TRINIDAD

EJIDO CARDENAS

0   5   10 MILES

0   5   10   15 KM

EJIDO SAN MATIAS

To San Felipe

ROADLOG 15

ENSENADA-SAN FELIPE...154 miles, 218 kilometers.

K0   The road to San Felipe from Ensenada is México 3. This part of México 3 begins from the intersection of Calzada Cortez, Ave. Reforma and Ave. Juarez where you go east to San Felipe. Go up long grade through rural section of Ensenada. (Refer to the city map in this book.)

K8   **Propane** station, "Gas Silza" on right behind blue block wall.

K14   Enjoy big frog rock on the left. One of the biggest we have ever seen.

K26   Top of grade. Turn right for Agua Caliente Resort hot springs and motel.

K37   Entering the big beautiful wide valley of Ojos Negros. A prosperous farming community.

K39+   Paved road left goes to the community of Ojos Negros.

K56   Road left leads to Laguna Hanson, 22 miles, mostly washboard. At an elevation of 5500 feet, a refreshing fresh water lake provides a unique week-end getaway spot. For a small fee you can camp at the edge of the lake among the Ponderosa pines and huge granite boulders. The road up there is not recommended for RVs. Outhouses are the only convenience provided. The lake is located in the Parque National Constitución de 1857. A poor dirt road, 4WD only, continues north to La Rumorosa.

K66   Climbing up out of the valley. Notice how the plants and the terrain are changing. You are now on the other side of the peninsular divide. If it is summertime it's now starting to get very warm.

K86   Road right to El Alamo.

K92   Ejido Heroes de la Independencia is to the right. Town has limited services but there is a Pemex station and a few stores. The dirt road to the left leads to the site of Misión Santa Catalina.

K102   El Rodeo, small farming community.

K120   Entering Valle de Trinidad. This prosperous little community has all kinds of services, including a highway rescue vehicle.

K138   Mike's Sky Ranch 22 miles from here. An interesting loop trip for motorcycles and 4WD is to take this road all the way to San Telmo at Mex 1. Not recommended in the rainy season. The road is kept open to the ranch from here but is sometimes impassable the other side. The ranch is located on the edge of Parque National San Pedro Mártir. Trout fishing is a possibility here.

(continued on RL18)

Laguna Hansen

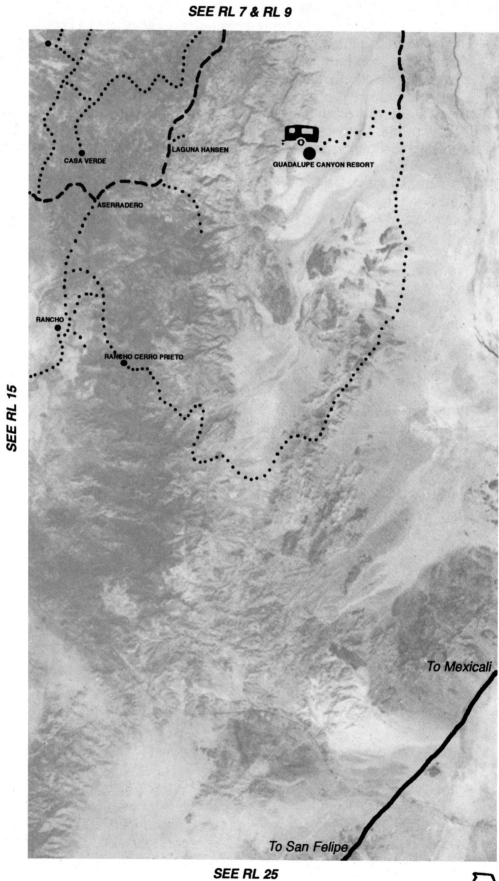

B
A
J
A

B
O
O
K

IV

SEE RL 15

SEE RL 19

CASA VERDE

LAGUNA HANSEN

GUADALUPE CANYON RESORT

ASERRADERO

RANCHO

RANCHO CERRO PRIETO

To Mexicali

To San Felipe

K154   At the top of the mountain to the right, if the sun is behind you, you can see the Observatory glistening among the pine trees. It is located on Picacho del Diablo at 10,156 feet, Baja's highest peak. This observatory has been used as a NASA tracking station. The skies are exceptionally clear from here.

K160   Valle de San Felipe. In 1967 a storm came through here and flooded this valley. A huge wall of water washed into San Felipe almost totally destroying the town. Many homes were totally destroyed and caskets from the graveyard were found floating in the surf. There is a poor dirt road through this valley down to San Felipe from here. Not recently traveled by author.

K196   Crucero Trinidad. Turn right for San Felipe, 28 miles. To the left, 88 miles, is Mexicali.

(continued on RL 26)

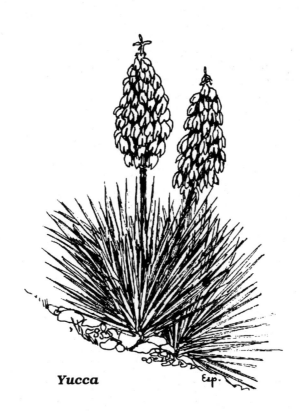

Yucca

YUCCA Spanish Bayonet. Yucca may be either short trees or shrubs, with simple or branched, woody stems. The beautiful cream-colored flowers are mildly fragrant and attract birds and insects. Yuccas are dominant in many desert areas of Baja. The flowers make an excellent salad when seasoned with a vinegar and olive oil dressing. Their flavor resembles avocados and almonds. Trunks are often used for fencing.

B A J A   B O O K   I V

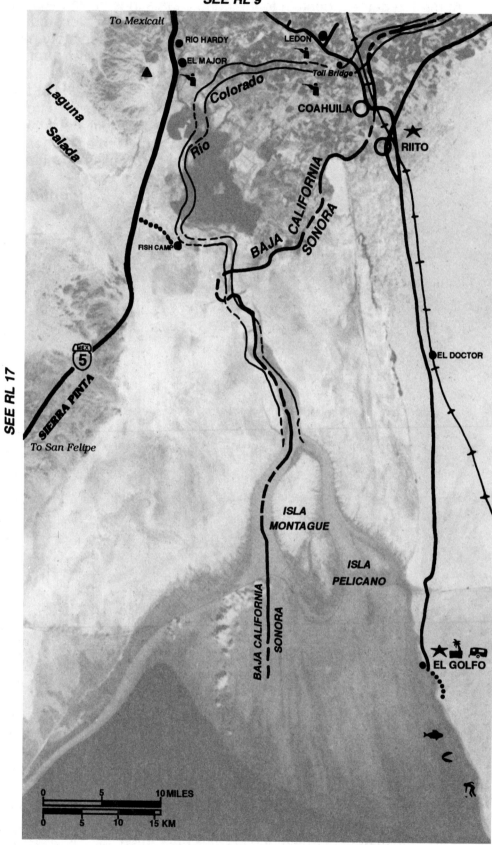

To Mexicali

RIO HARDY

EL MAJOR

LEDON

Toll Bridge

Laguna

Salada

Colorado

Rio

COAHUILA

BAJA CALIFORNIA

SONORA

RIITO

SEE RL 17

FISH CAMP

MEX 5

SIERRA PINTA

EL DOCTOR

To San Felipe

ISLA
MONTAGUE

ISLA
PELICANO

BAJA CALIFORNIA

SONORA

EL GOLFO

0   5   10 MILES

0   5   10   15 KM

N

ROADLOG 19

ENTRYWAY TO MISION SAN IGNACIO

CENTRAL BAJA CALIFORNIA

RL20

B A J A   B O O K   IV

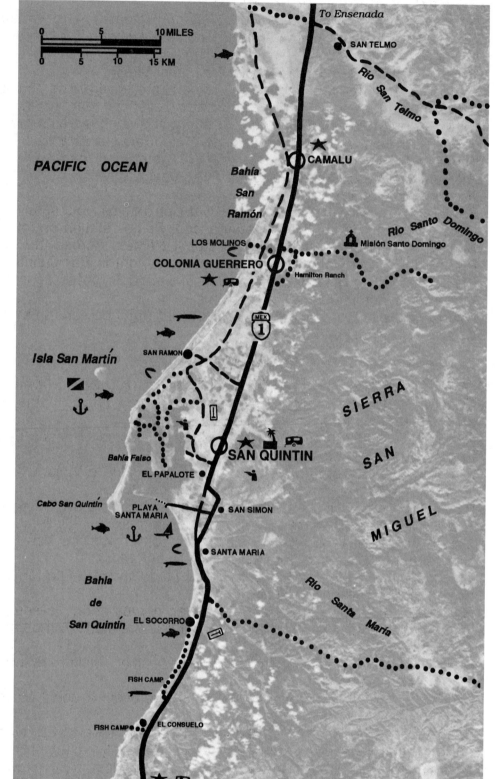

ROADLOG 21

ENSENADA-SAN QUINTIN...*(from RL14)*

K140+   Road left to San Telmo 8 km, Meling Ranch (40 miles) and Parque Nacional San Pedro Mártir (60 miles). México 1 continues south. For info on side trip to Meling Ranch see RL 24.

K149   Dirt road right to San Jacinto Trailer Park near beach.

K157   Camalú,a small farming settlement. To west are several fine fishing, camping and clamming beaches. Large Pemex has diesel and Magna Sin.

K169   Enter Colonia Guerrero. On right at signal is Distribudora Sanchez, a good auto parts place, same owner also has Motel Sanchez next to it. Just south is bridge over Río Santo Domingo. At K172+ is graded road right to Don Pepe RV Park and Posada Don Diego RV Park. Beach 2 miles.

K173   **Propane** station on right.

K190   **San Quintín.** Misión Santa Isabel Cafe on left as you enter town (about K188) is good and very reasonably priced. Pemex station on left has Magna Sin, Nova and diesel. Ice plant just past Pemex. Across the street "Agua Purificado", good water. South, one mile on right is Bar Quintín and Motel Chavez, cafe has good food, owner speaks good English. Tourist information. This area is famous for it's Pismo clams.

K195   Road right is to Old Mill Motel and RV park (full hook-ups), Rancho Sereño Bed and Breakfast and Ernestos.

End of log...

SAN QUINTIN-PARADOR PUNTA PRIETA...174 miles, 280 kilometers.

K0   Continue south on México 1 through the world's largest tomato producing area. Tomatoes are shipped world-wide from here.

K1   Road right to Old Mill Motel & RV Park, (full hook-ups), Rancho Sereño Bed & Breakfast and Ernestos Trailer park.

K4   El Papalote. Alternate right turn to Old Mill and Muelle Viejo. Continue S and SE past bridge over the Río Santa María flood plain.

K10   Paved road right 3 mi. to Hotel La Pinta and Cielito Lindo Motel, restaurant and campground. This restaurant is world famous for it's fresh stone-crab dinner, be early!. White sandy beach with sand crabs the size of your hand. Surf fishing and boats for hire. Light boat launch ramp.

K14   Junction with another road back to Cielito Lindo and Hotel La Pinta.

K16   Road right to El Pabellón campground.

K23   Road right to El Soccoro. Many American homes here. To south are a few unimproved campsites on small coves. At K35 the bluffs to the left yield many fossil shells.

K41+   Road right to old Rancho El Consuelo. Good fishing. Main road turns inland up arroyo. Many sharp curves.

K52   Las Brisas farming community. Just past here begin descent down Arroyo El Rosario.

K55+   Past Pemex with Magna Sin and into El Rosario. Meals at Espinosa's Place on left (before México 1 turns left) and supplies at market on right. Mission museum on right across from second gas station. Road right follows north side of arroyo to ocean, (7 mi). Sinai RV Park is located on the north side of the road after the road turns left.

(continued on page RL28)

**B
A
J
A

B
O
O
K

IV**

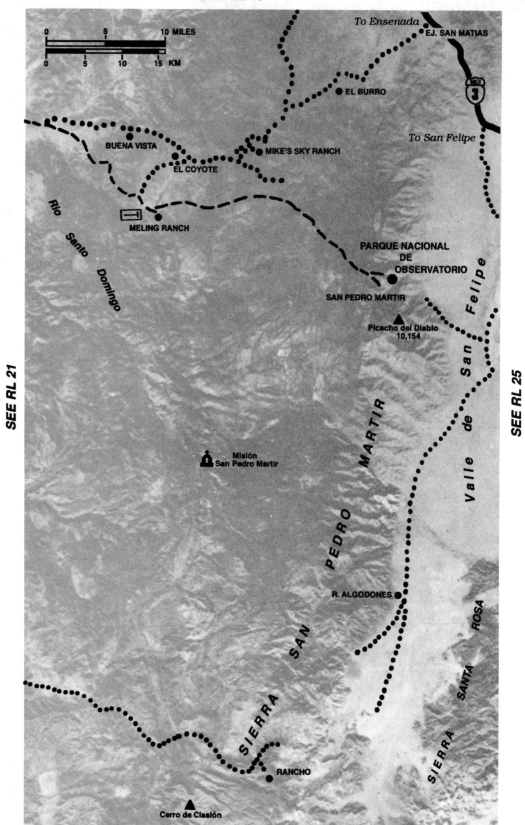

To Ensenada

EJ. SAN MATIAS

EL BURRO

3

To San Felipe

BUENA VISTA

MIKE'S SKY RANCH

EL COYOTE

Rio
Santo
Domingo

MELING RANCH

PARQUE NACIONAL
DE
OBSERVATORIO

SAN PEDRO MARTIR

Picacho del Diablo
10,154

Valle de San Felipe

Misión
San Pedro Martir

SIERRA SAN PEDRO MARTIR

R. ALGODONES

SIERRA SANTA ROSA

RANCHO

Cerro de Clasión

SEE RL 21

SEE RL 25

N

0   5   10 MILES

0   5   10   15 KM

SIDE TRIP TO MELING RANCH...

K140+   From K140+ of México 1 turn east for Meling Ranch. It is about 40 miles of dirt road to the ranch site. Beyond the ranch another 20 miles is the Observatory on Picacho del Diablo, Baja's highest mountain, 10,154 feet.

Meling Ranch. Originally a cattle ranch on the way to the observatory, it is located at 2200' elevation. Today the ranch is open to the public with comfortable accommodations and good ranch-style food. Horses and guides are available for pack trips to the Sierra San Pedro Mártir.

The ranch was originally founded by Harry Johnson in the early 1900's. He owned nearby gold and silver mines and built the ranch to supply meat to his workers. In 1922 the ranch was burned by bandits but rebuilt by Harry's daughter Alberta and her husband Salve Meling. Their daughter Aida ran the ranch as a guest lodge for many years. On her ham radio she relayed many a desperate message for Americans stranded in Baja and has helped with communications of all kind over the years.

Today you can book for Wilderness Baja trips from the Meling Ranch. They offer mountain lion hunts, saddle trips, trout fishing, quail hunting, cattle drives and gold prospecting trips. For information, call 01152-617-76223 in Ensenada (early morning or after 6 P.M.) or write to Meling Fishing and Hunting Services, P.O. Box 189003-73, Coronado, CA 92178

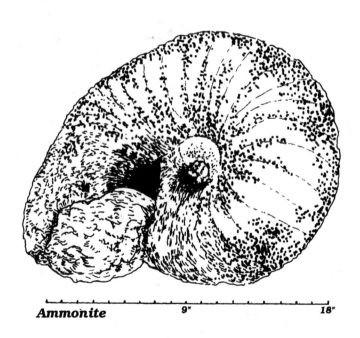

Ammonite   9"   18"

Ammonites are ancient giant snails (cephalopods) that have turned to stone. They lived at the same time as the dinosaurs and are found in Baja not far from the Pacific Ocean near Puerto Santa Catarina.

BAJA BOOK IV

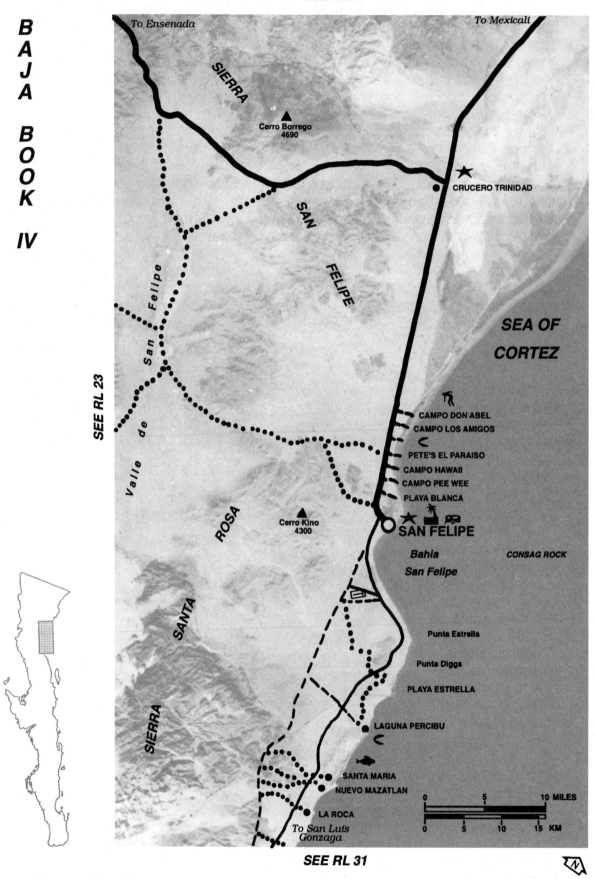

To Ensenada

To Mexicali

SIERRA

Cerro Borrego
4690

SAN

FELIPE

CRUCERO TRINIDAD

San Felipe

SEA OF

CORTEZ

CAMPO DON ABEL

CAMPO LOS AMIGOS

PETE'S EL PARAISO

CAMPO HAWAII

CAMPO PEE WEE

PLAYA BLANCA

Valle de

ROSA

Cerro Kino
4300

SAN FELIPE

Bahia
San Felipe

CONSAG ROCK

Punta Estrella

Punta Diggs

PLAYA ESTRELLA

SANTA

LAGUNA PERCIBU

SIERRA

SANTA MARIA

NUEVO MAZATLAN

0   5   10 MILES

LA ROCA

0   5   10   15 KM

To San Luis
Gonzaga

N

MEXICALI-SAN FELIPE *AND* ENSENADA - SAN FELIPE
        ...(continued from   RL10 & RL18)

K140   El Crucero. Paved road coming in from West is Highway 3 from Ensenada. Just past is small trading post with gas and diesel available from old-fashioned round gas pump.
K172   Campo Don Abel.
K175   Campo Los Amigos.
K178   Pete's Camp, Campo El Paraíso.
K180   Campo Hawaii.
K183   Campo Pee Wee.
K186   Playa Blanca.
K188   Entering the outskirts of **San Felipe**. Road turns left into town. To continue south, follow road to left then turn right where divided road has a circular park in the middle. Supplies and gas are available here. Diesel fuel is available south of town in front of the marina at the water's edge.

End of log...

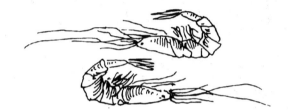

SAN FELIPE-MEXICO 1 AT CHAPALA...81 miles, 130 kilometers.
        As many of you will be trying to find your friend's "villa" (or your future one) along this route, we have listed most of the camps to assist you. We do not use the kilometer reference on this trip as many of the markers are missing; all reference is in miles. Set your odometer to zero.
M0.0   We begin this part at the first fork in the road south of town. Go left here; if you go straight you will go to the airport. Watch out for the **terrible dips** after mile 22.6. They are killers and most are unmarked.
M1.2   Ugly, barren desert.
M3.4   Campo San Fernando RV park.
M4.0   Faro Beach Residential area.
M5.3   Vista Hermosa, beach camping.
M5.4   Punta Estrella
M7.9   Beach Club Patty.
M8.0   Panchos Place.
M12.7   Rancho Percebú.
M13.5   Isla San Martín.
M18.9   Campo Santa María.
M19.2   Campo Mayma.
M19.3   Nuevo Mazatlán.
M19.6   Campo La Jolla.
M19.8   Playa Linda.
M21.0   La Roca.
M21.4   Campo San Pedro.
M21.9   El Vergel.
M22.0   Campo Lupita.
M22.5   Campo Esmeralda.

(continued on RL32)

B A J A

B O O K

IV

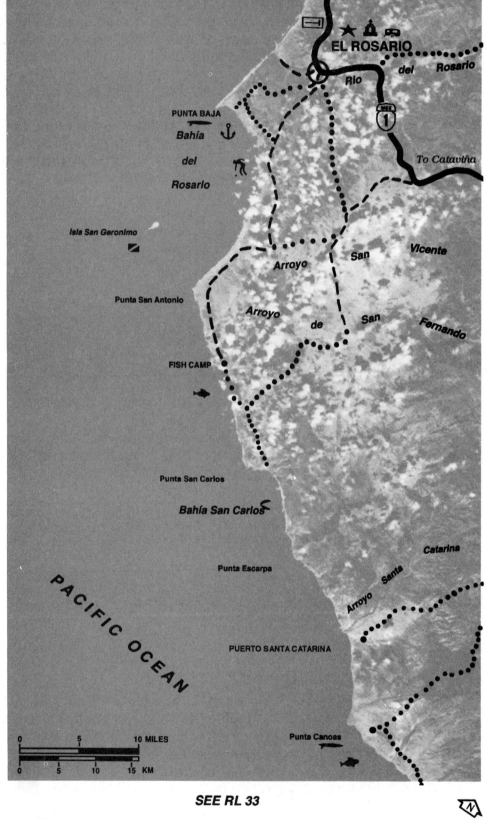

EL CONSUELO ● *To San Quintín*

EL ROSARIO

Rio *del* *Rosario*

MEX 1

To Cataviña

PUNTA BAJA

Bahía

del

Rosario

Isla San Geronimo

Arroyo *San* *Vicente*

Punta San Antonio

Arroyo *de* *San* *Fernando*

FISH CAMP

Punta San Carlos

Bahía San Carlos

Catarina

Punta Escarpa

Arroyo *Santa*

PUERTO SANTA CATARINA

PACIFIC OCEAN

Punta Canoas

| 0 | 5 | 10 MILES |

| 0 | 5 | 10 | 15 | KM |

SEE RL 29

SEE RL 33

N

ROADLOG 27

SAN QUINTIN...PARADOR PUNTA PRIETA...*(from page RL22)*

K62　　Highway crosses the wide arroyo on a large new bridge and climbs into the hills. Back up arroyo on left side is interesting rock formation called "El Castillo" - the castle. Before this bridge was built, floods in this valley were common and traffic was held up for as much as twelve days at a time.

K75　　You are now entering the "real" Baja with it's unusual plants; the cirio tree - those funny looking upside down carrots, pitahaya cactus with it's fabled fruits, elephant trees with their twisted trunks and the giant cardóns, the sergeants of the desert. You will see many of these before leaving Baja.

K78　　Signed, graded road south to Puerto San Carlos, 38 mi. Good surf fishing and several tiny coves where inflatable boats or car-toppers may be launched. Quite windy in spring and summer. At km. 82 there is a good view to the north of Baja's highest peak, Picacho del Diablo at 10,154 feet.

(continued on page RL30)

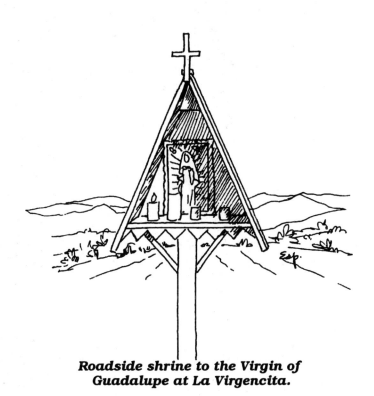

*Roadside shrine to the Virgin of
Guadalupe at La Virgencita.*

Shrines along the roadside exist throughout Baja and México. Most of the shrines are in honor of the Virgin of Guadalupe, the patron saint and protector of México. In 1531 an apparition of the Virgin is said to have appeared to an Indian in the city of Guadalupe Hidalgo near present day México City. Each year thousands of pilgrims from all over the world go to the shrine, holiest in México. Here in Baja many of the shrines have candles burning and a jar filled with a few coins.

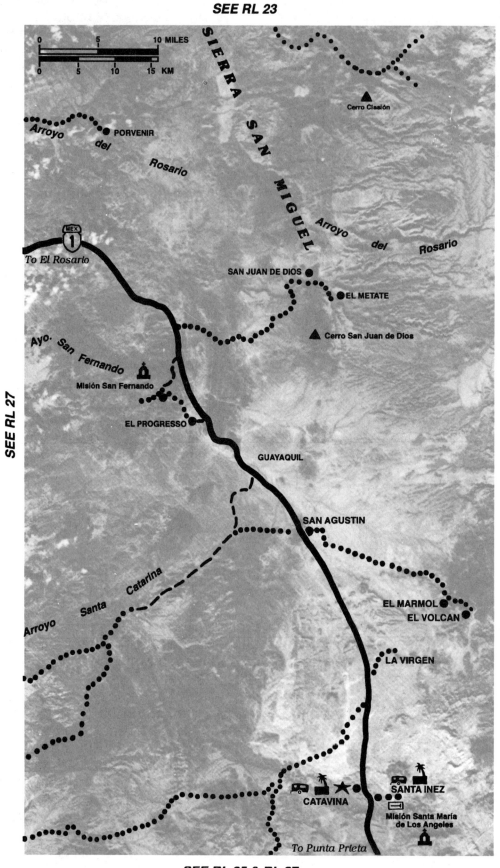

BAJA BOOK IV

ROADLOG 29

SAN QUINTIN-PARADOR PUNTA PRIETA...*(from RL28)*

K88+   Down hill to south is La Turquesa, a working turquoise mine. Some fine stones have come from here. The area is closed to the public.

K114   Dirt road right leads to ruins of Misión San Fernando Velicatá. The ruins are located about 3 miles from the highway.

K116+   El Progreso just off highway. On left is barren campground where proprietor sometimes sells agatized ammonites. They are found in the canyon on the way to Puerto Santa Catarina.

K125   Los Cuates, the twins. Two seasonal rivers meet here and run together beyond. Just beyond here an enterprising family has set up a 24 hour tire repair shop.

K127   Graded road south to seasonally occupied fishing village of Puerto Santa Catarina approximately 33 Km. from the highway. Guayaquil 1 Km. to the left. an agricultural settlement.

K140+   San Agustín. Road crews stay here temporarily while working on the road. Nothing else here, well went dry.

K142   Rancho Sonora restaurant.

K144   Signed graded road left to El Mármol. About 15 Km from the highway is what is left of a very productive onyx mining settlement. In the early 1900's onyx was cut from the area and trucked to Santa Catarina Landing where it was loaded onto ships. In the 1940's, when my father visited this town, the onyx school house was actively filled with lots of children and the mine was still being worked. Today, no one lives there and the onyx school house is slowly disappearing. Still it is an interesting side trip. You can also go on a 3 mile hike northeast to El Volcán and actually witness mother nature at work as she makes more onyx for generations to come to enjoy.

K161   This region is known as Las Vírgenes, an area of spectacular rock formations and huge boulders of all shapes and sizes interspersed with cactus and unique Baja plants. To the right, off the highway, is a shrine to the Virgin of Guadalupe. At km. 162 is unmaintained dirt road right to El Faro on the west coast, 45 mi. 4WD, 2 vehicles recommended.

K171+   Dip into Arroyo de Cataviñacito with fresh water that runs across the road almost all year. Notice the blue palms. Up the canyon are Indian rock paintings.

K174+   Cataviña. Gas and diesel available here. The diesel pumps are in the rear. The electricity is off in the afternoons and they cannot pump gas during this time. Between the gas station and the highway, the small cafe, La Enramada, also has a small grocery store in the rear. Cafe has very good food at quite reasonable prices. Hotel across street has all the amenities. There is an RV park, Trailer Park Cataviña, just north of the hotel (hook-ups don't always work). Across from RV Park, a small grocery - snack store, El Tonche.

Misión Santa María de Los Angeles (ruins) is 15 miles east of here. Access to the road to the mission must be obtained from the family who owns the property. The trip is very rugged and not passable to vehicles for the last few miles.

(continued on RL38)

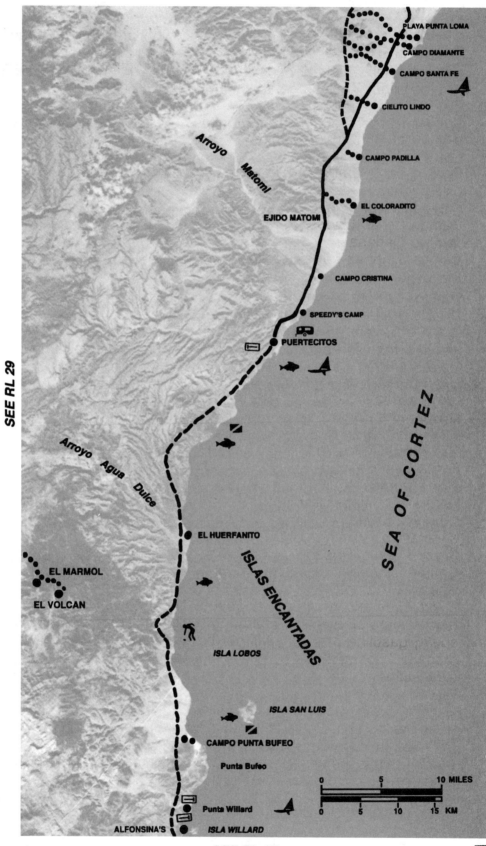

B A J A B O O K IV

SEE RL 29

PLAYA PUNTA LOMA

CAMPO DIAMANTE

CAMPO SANTA FE

CIELITO LINDO

CAMPO PADILLA

EL COLORADITO

EJIDO MATOMI

Arroyo Matomi

CAMPO CRISTINA

SPEEDY'S CAMP

PUERTECITOS

Arroyo Agua Dulce

EL HUERFANITO

EL MARMOL

EL VOLCAN

ISLAS ENCANTADAS

SEA OF CORTEZ

ISLA LOBOS

ISLA SAN LUIS

CAMPO PUNTA BUFEO

Punta Bufeo

Punta Willard

ALFONSINA'S

ISLA WILLARD

ROADLOG 31

SAN FELIPE-MEXICO 1 AT CHAPALA...*(continued from RL26)*

Note: We continue listing the various camps of American home sites until Puertecitos. Distances are in miles.

M22.6	Playa Punta Loma. South of here there are some **terrible dips** in the road. Use caution; there are quite a few of them. Larger vehicles might have to take these dips at an angle.
M22.9	Campo Diamante
M23.4	Campo Santa Fe
M24.0	Campo Villa Del Mar.
M24.1	Campo San Martín.
M24.2	Campo Garcia
M24.7	Playa México.
M25.3	Campo Cielito Lindo.
M25.8	Campo Cadena.
M26.3	Campo Jimenez y Los Gorditos.
M26.7	Playa San Antonio.
M27.2	Campo Padilla.
M27.8	Playa Adriana
M28.2	Playa Sol y Mar & Campo Los Burritos.
M28.5	Campo San José.
M29.0	Campo Feliz.
M29.2	Campo San Francisco.
M30.1	Playa Xanic.
M30.4	Campo Los Pulpos.
M30.6	El Coloradito.
M30.7	Campo El Consuelo.
M31.2	Punta Baja Beach.
M31.5	Playa Dorada.
M31.6	Campo Turistico Vallarta.
M34.0	Campo Cristina,
M38.0	Matomí wash on the right. Great boondocking.
M40.5	Campo Santa Teresa.
M41.2	Campo Toba.
M43.4	Speedy's Camp.
M46.0	Puertecitos and rough roads ahead! There are sulfur pools here, they have fenced them off and now charge for a dip but it's worth it. If you are continuing south, gasoline probably will not be available until you reach México 1, nor groceries, nor fresh water. Mileages start back at zero.
M0.0	Puertecitos.
M5.5	La Costilla.
M17.6	Nacho's camp. More American "Villas by the Sea".
M39.0	Road left to Punta Bufeo. Airstrip, meals, homes.
M42.0	Road left to Papa Fernandez' camp. Meals. Camping. Boats for rent and a nice beach. This is the desert; critters are likely here. In the summer, huge gusts of wind come off of the desert so tie everything down.

(continued on RL36

B A J A   B O O K   IV

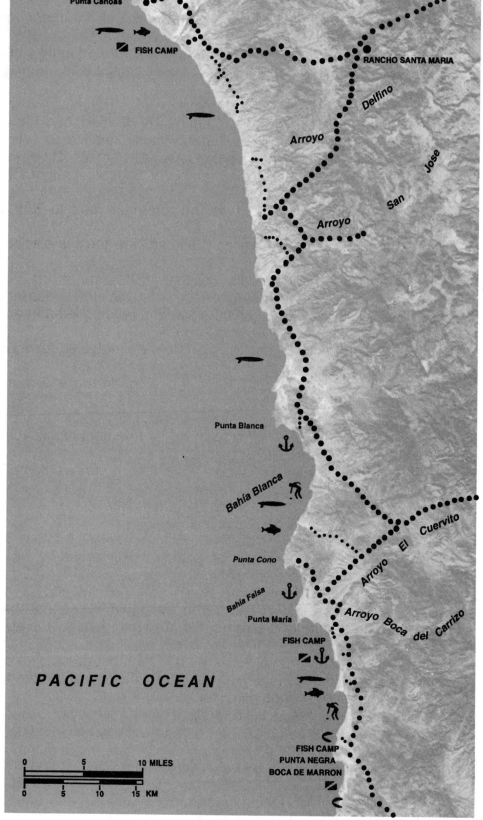

SEE RL 35 & 37

Punta Canoas

FISH CAMP

RANCHO SANTA MARIA

Delfino

Arroyo

Jose

San

Arroyo

Punta Blanca

Bahía Blanca

El   Cuervito

Punta Cono

Arroyo

Bahía Falsa

Arroyo   Boca   del   Carrizo

Punta María

FISH CAMP

PACIFIC   OCEAN

FISH CAMP
PUNTA NEGRA
BOCA DE MARRON

0   5   10 MILES

0   5   10   15 KM

N

PUNTA CANOAS-SANTA ROSALILLITA SIDE TRIP...159 miles, 255 km.

This off-road adventure begins at Km 127 near Guayaquil of the San Quintín-Parador Punta Prieta log. Route is for 4WD vehicles and it is recommended that two vehicles travel together. Very rough roads no gas stations, no grocery stores, no water and sometimes no people. Stay on the most well-traveled road at all times. There are no kilometer markers so we go by miles. This route encompasses maps on RL27, RL29, RL33 and RL45.

M0.0	Leave México 1 at K127 heading west.
M7.1	Road comes in from right rear. Continue on graded road through valley. After about 12.5 miles you will pass Rancho Santa Catarina on your right.
M20.7	Take left fork. Right goes to Santa Catarina, 16 miles. Do not attempt this side trip to Santa Catarina if its been raining or appears it might. The bottom of the valley turns into a sea of mud.
M35.0	Road comes in from right. It is the alternate road to Santa Catarina. We continue straight.
M41.2	Right fork goes to Punta Canoas. You can view the sea elephants from the top of the cliffs out there.
M43.6	Right road leads to seasonally occupied fish camp on the beach - about 1.4 mile. Just beyond, 2 other side roads lead to isolated beaches; seen a few die-hard surfers out here. We continue straight, bearing left and inland.
M57.6	Rancho Santa María, sometimes occupied.
M60.1	At intersection turn right and stay on most well-traveled road. Left goes back to México 1 near Cataviña, 25 miles, usually passable.
M77.3	Road to left continues south. Right road goes to the beach at 3 miles. We go left.
M82.8	Turn right. Follow Arroyo San José to beach.
M88.0	Road follows the shoreline for 16 miles. Some great campsites.
M104.0	Punta Blanca to right .8 mi. we go left.
M115.2	Turn right at the fork. This is a very bad stretch of road. If you have 4WD, now you know why you spent the money.
M120.2	Road right goes to Playa Blanca. We go straight.
M125.2	Road right to Punta Cono, 3.5 miles.
M128.5	Road right leads to Playa María fish camp, about 2.5 miles. This is the top of Playa María Bay. Clamming is great here as witnessed by the shells.
M132.5	Road right leads to nice campsite.
M135.5	Seasonally occupied fish camp.
M144.0	Road right leads to Boca de Marrón. Beautiful wide sandy beach with lots of pismos. The people of the fish camp are very friendly. It is about 9 miles from the fish camp to...
M153.0	Road right leads to Punta Santa Rosalillita and a graded road to the highway. Road left leads back to the highway but it is longer and more treacherous than the one further on. We go right.
M156.6	Turn left. Straight ahead is Alejandro's camp - surfing.
M160.6	Turn left to return to México 1. A right turn leads you into the fishing village of Santa Rosalillita, 1.5 mi.
M168.8	México 1. You are at Km 38 between Parador Punta Prieta and Jesús María. It is 36 miles to Jesús María to the south, or, to the north it is 24 miles to Parador Punta Prieta. Gas is generally available in Jesús María and seldom available at Parador Punta Prieta.

End of side trip...

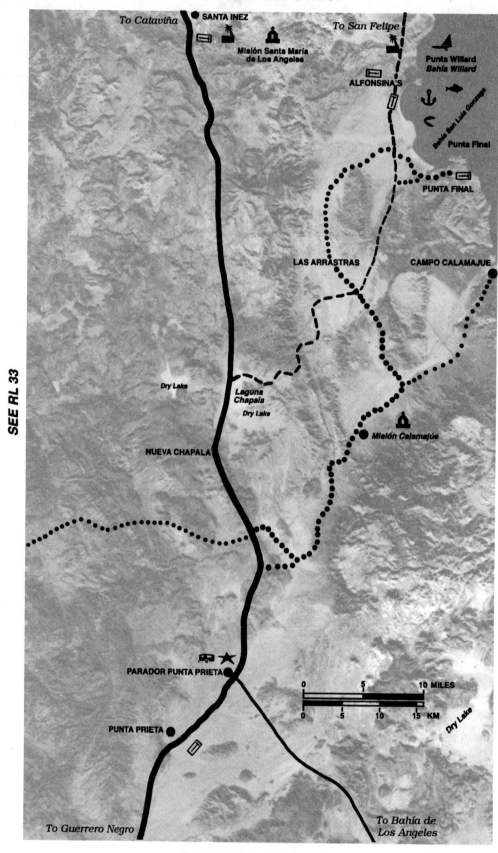

BAJA BOOK IV

To Cataviña
SANTA INEZ
Misión Santa María de Los Angeles
To San Felipe
Punta Willard
Bahía Willard
ALFONSINA'S
Bahía San Luis Gonzaga
Punta Final
PUNTA FINAL
LAS ARRASTRAS
CAMPO CALAMAJUE
Dry Lake
Laguna Chapala
Dry Lake
Misión Calamajúe
NUEVA CHAPALA
PARADOR PUNTA PRIETA
0   5   10 MILES
0   5   10   15 KM
Dry Lake
PUNTA PRIETA
To Guerrero Negro
To Bahía de Los Angeles

SAN FELIPE-MEXICO 1 AT CHAPALA...*(continued from RL 32)*

M44.6   Road right to Alphonsinas, 2 miles. A restaurant, modest rooms for rent. More villas. Gasoline is sometimes available.

M56.3   Road right to Punta Final. There are quite a few homes out there now. It is almost 10 miles out and they don't welcome strangers.

M64.0   Las Arrastras de Arriola. Here is where we used to dump out our stateside water and refill our tanks with the sweetest water we had ever found. The man who lived here and supplied the water to us wanted no money for his efforts to haul the bucket up from the deep well but he sure welcomed the fresh oranges we gave him. The water from here is now not as sweet as it was and it is no longer free.

M68.0   Road right goes 12.5 miles to México 1 at Km 229 just north of Laguna Chapala.

A left turn here at M68.0 leads to Arroyo Calamajué, about 5 miles. This is a good side trip for 4WD vehicles. When you get to Calamajué canyon a left turn will lead you 10 miles to the gulf at Bahía Calamajué. This small bay provides some good fishing at high tide on either end. If you have a small boat you can carry over the rocky shoreline to the water just off shore are white seabass and large grouper. There are also totuava here; they are endangered, please don't take them.

A right turn at the intersection with the canyon will lead you down through Calamajué canyon. The canyon is narrow with high walls of shale, shist and slate. In areas where the walls recede you can look back up and see green meadows with deer feeding. Small holes in the canyon walls harbor many more animals including giant owls that fly out when they hear your car coming. You will drive through water in many places and there are pools large enough for swimming next to the road. Look for snakes before attempting this cool respite. They live here too. Quail and dove are prolific here. Once we picked up an injured eagle the other birds were tormenting. We took it out to the bay and attempted to assist its survival. In the morning it was gone. If you take this "road" south all the way back out to the highway you will come out at Km 259 south of Laguna Chapala and north of Parador Punta Prieta.

Upon coming up out of the canyon the ruins of Misión Calamajué are visible off to the right. This site was never actually a formal mission site but just a *Visita* or visiting station. It was abandoned quickly when they discovered the water to be so highly mineralized that their crops would not grow.

End of log...

Peregrine Falcon

BAJA BOOK IV

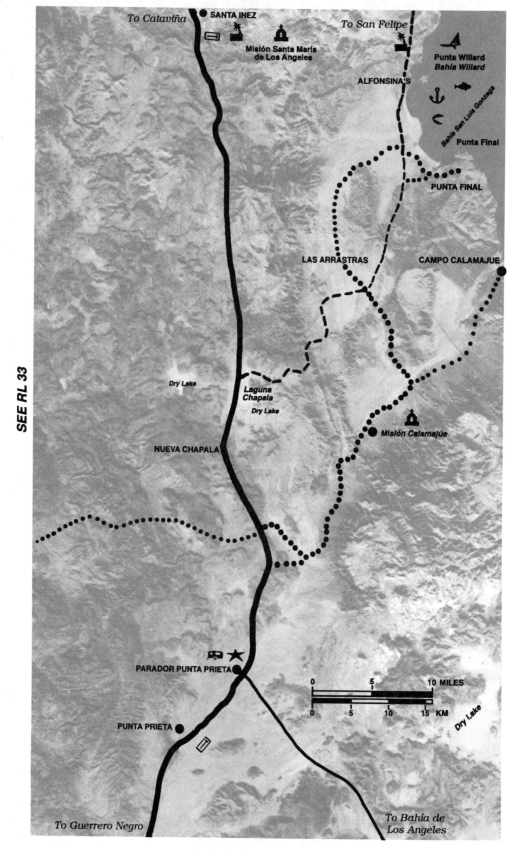

To Cataviña
SANTA INEZ
Misión Santa María de Los Angeles
To San Felipe
Punta Willard
Bahía Willard
ALFONSINA'S
Bahía San Luis Gonzaga
Punta Final
PUNTA FINAL
LAS ARRASTRAS
CAMPO CALAMAJUE
Dry Lake
Laguna Chapala
Dry Lake
Misión Calamajúe
NUEVA CHAPALA
PARADOR PUNTA PRIETA
PUNTA PRIETA
0   5   10 MILES
0   5   10   15 KM
Dry Lake
To Guerrero Negro
To Bahía de Los Angeles

N

ROADLOG 37

SAN QUINTIN-PARADOR PUNTA PRIETA...*(continued from RL30)*

K176   After crossing arroyo, paved road left leads to Ranch Santa Inés, an airstrip, very modest motel, campground, and restaurant. Road now heads south through stands of elephant trees and more unique plants.

K187   Rancho San Ignacito restaurant. Good food. It was here that the highway from the north and the highway from the south met thus completing México 1. Plaque commemorating this event is across the road.

K191   Rancho Jaraquay off to the left. Before this highway was built, travelers could stop for a bath here. Begin steep climb onto plateau. Road on top is easy driving with good visibility. At km. 196 larger vehicles should take caution as winds coming off of this dry lake have tumbled many a semi-truck.

K229   Graded road east skirting north edge of Laguna Chapala is to Bahía San Luis Gonzaga and points north. Beyond at km 230+ is restaurant at Rancho Nuevo Chapala, a true Baja experience.

K258   El Crucero. This is the old gulf road through Arroyo Calamajué from San Felipe and Bahía San Luís Gonzaga. After a few miles the road runs through a deep, narrow canyon where a large assortment of different animals and birds live. The walls of the canyon are of metamorphic rock and the green shist glistens. The canyon has freshwater pools where we have stopped for a dip.

K280   Parador Punta Prieta. Gasoline (sometimes) and, on occasion, diesel. At the junkyard on left is the only federal policeman for miles around. They have a small grocery store, public telephone and tow-trucks. On the west side of the road is an RV park, (no hook-ups). Paved road east leads to Bahía de Los Angeles, 42 miles (see RL48).

The Paradors of Baja. In 1973, when the highway was first opened these large buildings housed big cafeterias for travelers. There are quite a few, here in Punta Prieta next to the gas station; Cataviña, San Quintín, San Ignacio, Guerrero Negro, etc. A look inside reveals the large expense the Mexican government went to in trying to provide a place for the traveler to eat. The La Pinta hotels, originally called the Presidente Hotels were built at the same time for the travelers to have a place to rest - but then came the motorhomes. The Parador cafeterias lasted only a short time; the hotels were sold to private concerns and have been resold, divided, closed and opened in their effort to survive.

End of Log...

PARADOR PUNTA PRIETA-GUERRERO NEGRO;...80 miles, 128 km.

K0   Continue south from intersection with L.A. Bay road through fairly dense Vizcaino Desert flora. In late summer the fruit of the pitahaya cactus, abundant here, is ripe, sweet and dangerously difficult to pick.

K13   Pass through the edge of the small community of Punta Prieta. There is a small store, restaurant, mechanic and tire repair place here.

K24   La Bachata. Dirt road to right leads to coast; great surfing, fishing, diving and clamming. Road is poor, 4WD recommended. A better graded road is further south at Km 38 to Santa Rosalillita. From there you can drive north or south along dirt roads that follow the coast with many nice isolated camp spots.

(continued on Page RL46)

B A J A   B O O K   IV

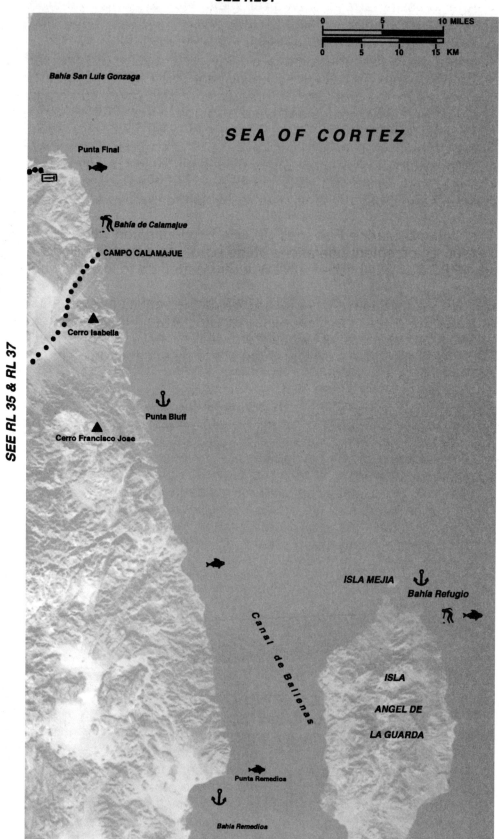

0   5   10 MILES

0   5   10   15   KM

Bahía San Luis Gonzaga

SEA OF CORTEZ

Punta Final

Bahía de Calamajue

CAMPO CALAMAJUE

Cerro Isabella

Punta Bluff

Cerro Francisco Jose

Canal de Ballenas

ISLA MEJIA

Bahía Refugio

ISLA

ANGEL DE

LA GUARDA

Punta Remedios

Bahía Remedios

ROADLOG 39

TOTUAVA - AN ENDANGERED SPECIES...

Fished for years for their livers, thousands of totuava were left to rot on the beach. The meat is delicious but these liver fishermen had no market for the tasty meat. Livers were used to make vitamins that are today made synthetically.

A prized sport fish, the totuava closely resembles the white sea bass and the orange-mouth corvina. Totuava may be distinguished from the other members of its family of croakers by the presence of three pairs of chin pores and the shape of the tail. Totuava can grow to 300 pounds and were common in the 100 to 200 pound range.

Both México and the U. S. have enacted laws to protect the totuava. México realized the problem and enacted laws in 1975, but today fishing with gill nets has continued. There has been a moratorium placed on fishing of any kind in the upper gulf north of a line that runs north of San Felipe to Puerto Penasco. Shrimp boats were allowed to drag this prolific area without restriction for many years and it is now literally fished out.

The National Marine Fisheries Service in cooperation with U.S. customs officials has increased enforcement operations at the border to detect the illegal entry of totuava. Also, the NMFS has established a NEW forensic method to identify whole or processed totuava.

Gillnets set for totuava have also killed off the vaquita porpoise. The vaquita is the smallest porpoise of all the cetaceans, rarely growing to over 4 feet in length. An estimated 30 to 40 vaquitas incidentally drown in gill nets in the northern Sea of Cortez each year. They reproduce slowly and are seriously endangered with only an estimated 300 to 500 individuals remaining.

Both of these species are endemic to the northern Sea of Cortez. Our awareness of their endangered status should assist their survival. If you should catch a totuava accidentally, release it immediately. If you see gill nets set - report it to the Mexican Department of Fisheries at the border.

TOTUAVA

The color of adult totuava is dull silver, burnished with iridescent copper and overlaid with minute dark spots. Juvenile totuava appear darker and more speckled.

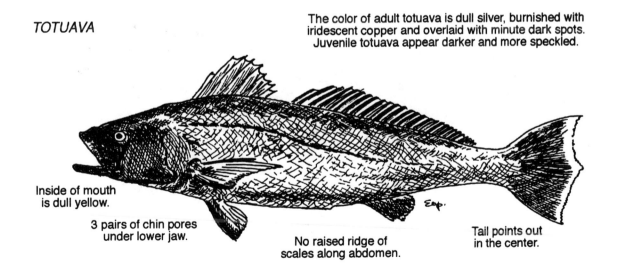

Inside of mouth is dull yellow.

3 pairs of chin pores under lower jaw.

No raised ridge of scales along abdomen.

Tail points out in the center.

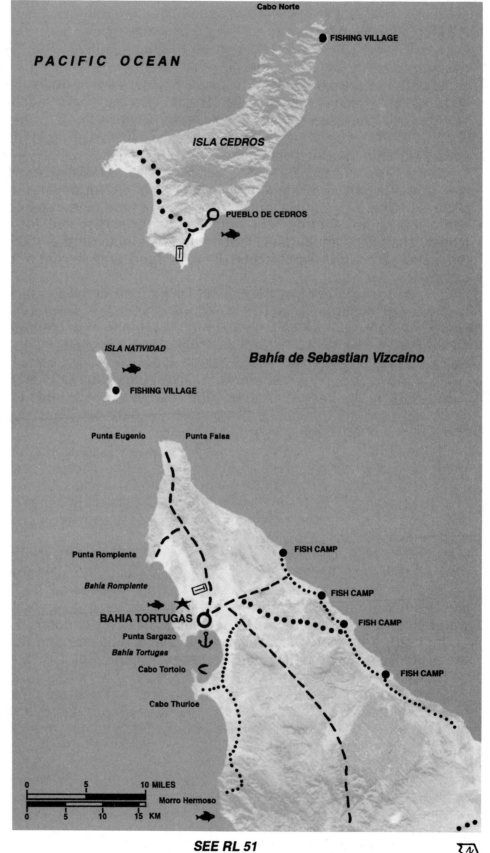

BAJA BOOK IV

Cabo Norte

● FISHING VILLAGE

PACIFIC OCEAN

ISLA CEDROS

⊙ PUEBLO DE CEDROS

ISLA NATIVIDAD

● FISHING VILLAGE

Bahía de Sebastian Vizcaino

SEE RL 43

Punta Eugenio   Punta Falsa

Punta Romplente

Bahía Romplente

BAHIA TORTUGAS ⊙

FISH CAMP

FISH CAMP

FISH CAMP

FISH CAMP

Punta Sargazo

Bahía Tortugas

Cabo Tortolo

Cabo Thurloe

0   5   10 MILES

0   5   10   15 KM

Morro Hermoso

SEE RL 51

N

ROADLOG 41

CEDROS ISLAND...

Jutting up out of the Pacific Ocean, this rugged and mountainous island measures 23 miles long and varies in width from 4 to 11 miles. High cliffs dominate most of the coastline with only a few arroyos reaching the sea where small pebbly beaches have formed. The two highest peaks reach about 4000 feet and on both are found forests of pine trees. Bubbling fresh water springs supply water to the town and have supplied water to whaler's ships in the past and today supply water to passing yachtsmen.

Cedros Island has played a major role in the subsistence and discoveries of man since the days of the Manila galleons. It was discovered by the Spaniard, Ulloa, in 1540. Ulloa mistakenly called some of the pine trees cedars and hence came the name, Cedros. The island became a resource for water, firewood, timber, shell fish, mule deer, rabbits and pine nuts. In the 1800's whaling ships left pairs of goats to proliferate on the island and increase their future meat supply.

The island was originally inhabited by a group of the Cochimí Indians. When the Spanish explorer, Ulloa, first encountered these Indians he noted that the women wore skirts made of whale tendons and the men used whale tendons for the strings of their bows. A search of the history reveals the Indians of this island were the only ones in Baja to actually hunt whales. With large rafts made of pine logs lashed together they proved to be adept mariners. Their spears, nearly three yards long, would have been capable of killing small whales. Father Taraval, in 1732, removed all of the Indians from the island who had not died from small-pox and took them to the mission at San Ignacio.

In the early 1800's, the island was a temporary base to whalers taking not only whales but elephant seals, sea lions and sea otters. The sea otter population was completely wiped out and has not returned. In the 1840's Chinese and American abalone fishermen from the coasts of upper California extended their operations to Cedros. The Chinese developed a way to cure the abalone and were able to ship tons of abalone all the way to China.

In 1857, when Captain Charles Scammon first entered the large Laguna Ojo de Liebre (later called Scammon's Lagoon) about fifty miles from Cedros, word spread world-wide of his find of the calving grounds of the grey whale and whalers from afar came here. Cedros Island was their fresh water source until a water hole was discovered at the back of Scammon's Lagoon.

In 1920, a cannery was built on the island. Abalone and fish were the main products. Turtles were also caught in great numbers and shipped live to foreign ports.

Today abalone are still taken on the island, however their numbers have greatly decreased. Poachers from the mainland steal over under cover of darkness for the valuable catch. During the summer the eastern shoreline provides good sportfishing. Lobster is still fairly abundant and harvested commercially.

1967 brought the building of the salt re-loading dock on Cedros and with it the first economic stabilization the island had seen. Today the salt works is well established on the island. There is a large airport and planes fly from here to Ensenada.

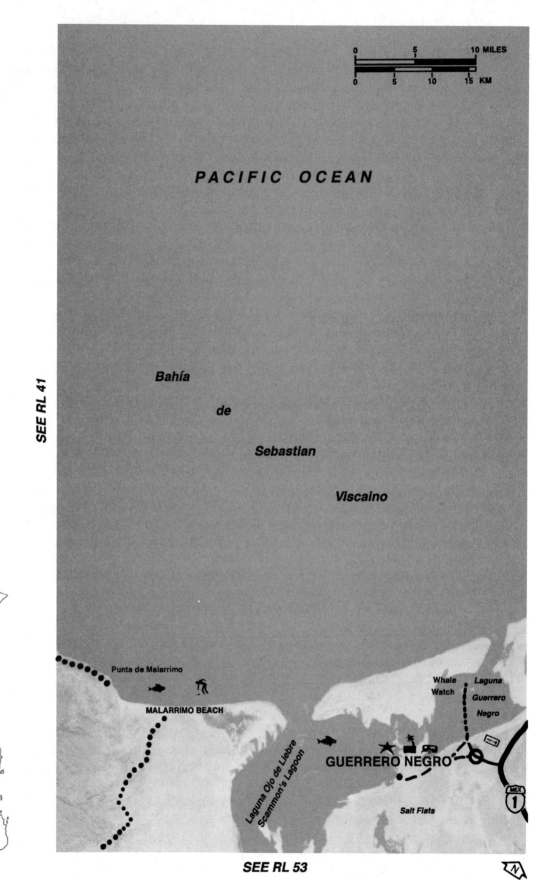

PACIFIC OCEAN

Bahía

de

Sebastian

Viscaino

SEE RL 41

SEE RL 45

SEE RL 53

Punta de Malarrimo

MALARRIMO BEACH

Whale
Watch

*Laguna
Guerrero
Negro*

*Laguna Ojo de Liebre
Scammon's Lagoon*

GUERRERO NEGRO

Salt Flats

MEX 1

ROADLOG 43

MALARRIMO BEACH - Beachcomber's Paradise

In my father's early travels to Baja he noticed that the fences and buildings at the ranch at San José de Castro were made from hatch covers of old ships and "lumber" that was obviously water-washed and printed with foreign names from all over the world. He inquired as to the origin of the wood and was told it came from down the canyon at a beach they called Malarrimo.

Without hesitation they planned a special trip to this beach of 'dangerous approach', the 26 miles down the canyon was a treacherous drive. They skirted around and down into a miniature grand canyon. (Photos of the canyon actually look like the Grand Canyon.) The last five miles was very soft sand and even with their 4WD vehicles they dared not slow down or they would sink into it.

They made camp just back from the water behind the rise of the sand. The wind blew hard and their skin became chapped and cracked from the blowing fine sand. Every bite of food was crunchy with more sand. Their sleeping bags absorbed it.

But the adventure and it's accompanying misery were well worth the effort. Getting out on the beach they found piles of debris three or more feet deep, all sizes and colors of Japanese glass fishing floats, packing crates with lettering in many languages, hatch covers everywhere, an abundance of C-rations, bottles with notes in them, a U.S. Navy torpedo (later reported to and dis-armed by the U.S. Navy), pieces of airplanes (both test planes and real ones), whole sides of old ships with copper on their bottoms, remains of recent ships, almost whole yachts and a case of scotch.

I joined my Dad on his next trip to Malarrimo. I spent 5 days beachcombing 17 miles of beach on foot. We piled up all of our booty in camp and then came the time to pack-up and leave. Obviously we had to leave most of it behind, and I was crushed at the thought of leaving anything. The beachcombing bug had bitten me.

In particular, one thing we found quite a number of were the bottles put out by the Scripps Institute of Oceanography to study ocean currents. These drift bottles are put to sea along the Pacific coast from Washington to México at varying distances from shore. Inside each is a numbered post card and some sand so it would follow the currents instead of the wind. I reported these numbers, saving the bottles intact. Scripps sent me maps showing the locations of the drops. I studied these maps and the dates, determining the best time to go to Malarrimo was February or March.

For eight years we went every year, sometimes twice a year. It was usually too windy for a tent so we would build a temporary 'house' from the sheets of plywood and debris we found on the beach. Taking a hammer and nails instead of a tent also made more room to take home more goodies. I now have so much beach 'junque' on my patio I can't even think about moving. What does one do with over 200 Scripps bottles, 75 glass balls, a few hundred beautiful old bottles, hatch covers, portholes, oars and a dugout canoe.

In 1965, Dad wrote A Beachcomber's Unplundered Paradise in Baja. San Diego Magazine made it their cover story. The word was out. To make things even worse, in February of 1972 a freak hurricane hovered over the area. Everything was washed back out to sea or covered up. The accessible 17 miles of beach was shortened to 9 miles when a new lagoon was formed by the storm and a tidal lake was formed in our camping area.

Today there is not much left at Malarrimo Beach. Someday a big storm will come from the other direction and plant mother nature's and man's flotsam and jetsam back up on the beach. I wait.

Instructions on how to get there are on page RL 52.

B
A
J
A

B
O
O
K

IV

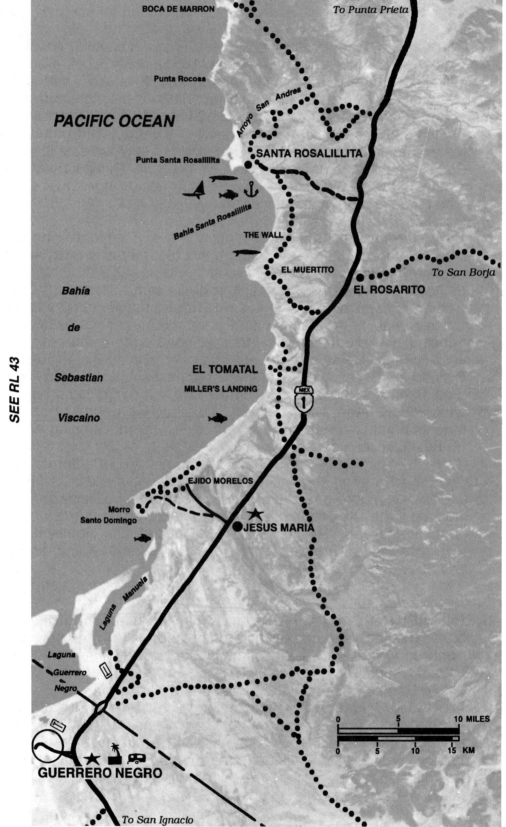

BOCA DE MARRON

To Punta Prieta

Punta Rocosa

Arroyo San Andres

PACIFIC OCEAN

Punta Santa Rosalillita

SANTA ROSALILLITA

Bahía Santa Rosalillita

THE WALL

Bahía

de

EL MUERTITO

To San Borja

EL ROSARITO

Sebastian

EL TOMATAL

Viscaino

MILLER'S LANDING

MEX 1

EJIDO MORELOS

Morro
Santo Domingo

★
●**JESUS MARIA**

Laguna Manuela

Laguna
Guerrero
Negro

0   5   10 MILES
0   5   10   15 KM

★ 🏕️

GUERRERO NEGRO

To San Ignacio

ROADLOG 45

PARADOR PUNTA PRIETA-GUERRERO NEGRO...*(from RL38)*

K25   Many of the cirios along here have Spanish moss growing on them. Ahead begins a steep, winding ascent. Follow along top for about 2 miles, then down into valley.

K38   Graded road right is to fishing village of Santa Rosalillita, 10 mi. A favorite spot for surfers is just south of the village. To the north of the village we have seen surfers on every accessible south facing beach (and a few in some inaccessible places). A turn right just before entering Santa Rosalillita leads north to San José de Las Palomas, 60 Km. 4-WD recommended.

K53   El Rosarito, small town on east side of highway. The hub of many ranches strewn about the mountains. A rugged dirt road to the east leads to Misión San Borja, about 21 miles. Inside the truck-stop cafe, Restaurant Mauricio, on left of highway, the owner displays some interesting large mutated agave plants. Good food at reasonable prices.

K61   Road right is alternate to surfer's beach.

K66   **Very dangerous blind curve,** slow down. Thirty-three people were killed on this curve during the first month this highway was open and accidents still happen frequently here.

K69   El Tomatal. Road right to beach and fish camp. Reach the beach at 3.1 mi. Good, dry camping in the dunes. We have a trailer out here on the point south of the camping area. Just south of here about 3 miles is what once was Miller's Landing, an onyx loading site; there is nothing there now.

K95   Jesús María. Pemex station with gas and diesel. Paved road west leads to Ejido Morelos and Laguna Manuela Morro Santo Domingo. For Manuela, turn right on paved road after 1 mile turn off to left on graded washboard road then go 5.5 mi. (heading to the left of Morro Santo Domingo, the large black mountain in the distance) to the beach. Excellent camping and fishing. Boats for hire; launch site for lightweight boats.

K128   The 28th parallel is the boundary between Baja California Norte and Baja California Sur. The huge statue is a stylized eagle and marks the state line. On right is La Espinita restaurant and soon-to-be trailer park. Until the park is finished the owner, Kiko, will allow you to park here free. Just past the "eagle" is the Hotel La Pinta Guerrero Negro and Las Dunas Trailer Park. The **agricultural inspection station** is just beyond. About 1 mile further is a **propane** station on the right.

End of Log...

GUERRERO NEGRO-SANTA ROSALÍA...137 miles, 220 kilometers.

    Note: The kilometer markers in the southern half of the peninsula run south to north so our logs in Baja California Sur generally begin with high kilometer values and decrease as we go south.

K220   Leave Hotel La Pinta Guerrero Negro and head south.

K217   Main road curves left at intersection with paved road right into **Guerrero Negro**, 2.5 miles, gas, food, lodging, whale-watching trips (inquire at the Malarrimo Restaurant and RV park). The Mercado La Ballena grocery store in town has a complete selection. Back on México 1 the road turns ESE through low dunes with a sparse covering of salt bush (brought here from Australia many years ago as cattle food).

(continued on RL56)

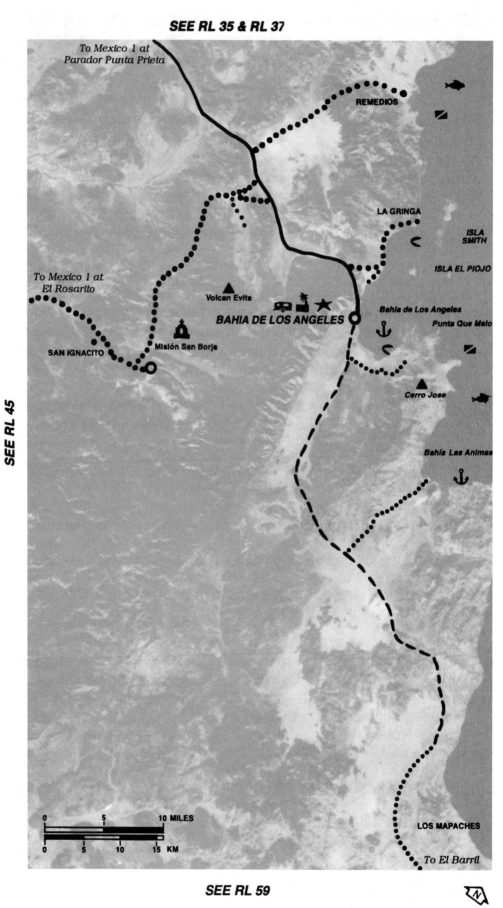

**B
A
J
A

B
O
O
K

IV**

To Mexico 1 at
Parador Punta Prieta

REMEDIOS

LA GRINGA

ISLA
SMITH

ISLA EL PIOJO

To Mexico 1 at
El Rosarito

Volcan Evita

BAHIA DE LOS ANGELES

Bahia de Los Angeles

Punta Que Malo

SAN IGNACITO

Misión San Borja

Cerro Jose

Bahía Las Animas

SEE RL 45

SEE RL 49

0   5   10 MILES

0   5   10   15   KM

LOS MAPACHES

To El Barril

SEE RL 59

N

ROADLOG 47

BAHIA DE LOS ANGELES...

The road to L. A. Bay is paved but not well-maintained so use caution. If you venture out there, you will remember forever the beauty of that first glimpse of the bay, dotted with islands big and small.

The 41 mile paved road from Parador Punta Prieta into Bahía de Los Angeles brings the traveler to one of the most interesting and accessible recreation areas in Baja. Rewards for visitors are many. Besides the sometimes-good fishing, shelling and clamming, diving and windsurfing are popular pastimes. There are old mining sites to be explored, 4-WD roads to follow, including one south to Bahía San Francisquito, and trips to the adjoining islands. There are 2 motels, a couple RV Parks, a few restaurants, grocery stores, a unique museum that is well worth the visit and boats for hire to go out fishing for yellowtail etc. Scallops are still harvested commercially north of town a few miles. Turtles were commercially taken for many years.

Wind can be a real problem in L.A. Bay. The water can be calm and flat as glass and in what seems like seconds 15' swells and whipping wind are upon you. One afternoon the wind came up and in less than an hour 24 boats were either sunk, swamped or blown away. Attesting to the wind problem is the way people tie their airplanes down on the landing strip - securely.

Remedios, north of the bay, is one of those places I have always wanted to visit but everyone I have talked to has said they were blown away when they were there so I haven't pushed it to get there.

Should you happen to come to Bahía de Los Angeles when the wind is not blowing it is a great place. Snorkeling around the rocks offshore or out around the islands is a beautiful experience. Fishing can be fantastic too. For years there was a famous yellowtail tournament here. The best fishing is from mid-June through October. During these times the reefs around the islands often become jammed with all manner of private boats looking for the current "hotspot" for yellowtail, cabrilla or grouper. The channel separating Isla Angel de La Guarda and the peninsula often hosts large pods of porpoise and finback whales.

Mission San Borja

Side trip to San Borja

An interesting day's outing to San Borja mission is convenient from Bahía de Los Angeles. To get to the mission from here it is recommended you have 4-WD or a buggy with high clearance. Take plenty of water and food in case of emergency as the road is not frequently traveled. Go back out the paved road about 12 miles, turn left and the mission is 23 miles from the paved road. A rock-art site can be accessed from a side road to the left about 2.5 miles from the pavement.

BAJA BOOK IV

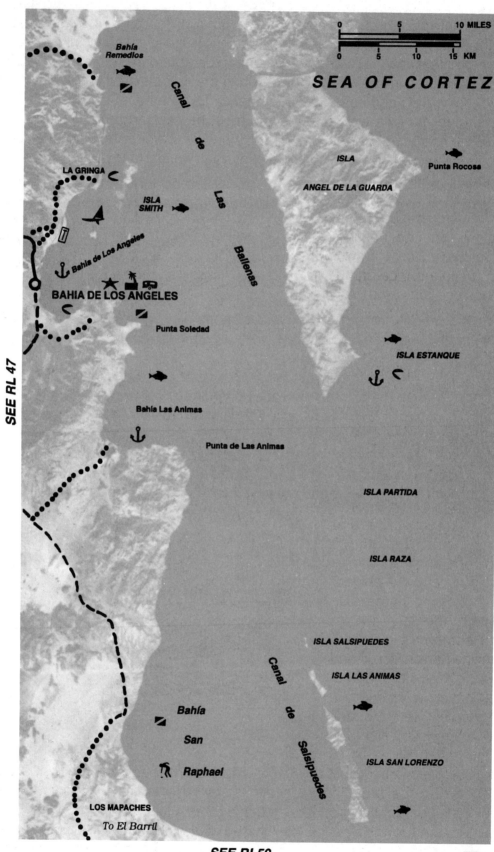

SEA OF CORTEZ

Bahía Remedios

Canal de Las Ballenas

LA GRINGA

ISLA SMITH

Bahía de Los Angeles

BAHIA DE LOS ANGELES

Punta Soledad

Bahía Las Animas

Punta de Las Animas

ISLA ANGEL DE LA GUARDA

Punta Rocosa

ISLA ESTANQUE

ISLA PARTIDA

ISLA RAZA

ISLA SALSIPUEDES

ISLA LAS ANIMAS

Canal de Salsipuedes

Bahía San Raphael

ISLA SAN LORENZO

LOS MAPACHES

To El Barril

SEE RL 47

SEE RL59

ISLA ANGEL DE LA GUARDA...

This is the largest island close by the Baja mainland. (Tiburón on the eastern side of the Midriff is the largest island in the Sea of Cortez.) It's 4000 foot plus mountains and 42 mile length makes it a prominent landmark whether boating or flying in the vicinity. The largely barren surface supports a few coyotes and rodents, plus abundant numbers of lizards and rattlesnakes. Several seal rookeries are found along the northeastern coast. Many schools of fish patrol the rocky reefs and coves of Isla Angel de La Guarda.

The highlight of a visit to the island must be exploring the almost-surrealistic Bahía Refugio at the north end. Here you will see a pinnacle of white and black rocks jutting from the water's surface, high cliffs of reds, browns, greys and whites. Many coves and lees afford refuge in any weather, thus the name, *Refugio.* Several of the small islands forming the bay also serve as early summer nesting grounds for the California brown pelican, (*pelícano.*) Later, in September, sea lions drop their pups, affording many opportunities for pictures.

ELEGANT TERNS

Snorkeling the shallow coves reveals a veritable smorgasbord of sea life; oysters, snails, lobsters and mussels on up to a variety of sub-tropical fish, much of which is edible.

ISLA RAZA...

Barely one-third of a square mile in area, this island is of prime interest to naturalists as it is the only known breeding place of the beautiful elegant tern. Ominously present are also the gallant looking, white-headed Heermann's gulls that dominate the barren little island with nests everywhere, sometimes less than a yard apart. Royal terns nest here too, and the fight for a nesting sight between the royal and elegant terns and the Heermann gulls is a never ending one. The cacophony of their squeals becomes deafening during the breeding season. Osprey's generally join the crowd, building their towering nests up from the ground as much as 3 or 4 feet.

In 1964, this low island was designated as a wildlife preserve. Several biologists have stayed on the island during the March to July breeding season to study and protect the nesting birds and their hatchlings.

B A J A   B O O K   I V

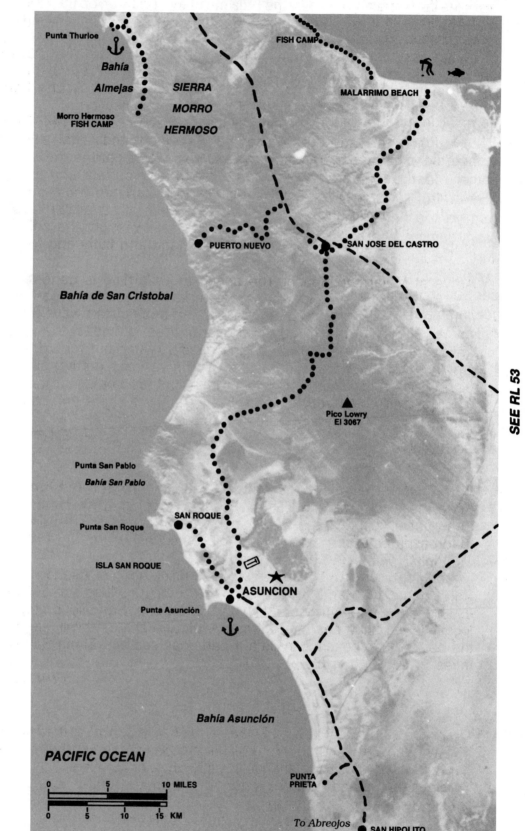

Punta Thurloe

Bahía

Almejas

SIERRA

MORRO

HERMOSO

Morro Hermoso
FISH CAMP

FISH CAMP

MALARRIMO BEACH

PUERTO NUEVO

SAN JOSE DEL CASTRO

Bahía de San Cristobal

Pico Lowry
El 3067

Punta San Pablo

Bahía San Pablo

Punta San Roque

SAN ROQUE

ISLA SAN ROQUE

ASUNCION

Punta Asunción

Bahía Asunción

PACIFIC OCEAN

0		5		10 MILES

0	5	10	15	KM

PUNTA
PRIETA

To Abreojos

SAN HIPOLITO

SEE RL 53

N

ROADLOG 51

MALARRIMO BEACH-SIDE TRIP...96 miles, 154 km from the highway.

This side trip is a rugged one. 4WD is highly recommended and having two vehicles is probably a very good idea. The road from the ranch to the beach is not an easy one. Although it is only 26 miles, you should plan on at least three hours driving time - before dark. There are many little roads branching off from the 'main' road; stay to the most well-traveled road. At the bottom of the canyon it is quite sandy for the last five miles, use caution.

M0.0   From the Guerrero Negro-Santa Rosalía Roadlog at Km 144, Ejido Viscaíno turn right on paved road to Viscaíno. Pavement ends after a few miles then road becomes graded and is generally very washboard.

M70   San José de Castro. A fairly large ranch with corrals and many small out buildings. Ask here for exact directions to Malarrimo; wash-outs change the situation from year to year. Fresh water is generally available here. The water is very sulfur smelling; however, if left to set overnight the odor leaves. It is fantastic to wash your hair with, leaves it soft and fluffy and feels great after seven days on Malarrimo Beach.

M96   Arrive at Malarrimo Beach. The beach at Malarrimo is generally very windy with lots of blowing sand. After an extreme high tide the area near the beach may be flooded, forcing you to make camp back quite aways from the beach. An ATC or a dune buggy with sand tires provides the best mode of transportation for getting out on the beach. Watch out for extremely soft wet sand. Surf fishing is good but the sting-rays keep getting your bait. We've found it is good fishing for corbina and spot-fin croaker at the mouth of the small lagoon about eight miles to the right from where you come out on the beach.

End of side trip...

BAHÍA ASUNCIÓN-SIDE TRIP...67 miles, 108 km from the highway.

M0.0   From the Guerrero Negro-Santa Rosalía Roadlog at Km 144, Ejido Viscaíno turn right on paved road to Viscaíno. Pavement ends after a few miles then road becomes graded and is generally very washboard.

M44.0   Turn left. Road is graded part of the way.

M67.0   Turn right for Asunción, 4 miles. About 8 miles north of Asunción is the town of San Roque. Isla San Roque, just off the coast, provides some very good sport fishing. Sometimes the sport fishing boats out of San Diego stop here. Hire a local with a panga and check it out. A left turn at M67.0 will lead you to one of the best surfing beaches in Baja. Road goes south to Bahía San Hipólito at 21 miles.

End of side trip...

BAHÍA TORTUGAS-SIDE TRIP...121 miles, 195 km from the highway.

Follow directions for side trip to Malarrimo Beach (above) but do not turn right at San José de Castro. Continue straight another 25 miles.

Tortugas, so named because there *were* so many turtles here, has a beautiful small deep harbor. Sport fishing is good from May to September. At one time there was an abalone cannery here. The piles of turtle shells are an overwhelming reminder of the slaughter that went on.

End of side trip...

**B
A
J
A

B
O
O
K

IV**

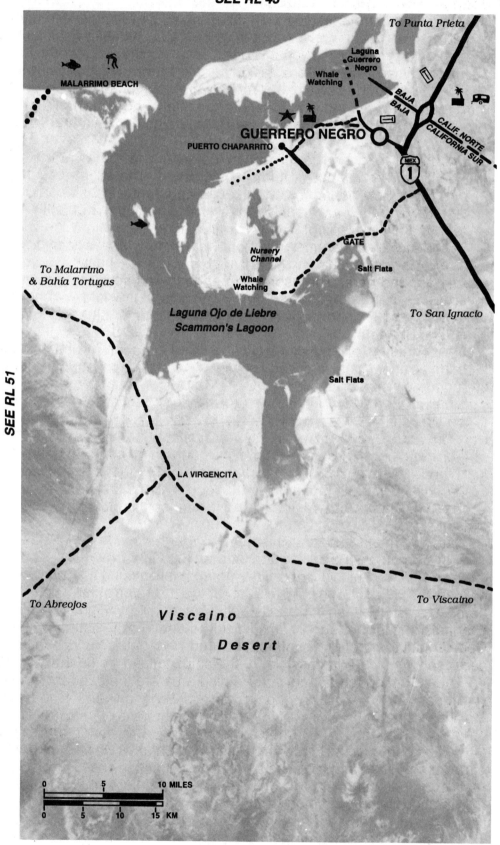

To Punta Prieta

Laguna
Guerrero
Negro

Whale
Watching

MALARRIMO BEACH

BAJA
BAJA

CALIF. NORTE
CALIFORNIA SUR

GUERRERO NEGRO

PUERTO CHAPARRITO

MEX
1

To Malarrimo
& Bahía Tortugas

GATE

Nursery
Channel

Salt Flats

Whale
Watching

To San Ignacio

*Laguna Ojo de Liebre
Scammon's Lagoon*

Salt Flats

LA VIRGENCITA

To Viscaino

To Abreojos

Viscaino

Desert

0   5   10 MILES

0   5   10   15 KM

N

ROADLOG 53

Scammon's Lagoon (Laguna Ojo de Liebre)

This lagoon stretches some 40 miles inland and has varying depths of from 10 feet to over 60 feet. The entrance is comparably small and shallow and the water inside the lagoon is somewhat trapped. The weather is generally cool and windy and it hardly ever rains. Because of the winds, the evaporation rate is quite high. This has caused the salt content of the water to average almost double that of the water outside of the lagoon. The water becomes more saline the further one goes inland from the mouth, and large natural salt flats dominate the eastern landscape of the lagoon.

Scammon's Lagoon is the winter home of the grey whale and is the place where they were almost brought to extinction. The initial slaughter of the grey whales took place during the late 1850's and early 1860's. Today the whales are protected when they are here in the lagoon. The number of boats in the lagoon is limited, and fishing is forbidden within the lagoon.

The Mexican government has set aside the whole lagoon and the adjoining Guerrero Negro Lagoon as a bird sanctuary. Ducks, geese, shorebirds and birds of prey abound here. The osprey, an endangered species, is found here in large numbers. I have seen avid bird watchers on whale-watching trips taking advantage of the opportunity to get out on the water and see some of the many unusual birds here.

Native Indians of Baja came here to fish. One account of the missionaries said the natives thought this lagoon to have more of a concentration of fish than any other area on the coast. Along with the fish were green sea turtles, clams, oysters, scallops and sharks. Twentieth century fishing with nets has depleted the fish. When the whalers were here they learned to appreciate the taste of turtle meat. Different parts of the turtle can taste like beef, pork, venison, or fish. Word spread of the abundance of this delicacy and soon shiploads of live turtles were taken from the lagoon. In 1869, one account revealed that 100 live turtles arrived in San Diego and 40 were shipped on to Chicago. It didn't take long to deplete the turtle population. Divers have wiped out whole beds of scallops. Clams are getting difficult to find.

The lagoon was never suitable as a port. In the late 1700's, it is recorded that Father Taraval went to Cedros Island (50 miles away), climbed up the big mountain, looked at the lagoon and thought it would be a good port for the Manila galleon. Luckily nobody took him at his word. A long sand bar forms a barrier on both sides of the entrance. The entrance is quite shallow and the deeper channels inside the lagoon are difficult to find. Today salt is hauled by barge to Cedros Island where it is off-loaded and reloaded onto ocean going freighters because it would be impossible for the ships to load inside the lagoon.

Today the lagoon and its surrounding area are the base for the world's largest industrial salt mine, Exportadora de Sal S.A., owned by Mitsubishi and the Mexican government. They ship 6 million metric tons of commercial salt from here annually. There are 30,000 hectares of evaporation ponds and 3000 hectares of crystallization ponds in continuous production. Twelve hundred people are employed by the salt works. The trucks that haul the salt are the biggest trucks in the world and each truck can haul 360 metric tons of salt at one time. Commercial salt is used mainly in the production of chlorine and soda, as a snow deterrent and in water softeners. Recently they have developed a process for making table salt here. The factory has been built and expected production is 100,000 metric tons annually. It will be marketed under the name Baja Pacifico Sal de Mesa and will provide 100 jobs.

**B
A
J
A

B
O
O
K

IV**

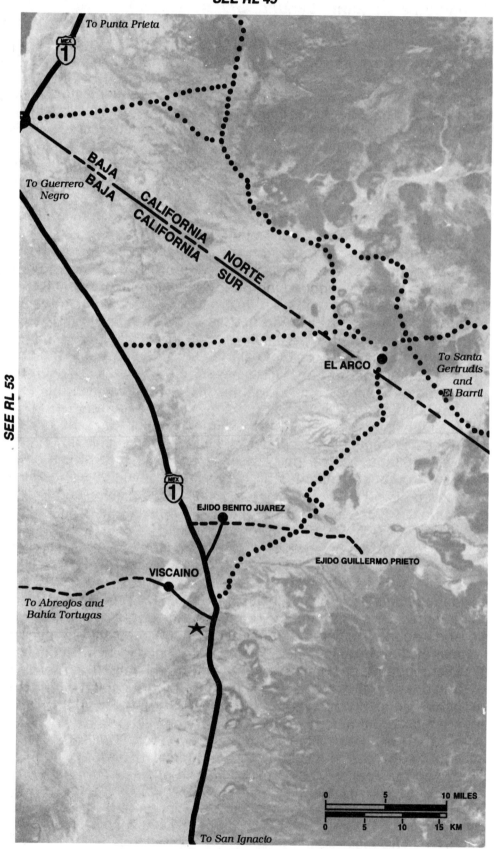

To Punta Prieta

To Guerrero
Negro

BAJA
BAJA
CALIFORNIA NORTE
CALIFORNIA SUR

EL ARCO

To Santa
Gertrudis
and
El Barril

EJIDO BENITO JUAREZ

EJIDO GUILLERMO PRIETO

VISCAINO

To Abreojos and
Bahía Tortugas

0   5   10 MILES

0   5   10   15 KM

To San Ignacio

N

ROADLOG 55

GUERRERO NEGRO-SANTA ROSALIA...*(continued from RL46)*

K208   Signed road right to Laguna Ojo de Liebre (Scammon's Lagoon) open to tourists during January, February, and March when the grey whales are present in the lagoon. It is closed to the public after the whale season. The road is graded at the beginning of each season. It is 16.5 m (27 Km) to the lagoon; the first half of the road can be quite rough but the last part is maintained by the salt works and is generally in very good shape. The road is well marked. In 1995 the fee was $3.00 per vehicle to enter and $10.00 U.S. per person to go whale-watching out in their pangas. There are some very nice dry camp spots on the edge of the lagoon. The road out is bumpy, washboard and sometimes sandy, but I have seen motorhomes and 5th wheels camped on the edge of the lagoon.

K189+   El Arco, 26 miles on graded road. In the 1920's, American's employed over 1000 miners to work in the gold mines of El Arco. There is gold, silver and copper there. A good dune-buggy side trip from here is to Misión Santa Gertrudis, an additional 24 miles east of El Arco. You can also reach the gulf-coast northeast of El Arco but it is a 4WD, 2 vehicle trip, over a very rough road, about 75 miles total. Check with the locals before attempting as it has been impassable at times.

K179+   Los Laguneros. Throughout this area there are numerous ranches sprouting up. Tomato are the main crop and farmers are reaping big crops. The water source is ancient water trapped many eons ago and it does not replenish itself.

K144   Viscaíno. Pemex, gas and diesel, several restaurants and stores, very modest "Motel Olivia" on left and RV park "Kaadekaman" past gas station on right. Paved road west past Ejido Viscaíno goes about 20 miles before turning into graded dirt. This is one entry into the very desolate part of the Vizcaino Desert. Bahía Tortugas is about 100 miles west. Malarrimo Beach is 95 miles (4WD recommended). Bahía Asunción is 66 miles. Some of these roads are graded and can be expected to be washboard. We've seen quite a few surfers at Asunción. Just ahead as you leave town on the right there is a family selling plastic buckets. One day in 1992, I stopped to purchase one. The husband wasn't home so a young boy waited on me. Not having any pesos at the time I gave him American money for my purchase. He went inside to get his mother and I soon discovered that neither he nor his mother had ever seen American money. It took quite a bit of talking to convince them my money had any value.

K123+   Microondas Los Angeles and several newer ranches. The dips, or vados, in this area flood easily during a storm. Be very careful when crossing if it has been raining. In the distance off to your right, if it is a clear day, you can see the Santa Clara Mountains. These jagged mountains are said to house the hidden treasures of the old missions of Baja. They are also said to be the source for the obsidian (volcanic black glass) the Indians made their arrowheads out of. The second is more likely.

(continued on RL64)

BAJA BOOK IV

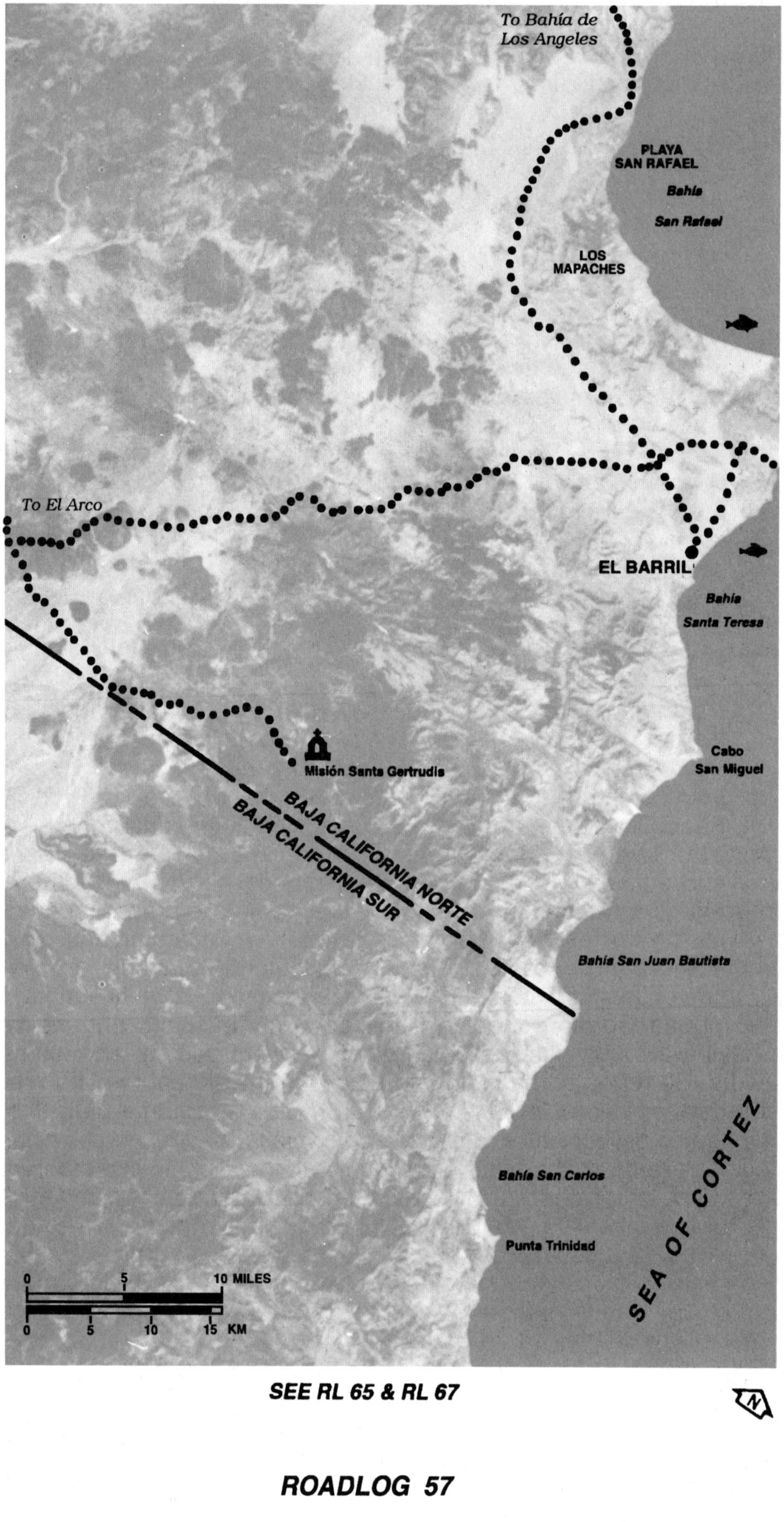

To Bahía de Los Angeles

PLAYA SAN RAFAEL

Bahía

San Rafael

LOS MAPACHES

To El Arco

EL BARRIL

Bahía Santa Teresa

SEE RL 55

SEE RL 59

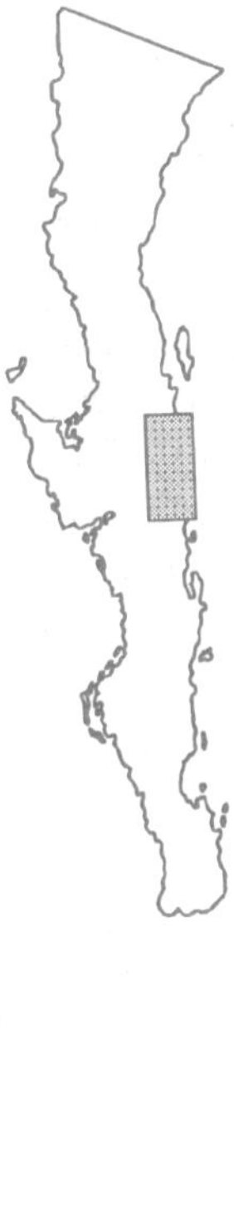

Misión Santa Gertrudis

BAJA CALIFORNIA NORTE

BAJA CALIFORNIA SUR

Cabo San Miguel

Bahía San Juan Bautista

SEA OF CORTEZ

Bahía San Carlos

Punta Trinidad

0   5   10 MILES

0   5   10   15   KM

SEE RL 65 & RL 67

N

ROADLOG 57

Giant Raccoon - El Mapache Grande

LOS MAPACHES...

Between Christmas and New Years in 1986 my husband and I were camped on the point at the south end of Bahía San Raphael. We took an evening stroll along the top of the cliff to the south of camp and saw a most unusual sight. The shore line along here is worn down lava flows and forms many tide pools on a receding tide. First we saw a coyote running very fast towards the north as if he were running from something. The cliffs meet the sea at the north and there would be no escape for him. While standing on the very edge of the cliff I looked down to see a strange large animal, a raccoon the size of my 95 pound German shepherd! I nudged my husband and we both stood there frozen having a tough time believing what we were seeing. The animal turned slowly and saw us. He retreated back up into a cave in the side of the cliff. Near his cave was an orange crate. I knew my friends would have a hard time believing this one, but I figured if I could get a picture of the raccoon next to the orange crate our story would be validated. Before dawn the next morning I went to the sight, camera in hand. I didn't get a picture. Had I seen the beast I probably wouldn't have gotten a good shot anyway because I was a little shaky and scared. His paw prints were all over the ground and his paws were as big as my hands. Upon my return to San Diego I looked in the encyclopedia and sure enough! - these animals do exist - on the shoreline of Chile in South America. I have named the place Los Mapaches (Spanish for raccoon) on my map in honor of my large furry friend.

B A J A B O O K IV

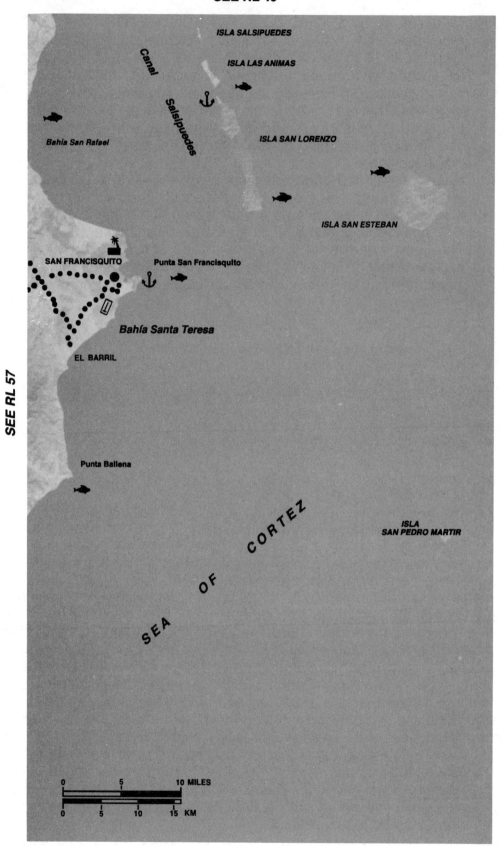

ISLA SALSIPUEDES

ISLA LAS ANIMAS

Canal

Salsipuedes

ISLA SAN LORENZO

Bahía San Rafael

ISLA SAN ESTEBAN

SAN FRANCISQUITO

Punta San Francisquito

Bahía Santa Teresa

EL BARRIL

Punta Ballena

ISLA
SAN PEDRO MARTIR

S E A   O F   C O R T E Z

0   5   10 MILES

0   5   10   15 KM

EL BARRIL AND BAHIA SAN FRANCISQUITO...

From México 1, just outside of Guerrero Negro, to El Barril and Bahía San Francisquito is 75 miles of some of the worst road in all of Baja. Even lightweight 4-WD pickups have trouble traversing this stretch of road. If your destination is El Barril and Bahía San Francisquito I suggest you enter from the north at Bahía de Los Angeles. This road is no picnic either but it is a lot better than the other route. Be prepared for washboard and dust. When you arrive you will be rewarded with a beautiful campsite, quite possibly some very good fishing and the remoteness you were looking for.

Here you will find good beachcombing; many rare and beautiful shells have been found along these beaches, especially the southern part of Bahía San Raphael. Diving is lucrative here. Surf fishing, if the tide is right and you watch for signs of bait jumping, can bring in a nice fresh fish dinner.

The Gulf is narrowest through here and consequently the area is popularly called The Midriff. The island of San Lorenzo offers good fishing on both sides but offers no safe harbor in case the unpredictable gulf wind comes up.

El Berrendo - Baja's Antelope

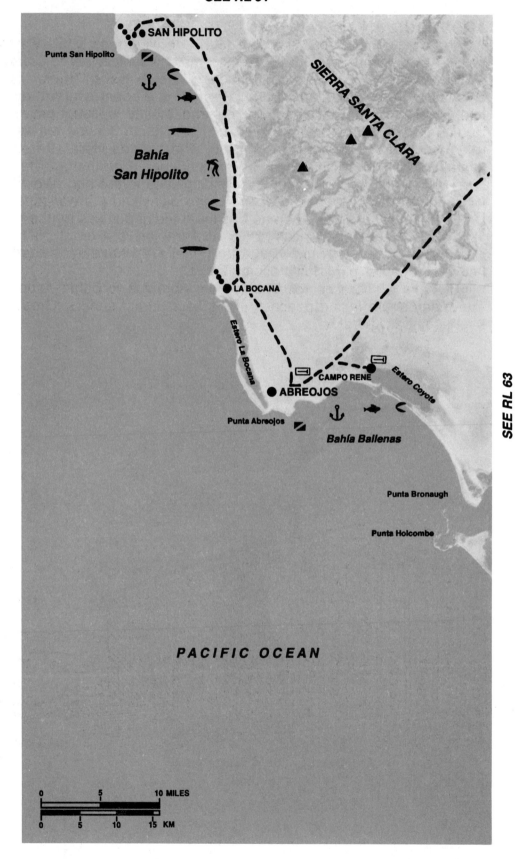

BAJA BOOK IV

SAN HIPOLITO

Punta San Hipolito

*Bahía
San Hipolito*

SIERRA SANTA CLARA

LA BOCANA

Estero La Bocana

CAMPO RENE

ABREOJOS

Estero Coyote

Punta Abreojos

Bahía Ballenas

Punta Bronaugh

Punta Holcombe

SEE RL 63

PACIFIC OCEAN

0   5   10 MILES

0   5   10   15   KM

ABREOJOS...

Abreojos, a small, isolated, fishing village with good whale-watching from the point. At one time there was a button-making factory here. Clam and abalone shells were cut by presses into thick, one-inch discs. These discs were then shipped by truck to Ensenada for export to the orient where they were finished into buttons. The operation, which hired mostly women, provided a meager income to residents for miles around.

We came into this village in 1966. The houses were all freshly painted in pastel colors and a lot of them were wall-papered on the outside! It was quite a site, with calico and gingham freshly displayed in the sun. We never found out who the contractor was who supplied the paint and the wallpaper but evidently his Spanish was lacking when he told them the paper was for the walls.

Campo René three miles south of Abreojos is a great place to dig hacha clams. Surf fishing isn't too bad either. Small RV's have been seen to access the beach at low tide, but I don't recommend it.

There is a shoreline road north from Abreojos to Bahía Asunción, 60 miles. The many south facing beaches along here attract surfers. Great surfing off the south point at Abreojos.

Abreojos

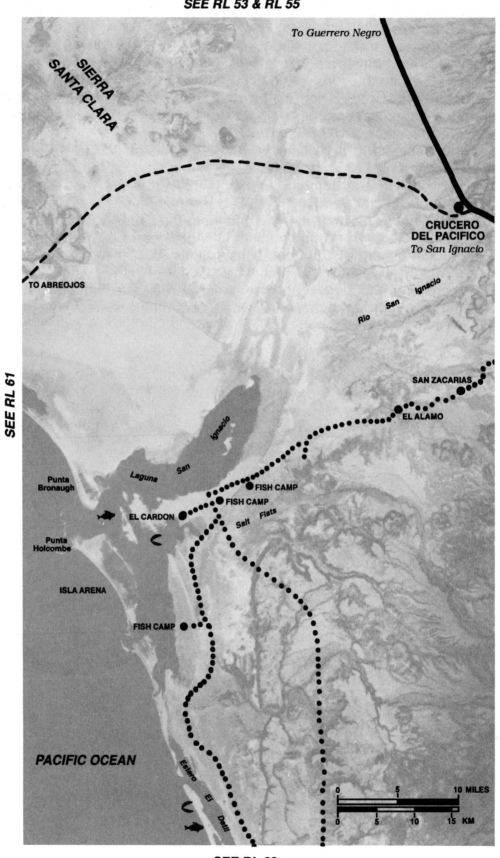

BAJA BOOK IV

To Guerrero Negro

SIERRA
SANTA CLARA

CRUCERO
DEL PACIFICO
To San Ignacio

TO ABREOJOS

Rio   San   Ignacio

SEE RL 61

SAN ZACARIAS

EL ALAMO

SEE RL 65

San   Ignacio

Laguna   San

Punta
Bronaugh

FISH CAMP

FISH CAMP

EL CARDON

Salt   Flats

Punta
Holcombe

ISLA ARENA

FISH CAMP

PACIFIC OCEAN

Estero

El   Datil

| | 0 | 5 | 10 MILES |
| 0 | 5 | 10 | 15 KM |

SEE RL 69

N

K118   Graded road left is to San Francisco de La Sierra, a rugged 24 miles. This is the access point for getting into view the ancient, renowned cave paintings (pinturas rupestres). There is a little village at the top where you can make arrangements to hire a guide and mules to go into the canyons to see the cave paintings. There is one small cave near the settlement. You can also make arrangements in San Ignacio for more extensive trips to see the major caves. The best time of year to view the paintings is the fall, after the hot and before the cold. You will go by mule back over some very precarious trails. A good trip will last three to six days.

        These "Great Murals" were made known by Erle Stanley Gardner in his book, "The Hidden Heart of Baja". The first recorded accounts occurred in the 1700's, when two Jesuit priests wrote about the sites. Today, these pictographs are world-famous. It has been said they were painted by a race of giants, for some of the human figures are depicted very large. There are many caves and sites with beautiful, colorful paintings. The exact age of these paintings has not been precisely determined but they are hundreds, perhaps thousands, of years old. In late 1994, 2 more large caves were discovered, and it is believed these are older than the others. It is well worth the trip to see them.

K108   Rancho Las Flores on right off highway.

K98   Graded road west leads to Abreojos, 53 mi. See previous page.

K84   On a clear day you can see the waters of Laguna San Ignacio to the south. There are some nice camp spots around the edge of the lagoon and good fishing around the mangroves. During whale season this is a fantastic place to go whale-watching.

(continued on RL66)

Pictographs

**B
A
J
A

B
O
O
K

IV**

To Guerrero Negro

Arroyo San Lino

SAN LINO

Rio San Ignacio

SAN IGNACIO

LAS TRES VIRGENES

6547

★

MEX 1

EL MESQUITAL

To San Ignacio Lagoon

To Santa Rosalía

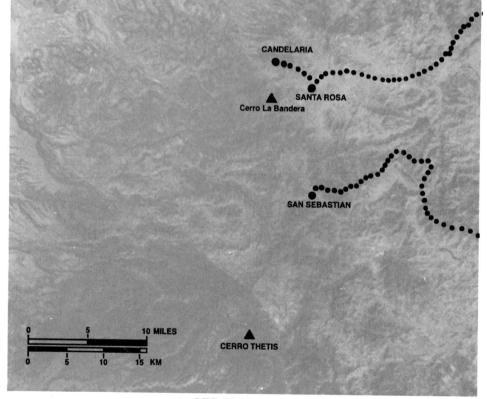

CANDELARIA

SANTA ROSA

Cerro La Bandera

SAN SEBASTIAN

0   5   10 MILES

0   5   10   15 KM

CERRO THETIS

N

GUERRERO NEGRO-SANTA ROSALIA...*(continued from RL64)*

K74   Entrance to **San Ignacio**. Pemex on left with Magna Sin and diesel. A right turn here takes you 3 Km. through the palms, across the river and into San Ignacio. Hotels, restaurants, RV park (full hook-ups). Visit the beautiful Misión San Ignacio. Continue straight through town to get to Laguna San Ignacio. Approx. 38 mi. of graded, sometimes washboard, road to great whale-watching in Jan., Feb. and March. Boats for hire to get closer to the whales. Inquire at El Padrino RV park in the palms on the road into town for more specific information on whale-watching trips.

K72   To the south is the upper end of this truly remarkable desert oasis. Road winds through hills, watch for oncoming traffic on the curves.

K67   The volcanoes, Tres Vírgenes, can be seen in the distance. There is a record of an eruption in the 1700's.

K62   A barely marked turn-off to the left leads to an ancient Indian site with hillsides literally covered with petroglyphs. This area has been designated as a National Park.

K60   Signed, graded road left to Santa Martha, and El Carricito in the southern San Francisco Mountains.

K39   Rancho El Mesquital. The road now begins winding around and over lava flows. Baja's elephant trees show their finest and largest specimens here, growing bravely on the lava flows.

K35   The top of Vírgenes Grade. Before this highway you ascended this grade via switch backs, some of which had turns so sharp you had to back up 2 or 3 times to make the turn.

K32   Road off to left leads to large government geothermal project.

(continued on RL68)

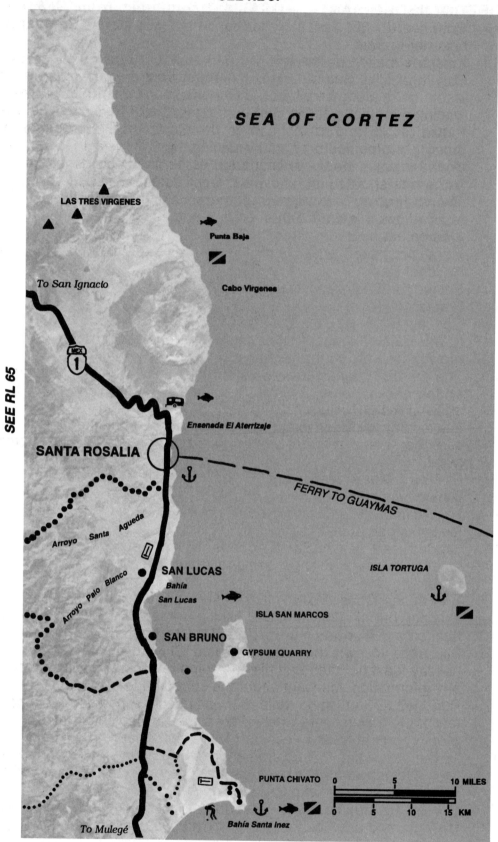

BAJA BOOK IV

SEA OF CORTEZ

LAS TRES VIRGENES

Punta Baja

Cabo Virgenes

To San Ignacio

MEX 1

SEE RL 65

Ensenada El Aterrizaje

SANTA ROSALIA

FERRY TO GUAYMAS

Arroyo Santa Agueda

Arroyo Palo Blanco

SAN LUCAS
Bahía San Lucas

ISLA TORTUGA

ISLA SAN MARCOS

SAN BRUNO

● GYPSUM QUARRY

PUNTA CHIVATO

0   5   10 MILES

0   5   10   15 KM

Bahía Santa Inez

To Mulegé

SEE RL 73

ROADLOG 67

GUERRERO NEGRO-SANTA ROSALIA...*(continued from RL66)*

K19 Your first view of the Sea of Cortez. A half-mile further, begin descent from 1500 feet to 300 feet in less than 4 miles. This is the steepest section of highway in Baja.

K12 **Propane** station on the left.

K7+ Bottom of hills. Sea of Cortez is right in front of you. Unimproved camping is just to north along beach called Playa Santa Maria. Yellowtail have been seen feeding right along shore here during months of November-February.

K0 **Santa Rosalía.** Turn right to go up into town. Great bakery, meat market, grocery stores, auto parts house, but you'll have to shop around to find everything you want - no superstores here. Almost all streets are one-way. Large rigs should park and walk. Don't forget to see the famous Eiffel metal church. If going to Guaymas on the mainland México side, confirm your ferry reservations in advance then enjoy sightseeing. Ferry terminal is just south of town on left.

End of log...

Sundial Shell

SANTA ROSALÍA-LORETO...122 miles, 197 kilometers.

K197 Leave town past ferry and gas station. Watch pumps at gas station to make sure they are at zero before filling up; government has closed this place down twice.

K195 El Morro Motel overlooking water. Good shelling on beach below. Arrange fishing trips here.

K194 Las Palmas RV park on right. Full hook-ups.

K189+ On left is new state prison.

K188+ Graded road west to Santa Agueda, 12 km. Beyond on rough road are several small ranchos and cave painting sites. The trip is an all day affair, but a rewarding one.

K182 San Lucas Cove. Follow sign to RV park on beach just past town. Minimal services but nice place. Good fishing in the cove. Restaurant Sara Reyna on right side of highway has very good food prepared by Jeff Alvarado. Jeff's dad, Bill, used to own the hotel at Punta Chivato and when there was to be a holiday feast he often had his son come to cook. Jeff will also provide you with any information you want about the surrounding area.

K174+ Road left to San Bruno trailer park on beach. A portion of this park and quite a few of the trailers were washed out to sea in September of '94.

K168 Side road right to San José de Magdalena, a farming community.

K162 To the east 2 km. the government has built an international airport to serve this area. Demand has not been as great as expected so they haven't opened it yet. However, they keep 3 guards on duty.

K156 Graded (sometimes very washboard) road left past houses leads to Punta Chivato, and shell beach, 20 km. Watch speed bumps as you pass between houses just after you leave the highway. A right turn here will take you to the cave paintings of San Borjitas.

(continued on RL74)

B A J A   B O O K   IV

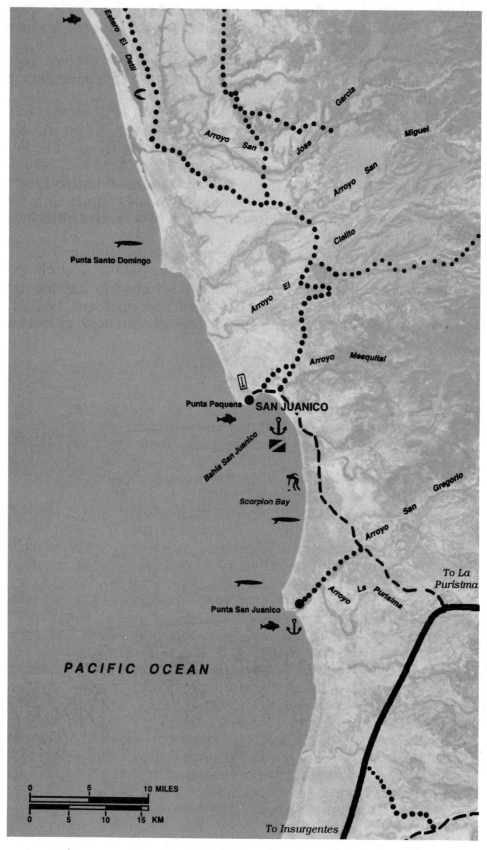

SEE RL 71

Garcia

Miguel

Arroyo   San   Jose

Arroyo   San

Cielito

Punta Santo Domingo

Arroyo   El

Arroyo   Mesquital

Punta Pequena   **SAN JUANICO**

San   Gregorio

Bahia San Juanico

Scorpion Bay

Arroyo

To La Purisima

Punta San Juanico

Arroyo   La   Purisima

PACIFIC OCEAN

0   5   10 MILES

0   5   10   15   KM

To Insurgentes

INSURGENTES-LA PURISIMA SIDE TRIP...65 miles, 101 kilometers

This side trip begins from K236 on Roadlog page 78.

K236   At the intersection turn right and continue north through Insurgentes. Distances are in miles.

M15.0   Dirt road coming in from the right is from Loreto via Misión San Javier. This 66 mile stretch of road is sometimes impassable and goes through some rugged country.

M17.0   Small farming community to the left is Santo Domingo.

M39.0   Ejido Francisco Villa.

M53.4   Road left, 5 miles to Las Barrancas. If you like to surf, this just might be your place.

M65.4   Junction with the road right to México 1 between Loreto and Mulegé at K59+. The road is paved for an additional seven miles through the communities of La Purísima and San Isidro. Beyond the road is graded dirt for approximately 34 miles before reaching México 1.

      A left turn here takes you 30 miles to Bahía San Juánico. This is a surfer's haven and rumor has it they are going to build a hotel out there. This poorly maintained dirt road continues on northward to Laguna San Ignacio and eventually to San Ignacio. There are no services and 4WD is recommended. The eventual plan is to pave this section of road north to meet with México 1.

End of trip...

-San Javier Mission

**B
A
J
A

B
O
O
K

IV**

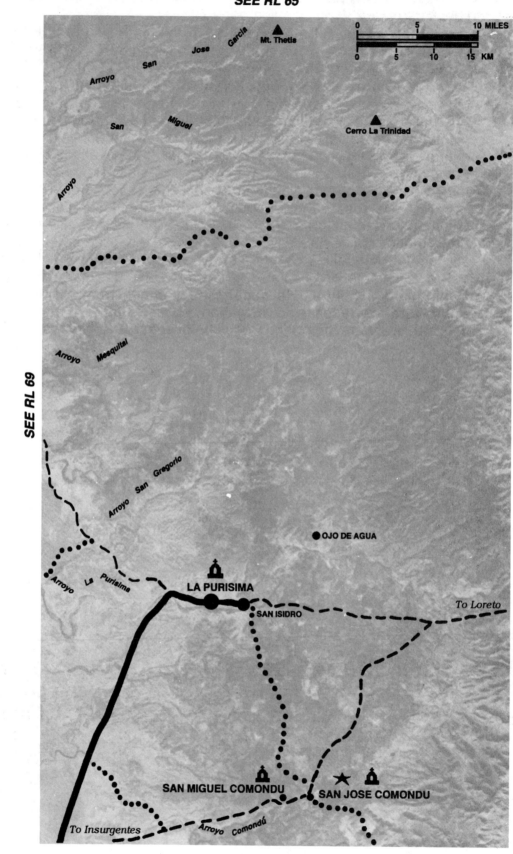

SEE RL 69

SEE RL 73

0   5   10 MILES

0   5   10   15 KM

Mt. Thetis

Cerro La Trinidad

Arroyo   San   Jose   Garcia

San   Miguel

Arroyo

Arroyo   Mesquital

Arroyo   San   Gregorio

●OJO DE AGUA

Arroyo   La   Purisima

LA PURISIMA

SAN ISIDRO

To Loreto

SAN MIGUEL COMONDU

★ SAN JOSE COMONDU

To Insurgentes   Arroyo   Comondú

LA PURISIMA...

        Access to La Purísima from the east is on Roadlog 70 at M65.4. To get there from the west see Roadlog 82 at K59 between Loreto and Mulegé.

        The trip through this valley is a beautiful one. A river flows between the mesas and the road winds back and forth over the river. The valley is not very wide, only 1/2 mile at La Purísima but is heavily planted with date palms, fruit trees, etc. The town of San Isidro, a farming community on the edge of a bluff overlooking the river, was established in the 1930's. The town of La Purísima was established in the 1700's as a mission site. The actual mission is now only a mound of adobe.

        To the south are San Miguel Comondú and San José Comondú, commonly referred to as "the Comondús." The mission site at San José de Comondú was established in 1708 by Father Julián de Mayorga. The site at San Miguel de Comondú never became an actual mission but was a visiting station. It was established by Juan de Ugarte, the father of California agriculture. He supervised the construction of important agricultural terraces and irrigation works. Both of the Comondú communities were important producers of sugarcane, grapes and fruit.

San José de Comondú

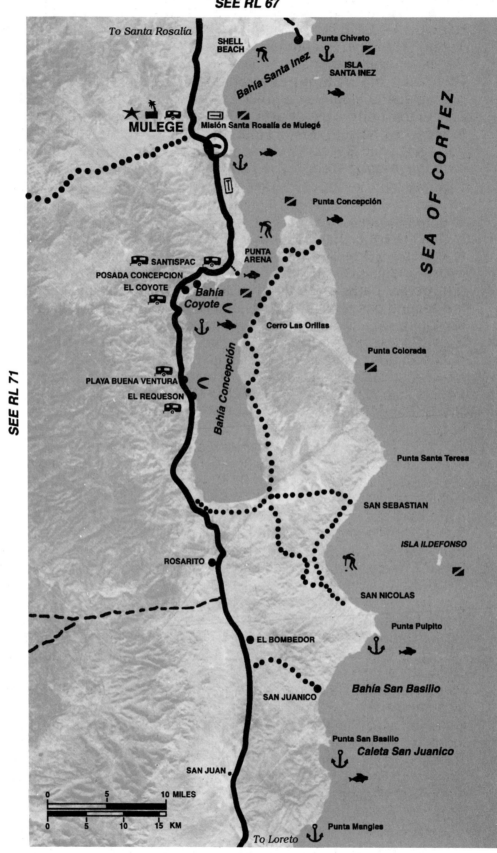

BAJA BOOK IV

ROADLOG 73

SANTA ROSALIA-LORETO...*(continued from RL68)*

K151   Turn-off for Playa Santa Inéz, dry camping; good shelling.

K143   Begin winding upgrade.

K135+   Road east into **Mulegé**. Several hotels, restaurants and markets make this a good place to stop. Large vehicles and those towing trailers will have difficulty driving the narrow old streets of Mulegé. La Almeja restaurant, on the beach, is great but hard to find (it's on the city map in this book). They don't mind if you park your RV on the beach for the night and after their margaritas it is probably a good idea. If you can't make it out there try Los Equipales or Las Casitas, both very good restaurants located in town having their own unique atmospheres. The Hotel Hacienda has an old-world atmosphere, good food and reasonable rooms. The Hotel La Siesta has very reasonably priced rooms. There is a good laundromat in town. If you spend a few hours in this town you will see why so many Americans call it home.

K135   Cross bridge over Río Santa Rosalía de Mulegé and continue south. There are two RV parks along the river to your left. The first is Orchard RV Park and the second one is Villa María Isabel RV Park (and great bakery). Both have full hook-ups. Villa María has all pull-through spaces.

K131   Hotel Serenidad 1 mile east. RV parking, a few spaces with full hook-ups, no pull-throughs, restaurant, pool and gift shop. Pig roast on Saturday night, Mexican fiesta dinner on Wednesday nights.

K130   Pemex station, magna sin, diesel, telephone office.

K126   View of sand dunes and Bahía Concepción. Just beyond is a dirt road to a sandy beach.

K119   To left of highway is a large stone corral, then road to secluded Playa Punta Arena. and Los Naranjos beach palapas. It is 3 miles to the beach.

K114+   On left is Playa Santispac. Popular with campers, windsurfers and boaters. Limited facilities, but a lady named Ana has a fine bakery and restaurant on north-east end of the beach.

K112   Bahía Tordilla and Posada Concepción. Many American villas here.

K110   Playa Las Cocas. We call this place Mosquito Beach.

K108   Bahía Coyote. Good public beach. During holidays hot-dog stands appear out of nowhere. Sometimes in the early mornings you can see giant manta rays jumping out of the water. Some of these animals are over twenty feet across and make a thundering splash.

K94.5   Playa Buena Ventura. RV parking on beach, limited services. Restaurant, George's Olé is owned by Mike. Motel was built here during the winter of 1994.

K91   Playa Armenta. Camping here and road goes around hill to south to another nice campsite.

K92+   Road left is to Playa Requesón. Fair clamming for chocolate clams. Up ahead there are several views of the old road.

K75   RV park on the water's edge has been abandoned.

K76   Bottom of Bahía Concepción. Bumpy dirt road east forks several times to a number of beaches and small ranchos.

(continued on RL82)

*B
A
J
A

B
O
O
K

IV*

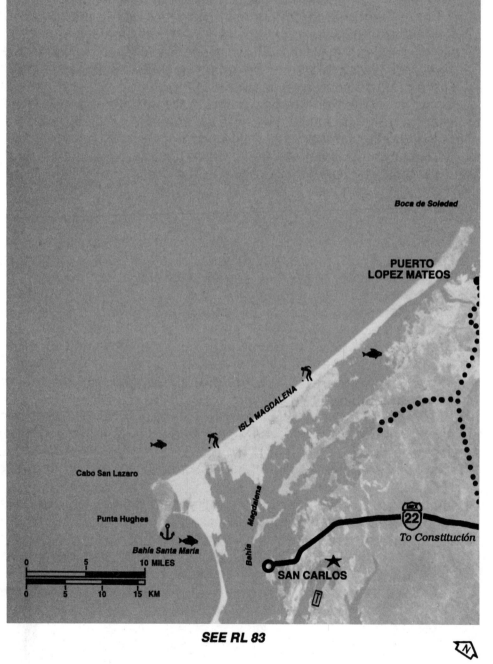

SEE RL 77

Boca de Soledad

**PUERTO
LOPEZ MATEOS**

ISLA MAGDALENA

Cabo San Lazaro

Bahía Magdalena

Punta Hughes

Bahía Santa María

MEX
22

To Constitución

★
SAN CARLOS

0   5   10 MILES

0   5   10   15 KM

SEE RL 83

ROADLOG 75

SAN CARLOS...
K211   Leave México 1 at northern end of Ciudad Constitución. From this intersection it is 36.8 miles, 59 Km, to San Carlos.

SAN CARLOS...
The paved and maintained road to San Carlos makes this an easy side trip. 3200 people live in San Carlos and the main source of income comes from the fish cannery. The only gas available in San Carlos is Nova. During the whale season there are many restaurants open and the hotels are also open. Services and supplies are very sparse at other times.

In 1991, we found one restaurant on a back street where we were offered a fresh lobster dinner. We accepted and were served 4 small lobster each! What a feed. It was delicious and the total bill for 2 people was only $10.00. This place is still doing a good business with the locals, and the prices are still quite reasonable.

San Carlos has a large commercial pier where deep-draft vessels can load and unload. We walked out there one day and watched them unload 260 metric tons of bluefin, yellowfin and big-eye tuna. They loaded it into open trucks and whisked it away to the cannery in Lopez Mateos. On this same pier there are large grain storage facilities. There are also some very large wharf rats.

Camping is allowed on the beach south of town about a mile. Many motorhomes and campers like the peace and quiet here on the edge of the lagoon. Personally I don't like the smell of the fish cannery just to the north of the camping area. If you can tolerate the odor the clamming is great; it's fairly easy to launch a small boat and there is some great fishing in the lagoon.

ISLA MAGDALENA...
Access to Isla Magdalena is best from Puerto Lopez Mateos. This island is a good place to go beach combing. If you desire to get out to the island you can hire one of the fishermen from Puerto Lopez Mateos to take you over in his panga. Determine the total price beforehand and pay him when he picks you up (you may have to give him money for gas before you go). It is only a 20 minute ride from Puerto Lopez Mateos to the back side of the island. From there follow the tracks (there are trucks on the island) over the dunes for about 1.5 miles and you're on the beach. The island is about 50 miles long. You will have about 40 miles of broad white sandy beach to comb. Remains of large ships lie deteriorating along the shore. Punta San Lázaro at the west end of the beach reaches far out into the sea and many an unwary captain has lost his ship along this shore. Yachts, paddle wheelers, whalers and all manner of ships are recorded to have been lost here.

The trucks on the island belong to the fishermen who have a camp down at the point. It is a dry camp (no liquor allowed) and there are no women allowed. Surf-fishing is good along the beach. During the winter months its fun to watch the humpback whales playing offshore. I have found many large grinning tun shells along the beach here.

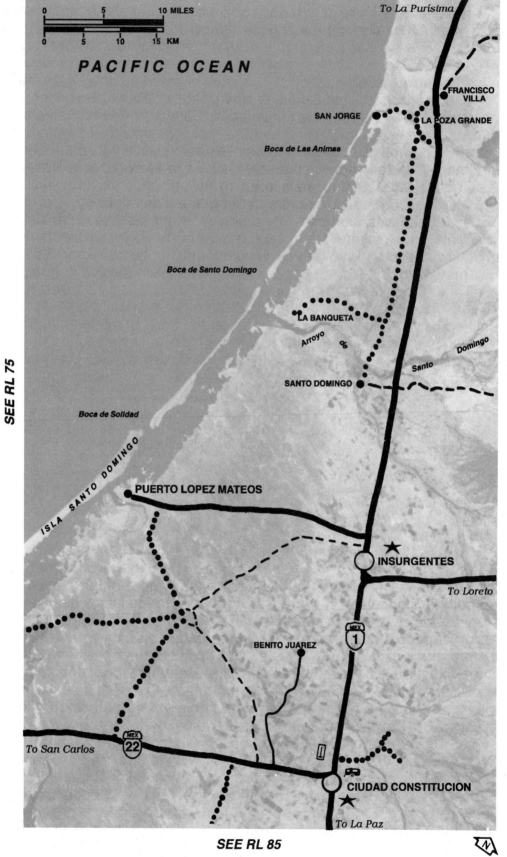

BAJA BOOK IV

ROADLOG 77

INSURGENTES-LA PAZ...147 miles, 236 kilometers.

K236   Intersection. Turn south and continue toward La Paz past numerous farms, small ejidos and narrow bridges. Watch for farm machinery and slow vehicles on highway. The community of Insurgentes is to the north and is described below.

K222   **Propane** station.

K213   Enter Ciudad Constitución. A new pre-pay Pemex is on right with Magna Sin and diesel. Just beyond, a paved road west to Puerto San Carlos and Bahía Magdalena (35 mi.). The hub for a growing number of farms, Constitución has little to show the tourist but supplies are relatively plentiful here. The "central market" (fresh vegies, cheeses, meats and seafood) is at Rosauro Zapata and Calle Bravo, off the main road to the left after the turn-off for Puerto San Carlos. Warning: do not turn left from the main highway, you must get into the road that runs alongside the highway on the right in order to legally turn left. Manfred's Trailer Park is on left side of the highway before you enter town. Just south of town a left turn takes you 31 miles to Misión San Luís Gonzaga, restored.

(continued on RL86)

INSURGENTES-LOPEZ MATEOS SIDE TRIP...21 miles, 34 kilometers

K236   From the top of this page - at this intersection turn right and pass through the town of Insurgentes. Mileages are in miles as kilometer signs are lacking.

M1.5   Turn right for Puerto Lopez Mateos. The road is paved all the way.

M21.0   Puerto Lopez Mateos. Watch for speed bumps as you enter town. Meager supplies available at a few small stores, no gas station.

LOPEZ MATEOS...

The population of Puerto Lopez Mateos is about 1500 people, most of whom work at the cannery. When the whistle blows they go to work, no matter the hour, day or night. The people are not prosperous. Except during whale season there is only one policeman in town. He has built a tree-house in front of the station. Perched up in his tree-house, binoculars in hand, he watches the incoming highway for speeders. There are no facilities such as hotels or RV parks but this will probably change soon. Thousands of people come here to see the whales. Two unions of *pangeros* hire out their boats to the eager whale-watchers. Planes fly people in from as far away as México City to view the whales. Restaurants open up. Motorhomes and campers fill the end of the runway at the water's edge. Over 20,000 people come here each year during the whale season which starts later here than in the north. The whales are here in number by February 20th. Kayaking is now forbidden during whale season.

Just outside of town to the north about 3 miles is what is left of a very expensive endeavor to mine phosphates. We heard it was the Japanese who built this huge machine. Obviously millions were spent. The machine started at the water's edge back in the lagoon. It was designed to dig a huge trench into the land, siphoning off the phosphates as it moved. Today, all that is left is one channel about 50 feet deep, over 100 yards wide and more than a half mile long - and the huge machine that created it.

B A J A

B O O K

IV

To La Purísima

SAN JOSE COMONDU

LA POZA GRANDE

Misión
San Javier

G I G A N T A

Domingo

Santo

de

Javier

Arroyo

San

PRESA VIEJA

Arroyo

PALO BLANCO

L A

SAN IGNACIO

D E

Arroyo

To Loreto

Santa

MEX
1

Cruz

To Insurgentes

S I E R R A

0   5   10 MILES

0   5   10   15   KM

LORETO-INSURGENTES...*(from RL82)*

K71   A microwave tower is on the left. Tall peaks are everywhere as road continues to wind. Watch for cattle in the road and large rocks after a rain.

K63+   Graded road south to Bahía Agua Verde, 40 km. This dirt road is now being occasionally maintained but it is still a rough one.

K45   A deep canyon is on south side as road continues along the edge of the mesa. Descent becomes more rapid. On a clear day the Pacific Ocean is visible ahead.

K39   Leave mountains and follow straight path in south-west direction across gently sloping plain and past growing numbers of deep-well irrigated farms. The water supply here is finite and not replaced by rains. Mexican eagles in this area.

K0   Another Pemex just before the intersection. To the north one mile is Ciudad Insurgentes and paved road to La Purísima (66 mi., 110 Km). One mile north of Ciudad Insurgentes is paved road to Puerto Lopez Mateos (21 mi., 34 Km) and good whale-watching in season. To the south, Ciudad Constitución and La Paz (236 km.).

End of log...

Bighorn Sheep

Baja's bighorn sheep. This beautiful animal survives well in the mountains of Baja. They are generally found on the eastern slopes of the mountain ranges all the way south to La Paz. They travel in groups and during the 1800's were slaughtered by the hundreds for their meat. Congregating at water holes on a daily basis they were an easy mark. Today the population is estimated at a conservative 4500 animals. Beef is more readily available today so they are not hunted continuously but still out back of almost every farmhouse the tell-tale curled horns lie baking in the sun.

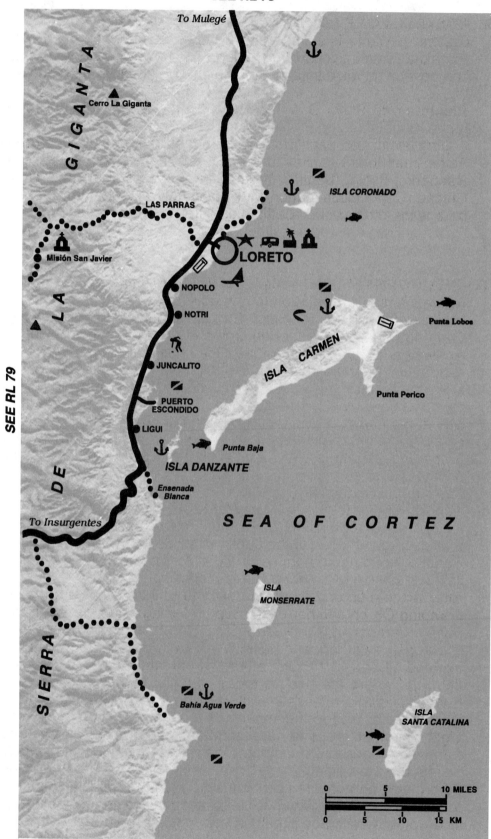

B A J A   B O O K   I V

SEE RL 79

To Mulegé

SIERRA DE LA GIGANTA

Cerro La Giganta

LAS PARRAS

Misión San Javier

LORETO

NOPOLO

NOTRI

JUNCALITO

PUERTO ESCONDIDO

LIGUI

Punta Baja

ISLA DANZANTE

Ensenada Blanca

To Insurgentes

ISLA CORONADO

ISLA CARMEN

Punta Lobos

Punta Perico

S E A   O F   C O R T E Z

ISLA MONSERRATE

Bahía Agua Verde

ISLA SANTA CATALINA

SIERRA

0	5	10 MILES

0	5	10	15 KM

SANTA ROSALIA-LORETO...(continued from RL74)

K62   Rancho Rosarito is to the right. Beyond, at K59+, road west goes to the La Purísima (34 mi.). Signed San Isidro, it is now widened and graded. This road can now be traveled by almost any vehicle with high clearance. It is a beautiful trip.

K48   Road east to Playa San Juanico, 10 mi. Good fishing out there around the rocks.

K6+   A fine view of Loreto and Isla Carmen before descending into valley.

K0   Paved road to left 2 miles to **Loreto**. All services, stores, gas stations, hotels, RV parks, fishing boats (Alfredos, on the waterfront) and Tiffany's Pizza, a Chicago style pizza parlor with absolutely scrumptious pizza. The mission here is the mother of all California missions and worth seeing.

End of log...

LORETO-INSURGENTES...74 miles, 119 kilometers.

K119   Leave intersection with Loreto and go south.

K118   Dirt road west leads to Misión San Javier (21.5 mi.) then on to San José de Comondú and San Miguel de Comondú reaching an extension of the paved highway at Ejido Francisco Villa. Road has been improved as part of mission restoration program; however, it is still rough. We rented a VW bug in town and took the bouncy trip in it. This mission is one of the most beautiful, well-preserved of all the missions in Baja. The side trip is recommended. There is a lady at the museum who can show you the old vestments in their "museum." A small donation is nice, or you could buy one of Hope's drawings. Hope (Esperanza) Bartmess is the lady who did the illustrations for this book. She donates her drawings to the museum.

K112   The airport is to the left.

K111   Nopoló. Site of Loreto Inn, large hotel on the water's edge with infrastructure for homes for Americans, convention center, etc. Large 18 hole golf course and club house, open to the public with club and cart rentals.

K102   Rancho Notrí. Ranch house on right; to left is beach where many species of fish come in close to shore. Great snorkeling!

K97+   After winding up and down, the entry to El Juncalito is at the bottom of grade. Camping OK on southern end. Superb fishing when the tide is high.

K94   Paved road on left is to Puerto Escondido (1.5 mi.) and the Tripui RV park (full hook-ups) restaurant and motel. Well worth the visit. The region abounds with fish and other sea life. One afternoon our family caught 21 different species of fish right where the dock is today. A major tourist development is underway here, including a high rise hotel, launch ramp and marina. Rumor has it that it is financed by a French company.

K84+   Liguí is a small group of houses set back from the sea. Beyond about 1 mi. is Ensenada Blanca fish camp and camping beach. Very crowded during major holidays.

K83   Turn inland and up into pass leading through the Sierra de La Giganta and on to Magdalena Plain. Watch for interesting remnants of the old road.

K77   The worst of the grade is behind you.

(turn back to RL80)

B A J A   B O O K   IV

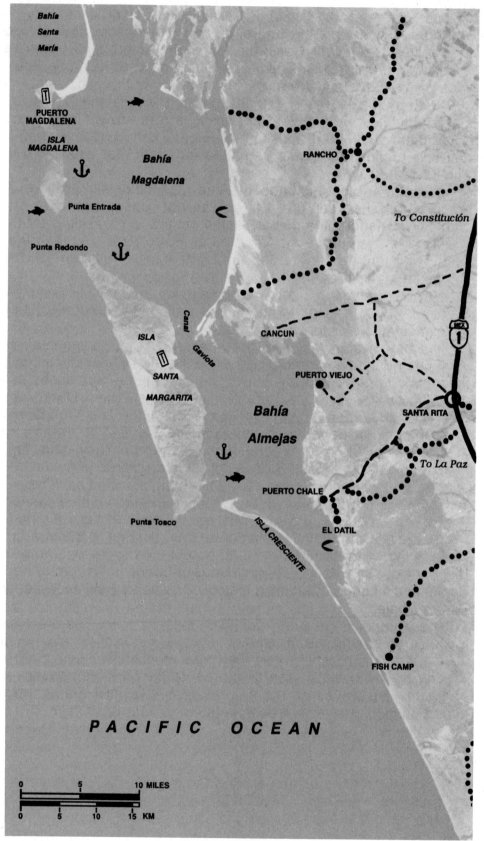

Bahía
Santa
María

PUERTO
MAGDALENA

*ISLA
MAGDALENA*

*Bahía
Magdalena*

Punta Entrada

Punta Redondo

*Canal
Gaviota*

ISLA

SANTA

MARGARITA

*Bahía
Almejas*

Punta Tosco

ISLA CRESCIENTE

RANCHO

To Constitución

CANCUN

PUERTO VIEJO

SANTA RITA

To La Paz

PUERTO CHALE

EL DATIL

FISH CAMP

P A C I F I C   O C E A N

0   5   10 MILES

0   5   10   15   KM

N

BAHÍA MAGDALENA...

From the beginning of the recorded history of this area there are records of groups attempting or planning to settle on Magdalena Bay. None of these attempts succeeded but there is one attempt worthy of mention. Calling themselves the Lower California Company, a group of American speculators obtained a grant from the Mexican government to colonize Baja in 1869. They were given 46,800 square miles or five-sixths of the peninsula. A scout was sent out to study the land and this area around Magdalena Bay was chosen as the place to begin their venture. Specifically, a place called Matancitas was selected. It is located about 15 miles south of where Puerto Lopez Mateos is located today and was originally a slaughter house for cattle that supplied the whaling ships with fresh meat.

In 1870, three shiploads of American colonists arrived. They were not prepared for their venture. Water was not readily abundant and the land not arable. For a short time they collected orchilla, a parasitic plant that grows in the area and is used in the manufacture of indigo dyes. But their venture didn't last long. They returned home and the grant was annulled in 1871. Today there is nothing at Matancitas.

In 1908, and again in 1912, the Japanese tried unsuccessfully to lease land at Magdalena Bay. Had either one of these efforts been successful it would certainly have affected our history as it is today.

The bays within the area are sheltered by large mountainous islands and have offered safe harbor for ships since the days of the Manila galleon - that is for those who made it into the bays. There are numerous accounts of ships going down here. One map calls the big bay "Wreck Bay." Diving around the many wrecks could be dangerous. Sharks are numerous and currents are strong. There is still lots of gold and silver out there though.

Today there is a marked channel in the main bay, and large ocean going freighters come to port at San Carlos to load grain and cotton. Commercial tuna boats also unload at the long pier. The mangrove lined back bays are charted but continually change as storms fill in the estuaries and create new ones.

Fishing for snook, croaker, corbina, halibut and bass is good inside the bay during the winter months. Outside the bay, during the summer months, is found some of the finest sport fishing on the west coast. The long-range boats from San Diego make stops here. Just south of San Carlos is the former home of the Flying Sportsmen's Lodge. Clamming is good in Almejas Bay, accessed from Cancún or Puerto Chale.

The weather is generally cool with fog and wind. There are lots of bugs and mosquitoes around the mangrove swamps, but if one makes camp close to the water there doesn't seem to be much of a problem.

Surfing on the outer shores of Isla Santa Margarita is popular. At the southern end when the waves are right, rides of over a mile are common. There is an airport on the island and surfers are flown in from San Diego.

**Knobbed
Whelk**

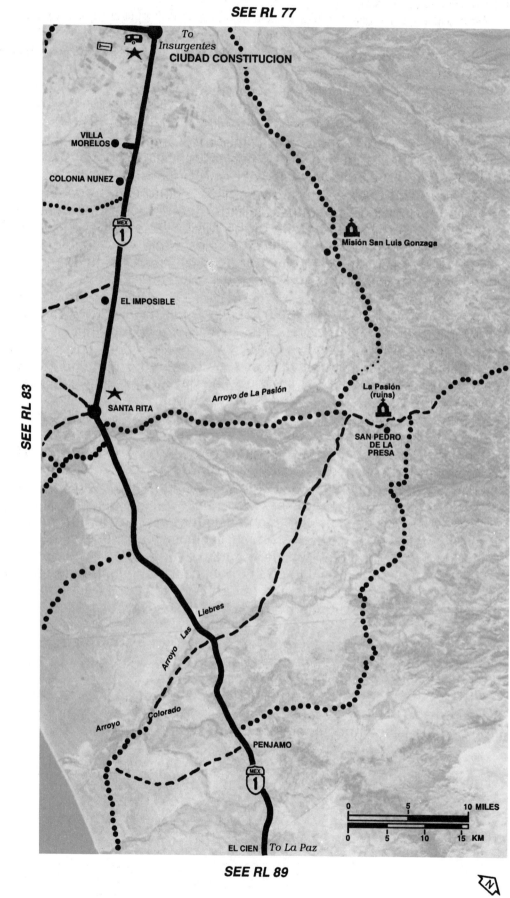

*B
A
J
A*

*B
O
O
K*

IV

To
Insurgentes
CIUDAD CONSTITUCION

**VILLA
MORELOS**

COLONIA NUNEZ

MEX
1

EL IMPOSIBLE

SANTA RITA

Arroyo de La Pasión

Misión San Luis Gonzaga

La Pasión
(ruins)

**SAN PEDRO
DE LA
PRESA**

Liebres

Las

Arroyo

Colorado

Arroyo

PENJAMO

MEX
1

0   5   10 MILES

0   5   10   15 KM

EL CIEN *To La Paz*

N

ROADLOG 85

INSURGENTES-LA PAZ...(*continued from RL78*)

K210   Radio tower on left. On right, off highway, is RV park, Campestre La Pila with a few places with hook-ups. They have a large swimming pool in a park-like setting with lots of grass and trees. The park is about a mile from the highway on a fairly good dirt road.

K198   Villa Morelos, a small prosperous farm community.

K183+   Rancho El Coyote. At K183, a sign, "Rancho El Imposible," and boy, does the surrounding area look it. Soon road will turn slightly to east.

K173   Graded dirt road leads west 20 miles to Cancún fish camp and an access point onto the Bahía Almejas portion of Magdalena Bay.

K135   Santa Rita. An extra dry portion of a very dry desert--less than 2 inches of rain per year. Dirt road south and west is to Puerto Chale about 15 miles. Good fishing and diving - no tourist facilities. The dirt road east from here leads 60 miles to the gulf and the site of the Misión Dolores del Sur (ruins). The dry washes along here start in the mountains at the very edge of the gulf side of Baja and eventually empty into the Pacific Ocean. Should a storm occur, this road can become impassable for days.

K156+   Microondas El Rifle. After reading <u>The Baja Highway</u> we decided to camp here and look for the petrified shark's teeth the book mentions. We stayed behind the microwave tower. The night sky was brilliantly lit with more stars than there are supposed to be. We stayed up late watching falling stars and satellites zooming every which way. Morning came and we spent a few minutes looking around but left without finding anything. Must go back there sometime!

K123   Lonchería San Antonio on the right side of the highway. Truckers stop here to eat - the food must be good.

K110   Rancho Pénjamo, typical little Baja cafe with fairly good food. Watch out for those tiny red chilis - they are fire!

K100   Shortly after entering the foothills you come to El Cien which is 100 km., or 62 miles from La Paz. The Pemex station here has Magna Sin, Nova and diesel. Some nice petrified sharks teeth can be purchased from the old man at the gas station. Road then climbs and for the next 20 miles meanders through increasingly heavy vegetation.

(continued on RL90)

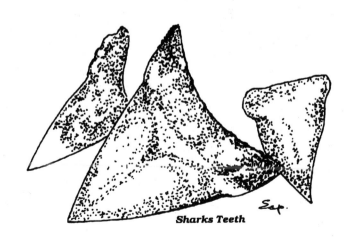

Sharks Teeth

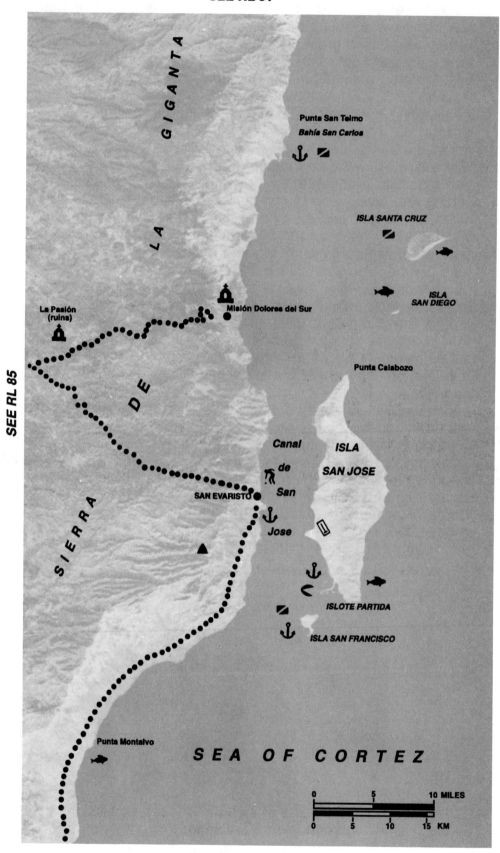

B A J A

B O O K

IV

Punta San Telmo

Bahía San Carlos

ISLA SANTA CRUZ

ISLA
SAN DIEGO

La Pasión
(ruins)

Misión Dolores del Sur

Punta Calabozo

DE

Canal

de

San

ISLA

SAN JOSE

SIERRA

SAN EVARISTO

Jose

ISLOTE PARTIDA

ISLA SAN FRANCISCO

Punta Montalvo

S E A   O F   C O R T E Z

0   5   10 MILES

0   5   10   15   KM

SEE RL 89 & RL 91

Misión San Luis Gonzaga Chiriyaqui

Misión San Luis Gonzaga Chiriyaqui, one of the missions that is intact. Exact location of this mission is on Roadlog map 85.

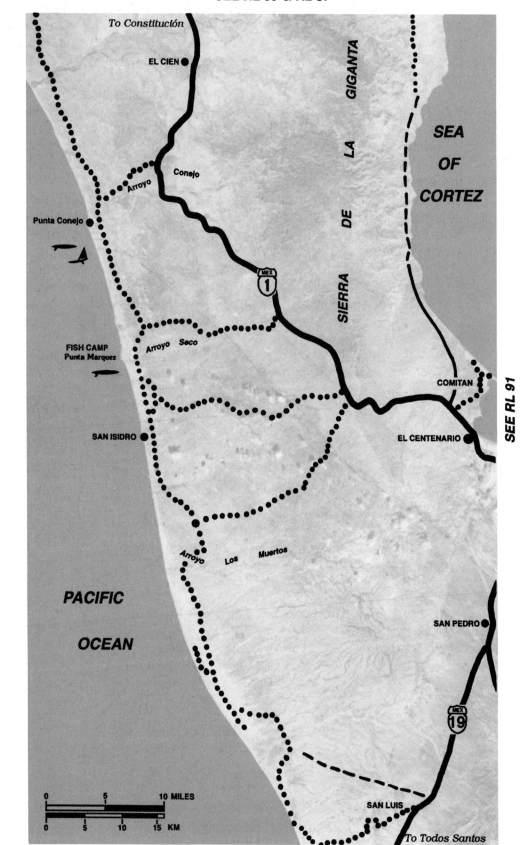

BAJA BOOK IV

To Constitución

EL CIEN

LA GIGANTA

SEA

OF

CORTEZ

Conejo

Arroyo

Punta Conejo

SIERRA

DE

LA

MEX 1

SEE RL 91

FISH CAMP
Punta Marquez

Arroyo   Seco

COMITAN

SAN ISIDRO

EL CENTENARIO

Arroyo   Los   Muertos

PACIFIC

OCEAN

SAN PEDRO

MEX 19

0   5   10 MILES

0   5   10   15   KM

SAN LUIS

To Todos Santos

ROADLOG 89

K80   Dirt road right, 17 km., is to popular surfing spot, El Conejo. Good rock oysters can be purchased from the commercial oyster divers at $5.00 a dozen, shucked. Surf fishing is so-so. There are some nice dry camp spots just back from the beach in the dunes. From El Conejo an unmaintained dirt road goes south along the coast to Todos Santos, about 75 miles. There are many beautiful isolated beaches along here. There is also an unmaintained very rough road to the north which eventually reaches the highway, but there are some very rough, almost impassable, spots on it. High-clearance vehicles recommended. No gas stations, no grocery stores, no telephones.

K77   Arroyo Conejo. Lots of fossils from an old sea here; it's worth a walk around the area.

K62   On the right is a strange white-washed cactus-shaped shrine. A longtime landmark it is a refreshing respite. I like the flowers in the belly-button.

K34   You are on the crest of the hills surrounding the La Paz valley and from here on a clear day you can see La Paz in the distance. Winding downgrade next few miles. About here you will start to see more and more traffic. La Paz is a big city and the people drive like city people, fast and with destination.

K22   **Agricultural inspection station.** They usually don't check you going south, only heading north. Mangoes, citrus and potatoes are not to be taken north of here.

K17   Paved road north is to San Juan de La Costa (25 mi.), site of a large phosphate mine. A very poor road continues on from there to many small beaches and San Evaristo (about 70 miles total).

(continued on RL92)

Coyote

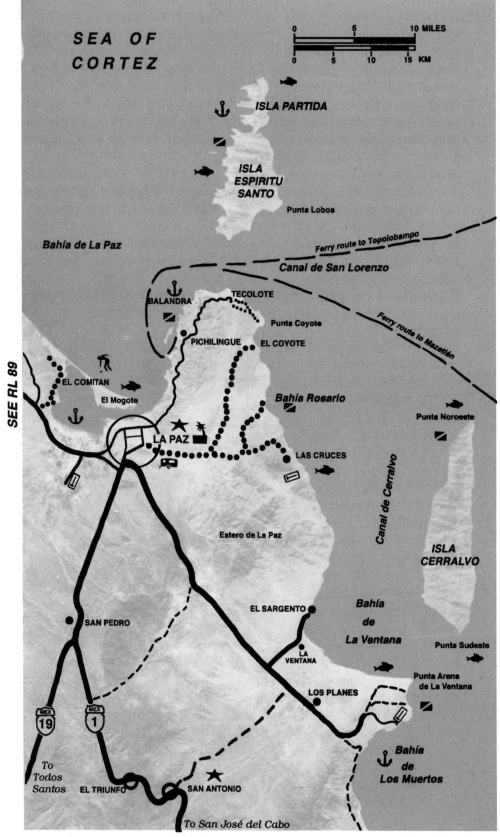

**B
A
J
A**

**B
O
O
K**

IV

SEA OF
CORTEZ

0   5   10 MILES
0   5   10   15 KM

ISLA PARTIDA

ISLA
ESPIRITU
SANTO

Punta Lobos

Bahía de La Paz

Ferry route to Topolobampo

Canal de San Lorenzo

BALANDRA   TECOLOTE

Ferry route to Mazatlán

Punta Coyote

PICHILINGUE   EL COYOTE

EL COMITAN

El Mogote   Bahía Rosario

Punta Noroeste

LA PAZ

LAS CRUCES

Canal de Cerralvo

Estero de La Paz

ISLA
CERRALVO

SAN PEDRO

EL SARGENTO   Bahía
de
La Ventana

Punta Sudeste

LA
VENTANA

Punta Arena
de La Ventana

LOS PLANES

MEX
19

MEX
1

To
Todos
Santos   EL TRIUNFO   SAN ANTONIO

Bahía
de
Los Muertos

To San José del Cabo

SEE RL 89

ROADLOG 91

INSURGENTES-LA PAZ...*(from page RL90)*

K16+   El Comitan turn-off.

K15   El Centenario. Trailer park on left side of road.

K12   Pemex on right has Magna Sin and diesel.

K9   Road right to La Paz International Airport.
Between here and downtown La Paz there are many RV parks both on the right and left sides of the highway. The oldest is the El Cardón on the right. It is our favorite because they have lots of pull-through spaces and we like the little palm shaded individual patios.

K6   The large statue appears to be a whales tail from a distance but on closer inspection becomes the doves of peace. (Peace in spanish is Paz). Turn right here and completely by-pass La Paz if you're heading straight for Cabo San Lucas.

K5   Department of Tourism on your right. Beyond here on left and right are the trailer parks. El Cardón on right is recommended, many pull-throughs, all facilities, older and has more character.

K0   Downtown **La Paz**. More specifically we are at the Pemex station at the corner of 5 de Febrero and Abasolo.

End of Log...

LA PAZ-CABO SAN LUCAS...via Mex 1, 132 mi, 213 km.

K213   From corner of 5 de Febrero and Isabela La Catolica, bear west and south.

K211   Road left to San Juan de Los Planes (30 mi.), Bahía de Los Muertos (42 mi. more) and El Sargento. The beach at Los Muertos faces south and is somewhat protected from winds in winter. Windsurfing is at its finest at El Sargento which has only dry camping. Surf fishing from Punta Arena de La Ventana has yielded many a nice roosterfish right out of the surf. Hotel Las Arenas (if open) has boats for hire.

K204   **Propane** station.

K191   Enter small community of San Pedro.

K185   Paved road to right leads to Todos Santos, El Pescadero and, ultimately, **Cabo San Lucas** via highway 19. We go left.

K165   Top of grade, excellent view of El Triunfo. Note well kept graveyard (panteón) on hill.

K164   Enter El Triunfo. Across bridge on right is a small basket shop. These baskets are made here by the locals. The shop is not always open but the children are most always selling baskets on the street. The small restaurant serves good food. Wow! Look at the paint job on the church. If you are in this area during October, you will see people selling buckets full of pitaya fruit. Try some, it is very different, kind of like a strawberry, raspberry and watermelon mixture. You will seldom see this fruit in the markets as it does not maintain it's sweetness very long. Pitaya keep fairly well in the refrigerator.
The brick chimney is a dominate reminder of the days when silver and gold were successfully mined in this area. In 1874, $50,000 worth of silver a month was taken from these mines. In 1918, a hurricane flooded the mines and they have not been successfully reopened since.

(continued on RL98)

B A J A   B O O K   IV

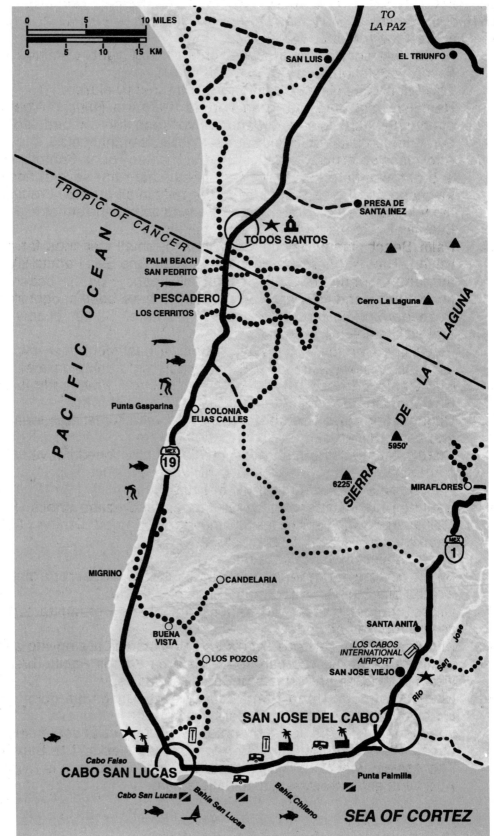

TO
LA PAZ

EL TRIUNFO

SAN LUIS

10 MILES
KM

TROPIC OF CANCER

PRESA DE
SANTA INEZ

TODOS SANTOS

PALM BEACH
SAN PEDRITO

PESCADERO

Cerro La Laguna

LOS CERRITOS

SIERRA DE LA LAGUNA

PACIFIC OCEAN

Punta Gasparina

COLONIA
ELIAS CALLES

5950'

MEX
19

MIRAFLORES

6225'

SIERRA

MEX
1

MIGRINO

CANDELARIA

SANTA ANITA

BUENA
VISTA

LOS CABOS
INTERNATIONAL
AIRPORT

LOS POZOS

SAN JOSE VIEJO

San Jose

SAN JOSE DEL CABO

Rio

Cabo Falso
CABO SAN LUCAS

Punta Palmilla

Cabo San Lucas

Bahia San Lucas

Bahia Chileno

SEA OF CORTEZ

N

CABO SAN LUCAS VIA TODOS SANTOS...80 miles, 128 km.

Note: This log begins 17 miles or 28 kilometers south of La Paz at K185 of México 1 where it intersects with México highway 19 .

K0   At the intersection of México 1 and 19 turn right. Continue through dense desert vegetation.

K7+   To west is Club Carrizal campground, frequently closed.

K26   Heading west is signed graded road, Ramál a Rancho Albanez. This road eventually gets to the ocean. We've seen lots of bird life through here, peregrine falcons, Mexican eagles, orioles, cardinals etc.

K53   After passing a number of ranches you enter Todos Santos. After left turn at end of town there is full service Pemex. There are several fine restaurants in town and the fish taco stands are the best in all of Baja. We like Pilars, where the telephone office is, and also the stand across the street.

K55+   Botanical gardens on left. Needs lotsa love.

K56+   Palm Beach, many palms, lovely beach, small clearings for camping. Good fishing. The next right turn (km 58+) leads to the San Pedrito RV Park, home of the famous Pancho's Sports Bar. Trailer park is on the beach; full hook-ups, good surfing and fishing. Small roosterfish have been caught in the surf here.

K60   Pescadero. Rich farms abound around here. Center of town is off to east around a small hill.

K64   Playa Los Cerritos to the right 1.6 mi., a beautiful beach protected on north end. Just below, a trailer park and impromptu camping area. Several times we've enjoyed good fishing off the rocks here. Frequently lots of humpback whales offshore.

K69   During rainy season a sizable fresh water lake sometimes forms between road and sand dunes.

K72+   Road west to southern end of same beach mentioned above. Watch for strong currents.

K71   Rancho Nuevo. New development going in.

K81+   Beautiful beach near road. Many small, interesting shells. Heavy surf and steep drop-off. Dangerous swimming, but good fishing. Cast lures past breaker line or use bait near rocks.

K97   La Candelaria, 4 km to the east.

K99   Begin curving downgrade with beautiful sandy beach in distance. Look for whales blowing. Soon you cross Puente El Pastor.

K107   Cross another bridge and begin long, gradual grade to top of hill before seeing the Sea of Cortez.

K111   At this point you can see "land's end." Americans are buying and leasing land out here as far as you can see. This area affords Pacific breezes and good views of the Sea of Cortez and Cabo San Lucas.

K122   Enter outskirts of **Cabo San Lucas**. New buildings are going up daily as this now world-famous resort prospers and grows.

K128   Intersection with México 1 on north end of the business district of Cabo San Lucas. Pemex on left. Turn left here to reach Mexico 1 to San Jose del Cabo. The easiest way to get into downtown Cabo San Lucas is to go left here and when you get to the first signal make a right.

End of log...

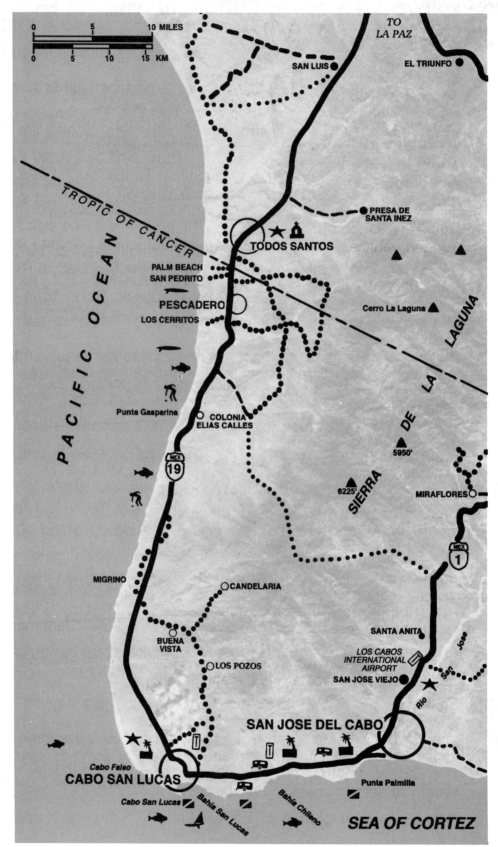

BAJA BOOK IV

LA PAZ-CABO SAN LUCAS via Mex 1...*(from RL98)*

K46+	Enter Santa Anita. This is one of several sleepy little towns that have changed little with time.
K44	Paved road west to Los Cabos International Airport (1 mi.). New four lane highway to Cabo San Lucas begins here.
K40	Pemex, Magna Sin, Diesel. Next door a large supermarket stocked with goods for Americans and Canadians to buy. Fresh seafood.
K38	San José Viejo, a long-established farming area. This area was well established until, in 1993, a storm brought almost 50 inches of rain in one night. Rebuilding is slow and mother nature can't be hurried when it comes to growing mango trees and banana palms. To the east of San José is a fairly well-maintained dirt road that follows the coastline up to La Ribera. All along this road are lots for sale and foreigners building beautiful homes along the shoreline. Fresh water is plentiful in the area. It is a nice side trip if you have a rugged vehicle. There are lots of beautiful lonely beaches and good fishing holes.
K33	Turn left on Zaragoza for **San José del Cabo**. Full service Pemex at intersection. México 1 continues toward ocean. Below town along the coast are a series of beach front hotels, a golf course and hundreds of Americans' homes.
K32+	Another turn into San José del Cabo.
K30+	Left turn here to the beach front hotels of San José del Cabo.
K30	Brisa del Mar RV Park (full hook-ups) on a beautiful beach. Open all year. Then we pass a beach which is often crowded with surfers during the late summer storm season. Are they waiting for a tropical storm to generate some nice big waves? Treacherous surf.
K27	Turn left to Hotel Palmilla with its beautiful meandering Jack Nicklaus signature golf courses. Across the street - **Propane** station.
K24	Entrance to the newest of the major hotels, the Westin Regina. Built with international conferences and symposiums in mind, this huge complex is bringing a new type of visitor to Baja.
K20	Entrance to the Melía Cabo Real.
K15+	On left is the Hotel Cabo San Lucas. Lush tropical gardens surround the cobblestone driveway to this exceptional resort. This place has it all, sport fishing, snorkeling, sunbathing - in a very peaceful setting. They have a large gift shop with some exquisite oriental antiques. Nearby Chileno Bay provides some of the best snorkeling and diving in all of Baja. Giant marlin are regularly caught just outside of this bay.
K12	Entrance to Twin Dolphin Hotel. Beautifully landscaped with native desert plants; this is a favorite with the affluent visitor.
K7.5	Villa Serena RV park on left, very nice park, reservations needed in the winter. Wonderful view of Baja's famous arch at land's end.
K5.5	El Arco RV Park on right.
K2.5	Vagabundos del Mar RV park on left.
K1	Full service Pemex with Magna Sin and diesel. Just before the gas station is road right (México 19) to Pacific side of peninsula and La Paz via Todos Santos.
K0	You are now in **Cabo San Lucas**. Enjoy!

End of Log...

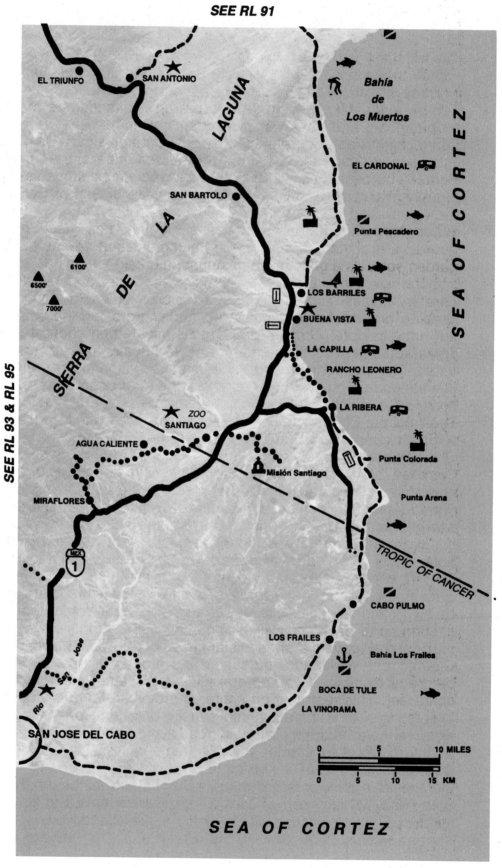

BAJA BOOK IV

SEE RL 93 & RL 95

EL TRIUNFO

SAN ANTONIO

LA

LAGUNA

Bahía de Los Muertos

EL CARDONAL

SAN BARTOLO

DE

Punta Pescadero

6100'

6500'

7000'

LOS BARRILES

BUENA VISTA

SIERRA

LA CAPILLA

RANCHO LEONERO

LA RIBERA

ZOO
SANTIAGO

AGUA CALIENTE

Punta Colorada

Misión Santiago

Punta Arena

MIRAFLORES

MEX
1

TROPIC OF CANCER

CABO PULMO

José

San

LOS FRAILES

Bahía Los Frailes

Rio

BOCA DE TULE

LA VINORAMA

SAN JOSE DEL CABO

0		5		10 MILES

| 0 | 5 | 10 | 15 | KM |

SEA OF CORTEZ

S E A   O F   C O R T E Z

N

LA PAZ-CABO SAN LUCAS...via Mex 1...*(from RL92)*

K160   Reach top of ridge after a winding ascent and drop into San Antonio Valley. Slow down and enjoy some of Baja's tropical greenery.

K156+   San Antonio. Mangoes, papayas, oranges, avocados and date palms are visible in this area. Dirt road down the canyon 14 miles (turn left at sharp left curve, high clearance vehicles recommended) intersects with La Paz-Los Planes road a few miles west of San Juan de Los Planes. Continue past small Pemex and begin to climb out of the canyon almost immediately. Road winds sharply in places. Shortly you will have views of Sea of Cortez as you pass through area of many flowers (in rainy season).

K129   Enter San Bartolo. This roadside settlement has many picturesque little houses with thatched roofs nestled along sides of arroyo. Long famous as a garden spot, it's a good place to stop for a break.

K110+   Los Barriles. Road left to Hotel Palmas de Cortez and Hotel Playa Hermosa (.4 and .9 miles respectively). Pemex is on right 1 mile further south in Buena Vista. A graded dirt road continues northward along the coast past beautiful and remote Hotel Punta Pescadero (9 miles), then about 4 miles further the small settlement of El Cardonál and eventually through to the Los Planes valley. The last portion of the road is not recommended for the fainthearted or ill-equipped. A better, paved and graded road goes to Los Planes from the south edge of La Paz.

K106+   Road right to El Coro, 10 km., a few remote ranchos in the sierras. Just beyond a road left is signed to Hotel Rancho Buena Vista resort

K105   Cross bridge, Puente Palmilla, and left into Hotel Spa Buena Vista.

K104+   Dirt road left to La Capilla RV park (full hook-ups) and Rancho Leonero. The Rancho invites last minute guests but the road out there is quite rough. Call first to see if they have space before driving all the way out and being turned away. The ranch, which encompasses over 350 acres, was originally owned by Gil Powell. The outside barbecue was built by him and is still used by the hotel today. Gil died, over the age of 60, while honeymooning with his fifth wife. They were on a safari in Africa.

K93   Paved road east to La Ribera (7.5 mi.), Hotel Punta Colorada (13 mi. total), Cabo Pulmo (24.1 mi. total), Los Frailes (29 mi. total) and on to circle the eastern tip to San José del Cabo (82 mi. total). At this writing the new paved road is only paved a short distance and large portions have already been washed out. Frequent hurricanes and storms in this area. Inquire locally before attempting. If you do make it out to Cabo Pulmo look for Baja's only coral reef. This reef, just off shore, is protected from fishing but makes very interesting diving. There is a dive shop in Cabo Pulmo.

K84+   Road right to Santiago. Paved road winds sharply down into Arroyo de Santiago and across to the town. The unsophisticated nature of the little zoo they have here makes the visit a very special experience.

K81+   Monument in form of large white cement sphere marks the Tropic of Cancer. Stand here at high noon on June 21 and you will have lost your shadow.

K71   Miraflores. Pemex station with Magna Sin, diesel and Nova.

(turn back to RL96)

ROAD SIGNS...

Road signs in Baja are fairly easy to figure out as they use the international symbols in many places and in the extreme north and south some of the signs are in both English and Spanish. However, in many places there are signs only in Spanish and they can be confusing. It can be easy to misinterpret a sign; a friend of mine thought *no tire basura* meant "no tire changing" (it means don't litter); another friend thought *arena* meant a place for a bull-fight when it meant "sandy"; and another friend thought *obedezca las senales* meant to slow down for the old people when it means to "obey the signs". Signs take planning and coordination - take them seriously. Following is a list of the more common signs that you should learn.

Acceso a la playa - beach access.
Agua para radiador - radiator water.
Alto - stop.
Area de ganado - cattle area.
Area de peatones - pedestrians.
Aeropuerto - airport.
Asfalto fresco - fresh asphalt.
Camino cuota - toll road.
Camino dividido - divided road.
Camino sinuoso - winding road.
Carga ancha - wide load.
Ceda el paso - yield.
Conceda cambio de luces - dim your
    lights.
Cruce de camiones - truck crossing.
Cuota - toll.
Curva peligroso - dangerous curve.
Derecha - right.
Derecho - straight ahead.
Despacio - slow.
Desviación - detour.
Disminuya su velocidad - slow down.
Doble remolque - double trailer.
Estacionarse - parking.
Este - east.
Faltas geologica - geological faulting.
Ganado - cattle.
Grava suelta - loose gravel.
Hombres trabajando - men working.
Izquierda - left.
Libre - free (non-toll road.)
Maquinas trabajando - machines
    working.

Maxima velocidad - maximum speed.
No deje piedres en el camino - don't
leave rocks in the road.
No hay paso - road closed.
No rebase - no passing.
No rebase con raya continua - don't
    pass over the white line.
No tire basura - don't litter.
No vuelta a la derecha - no right turn.
Norte - north.
Obedezca las senales - obey the signs.
Oeste - west.
Peligroso - dangerous.
Poblado proximo - town nearby.
Policia federal de caminos - highway
    patrol.
Prepare su cuota - prepare your toll fee.
Puente angosto - narrow bridge.
Ruta de camiones - truck route.
Salida de camiones - truck exit.
Semaforo - traffic signal.
Si toma no maneje - Don't drink and
    drive.
Solo izquierda - left turns only.
Sur - south.
Topes - speed bumps.
Un solo carril - one way street.
Vado - dip.
Velocidad limite - speed limit.
Zona de derrumbes - falling rocks.
Zona de escolar - school zone.

Chapter 7

ENJOYING BAJA

All the popular water sports are available to you in Baja. Swimming, snorkeling, diving, surfing, windsurfing, fishing, boating, kayaking and water skiing, are all enjoyed by many in the beautiful clear waters surrounding Baja.

The wave action on the Pacific side is quite strong and the weather generally cooler. There is very little wave action on the Sea of Cortez. Fishing is great on both coasts. Boat launch ramps are located throughout the peninsula. You'll get more of a variety of fish out of the gulf but generally catch larger fish on the Pacific side and at the tip. Surfing is limited to the Pacific side and great surf it is. Whale-watching to see the grey whale is confined to the Pacific side; however, there are finback, blue, minke and humpback whales almost all year round in the Sea of Cortez. Windsurfing is at it's peak in the East Cape area in the winter. Diving is good on both coasts but is best in the lower gulf area from the midriff south to Cabo San Lucas where the water is warmer and clearer. Beachcombing for the cast-offs of man and nature is best on the Pacific side; however, both coasts reveal beautiful and unusual shells. Both coasts have wonderful, secluded beaches for camping.

Almost all of the things you will do in Baja will be centered around her shores. Many of the things you do will be controlled by the height of the tides. Tides in the upper gulf near San Felipe and El Golfo sometimes surge for more than 30 feet. This is great for shellers and clammers but not so great if you are out swimming, your new 4-wheel truck is on the beach, and the tide starts coming in. Tides change from high to low in just under six hours The highest high tides of the month are during the full moon and the dark of the moon. Annually the highs and lows have extremes during June and December. If you plan to enjoy both coasts you will need two different tide tables, one for the gulf side and one for the Pacific side of Baja. Places to get these tide tables are listed under "Resources" in the back of this book.

Use caution while you enjoy the many water sports. Medical assistance is not always nearby. The Red Cross supplies the basic ambulance service in Baja. They have people collecting along the roadside as you go south. Contribute! Hospitals provide free emergency care in many of the larger cities.

WHALE-WATCHING...

Every year the grey whale returns to Baja to mate and calve in the lagoons. From near extinction, they have rebounded. In 1857, the count was estimated at 30,000, (down from perhaps 50,000). In 1953, the total number was estimated by count at under 3000. Today they estimate the total herd at over 20,000. It is believed the herd is increasing about 11% per year.

In December of 1857, Captain Charles M. Scammon, a whaler from San Francisco, followed the whales inside the large lagoon at the edge of Viscaíno Bay. Soon this lagoon became known as 'Scammon's Lagoon" and is still called this by many today. (The locals and the Mexican government refer to it as Laguna Ojo de Liebre, originally named so because of a local water-hole frequented by jack rabbits.) Captain Scammon's first year of whaling inside the lagoon was tremendously successful and upon his return to San Francisco the word spread of his bountiful catch. The following year others followed him. After only 4 years the cost of rigging for the trip became more than the potential income. They had almost totally wiped out the grey whale population.

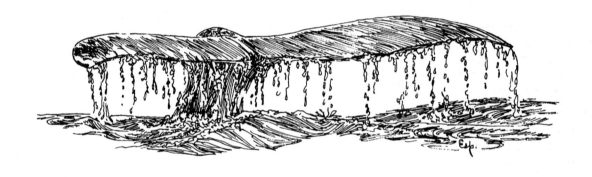

Over the years the slaughter of the grey whale continued. (Because migrations of this species follow the shoreline, seldom more than 10 kilometers out; the grey whale is easy to find and kill and thus very vulnerable.) Man's technology improved and in the early 1900's came the factory ships and powerful new harpoons. Part of the grey whale population that migrated to the shores off of Korea was virtually exterminated between 1899 and 1933. Fossils of recent times have shown these whales once existed in the Atlantic Ocean.

It was not until 1938 that something was done about the possible annihilation of the grey whales. The International Agreement for the Regulation of Whaling forbade the killing of whales. Sadly Japan and the Soviet Union ignored the agreement. Then, in 1946, a new convention was ratified and both Japan and Soviet Union were among the countries that agreed to this one; however, still there was killing. Only recently has the slaughter of this gentle giant been brought under control. The population has rebounded and in 1993, they were removed from the endangered species list. Today, they are protected.

Every year thousands of grey whales migrate from the farthest northern shores of the Bering Sea over 4000 nautical miles south to the lagoons of Baja. They are present in the lagoons from January through March. Here they calve, frolic and mate while enthralled tourists watch in wonder. They have shown very little fear of man, letting people pet them and rubbing their backs on the bottom of the boats. There appears to be an order in which they group for the migrations. In their southern migration the pregnant females come first, followed by non-pregnant females, mature males with the young and their mothers lagging behind. On the return trip up north it appears that the newly pregnant females leave first, then the adult males, with the mothers and their young following closely behind.

Upon arrival in the lagoons, the females bear their young in the calm back waters. Shortly thereafter, the new mothers take their babies out to the open ocean to teach them to swim and stay close to mom. Mating generally takes place in the shallower waters near the entrances to the lagoons. Groups of 2 or 3 males will assist each other with one female but only one will mate with her. Courtship may take hours but actual copulation takes about five seconds.

It has been estimated that a mature grey whale weighs about 14 metric tons and is about 40 feet long. Newborn babies are 15 feet in length and grow rapidly to 22 feet or so in just 6 months on the rich, 30% fat, mothers milk. The actual age a grey whale will grow to is still undetermined but methods of identifying certain whales by scars and marks will soon help us to know how old they can become.

It is interesting to note that the grey whale has had two different scientific names: *eschrichtius robustus*, eschricht referring to a nineteenth century Danish zoology professor and robustus is Latin for oaken or strong; *Rhachianectes glaucus*, which means "grey swimmer along rocky shores," was the name preferred by Dr. Raymond Gilmore of the San Diego Natural History Museum. The former name is the accepted one in use today.

Scientists continually study the affect the huge salt mining operation which encompasses Laguna Ojo de Liebre might have on the grey whale. No general consensus has yet been formed. There is concern about the salt barges moving through the water when the whales are present but the barges move slowly and infrequently. SEDESOL, the department of the Mexican government in charge of overseeing the protection of the grey whales has limited the number of whale-watching boats that are allowed in the lagoons at any one time. They have also limited the areas where the boats are allowed to go and the hours they can be in the lagoons. The Mexican government is actively enforcing every effort to protect the whales. Plans are now being made to mine salt in San Ignacio Lagoon.

Thousands come to watch the whales every year. Petting, actually touching, a whale is a thrilling experience. Can you imagine watching all of this up close? Mothers with their young sticking their heads out of the water and letting you pet them, whales so close you can smell their breath, splashing you and rubbing their backs on the bottom of the boat. It happens in the lagoons of Baja every year. Whale-watching for the grey whale occurs in the areas of Guerrero Negro, Laguna San Ignacio, Lopez Mateos, and San Carlos, all of which are situated on the Pacific side of Baja. Following are map overviews of these areas and maps of the cities where whalewatching is a business.

Guerrero Negro area...

Currently there are more than three people in the town of Guerrero Negro with permits to enter Laguna Ojo de Liebre (Scammon's Lagoon) with whale-watchers aboard. In 1995. the price varied from $10.00 to $35.00 per person. If price is your concern then shop around and ask what else you get for your money. I have found the most professional whalewatching trips start from the Malarrimo Cafe and RV park in Guerrero Negro. These trips leave from the restaurant by passenger van; you will ride through a part of the world's largest industrial salt mine to a place not far from the mouth of the lagoon. You will see many unusual ducks and birds including the osprey. An English speaking guide rides with you telling you what to expect while whale-watching, pointing out the various birds as you drive by and filling you in on some of the statistics about the salt mining operation. These tours take about 3 hours total and you are provided with lunch. The boats, customized pangas, take you right out among the whales at the mouth of the lagoon. There appears to be more mating behavior here than back inside the lagoon. You will also see mothers with their babies entering and leaving the lagoon.

Guerrero Negro, from the edge of the lagoon...

Southeast of town at kilometer 208 on México 1 is the turnoff to Laguna Ojo de Liebre (Scammon's Lagoon). It is 16.5 miles on graded dirt to the edge of the lagoon. Nearby is the entrance to the "nursery channel" where many of the babies are born. The boats that leave from here charge $10.00 U.S. per person and the trips last about an hour. There are some very nice dry camping spots on the edge of the lagoon. You can sit and watch whales blowing and breaching all day long. If you stay the night you might enjoy hearing the whales blow in the distance. A small cafe is the only service at the edge of this lagoon. The evenings are cool, the nights are damp and the days are generally nice.

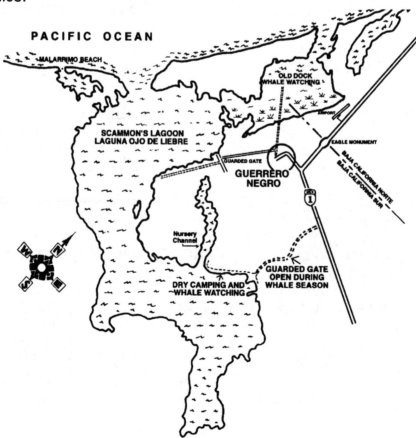

SCAMMON'S LAGOON - LAGUNA OJO DE LIEBRE
GUERRERO NEGRO AREA MAP

Lopez Mateos...

Lopez Mateos is a good place to whale-watch as the whales are very close to shore here. Whales are generally not in this area until mid-February. Access to Lopez Mateos is from Mexico 1 about 1 mile north of Insurgentes. It is 20 miles of 2-lane paved road from the main highway to town, watch speed bumps as you enter town. The town is located in the inside of Laguna Magdalena on the northern part of Magdalena Bay.

Camping is allowed in the field between the lighthouse and the edge of the water and also on the end of the airport runway at the water's edge. There is a fish cannery between these two camp sites; the airport runway is generally upwind from the cannery. Two different groups of *pangeros* run whale-watching trips out into the lagoon. The charge is $10.00 per person and the trips last about an hour. During February they have a big festival celebrating the whales and hundreds of locals come for the festive event. Stalls are set up on the end of the runway selling food and whale related merchandise. And the band plays on. In 1994, 24,000 people went to Lopez Mateos to see the whales. Whale-watchers are flown into here from as far away as México City. It should be mentioned that there are very few services here and there is no gas station. Gas is available in Insurgentes.

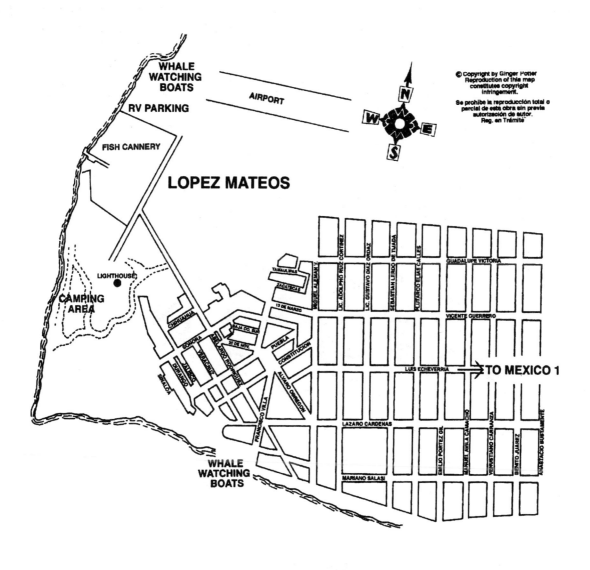

San Carlos...

San Carlos is accessed from México 1 by a paved highway from the town of Constitución. Whales are here from mid-February to mid-April. During this time when you drive into San Carlos you will see kiosks advertising whale-watching trips. If you camp south of town on the water's edge more than likely someone will come and ask you if you want to go whale-watching. In 1995, the charge was $25.00 U.S. for about 3 hours for a boat load of people. One enterprising family has built a ramada on an island on the other side of the lagoon and they sell fresh lobster cooked *al mojo de ajo* (cooked in the shell with butter and garlic) at a very reasonable price. There is a fish cannery immediately north of the camping area that can smell absolutely putrid - especially in the middle of the night. Facilities in this town include 3 or 4 hotels, a few restaurants and a gas station but the gas station only had regular gas in 1995. Diesel and Magna Sin are available in Constitución.

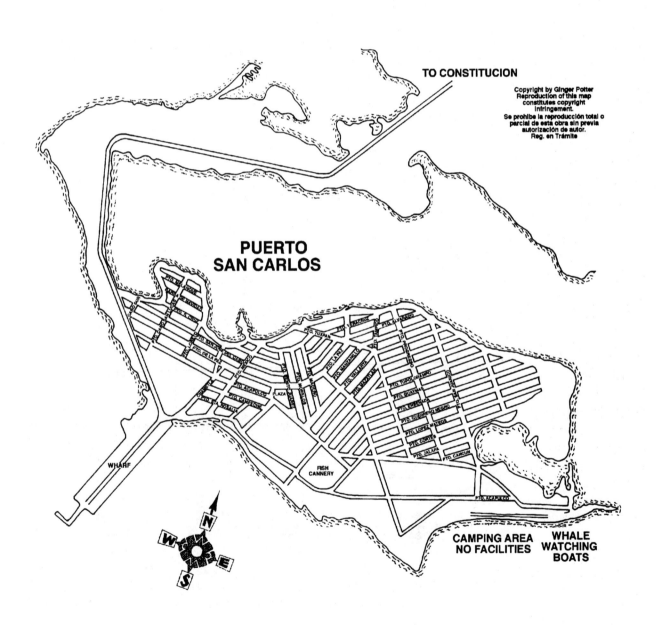

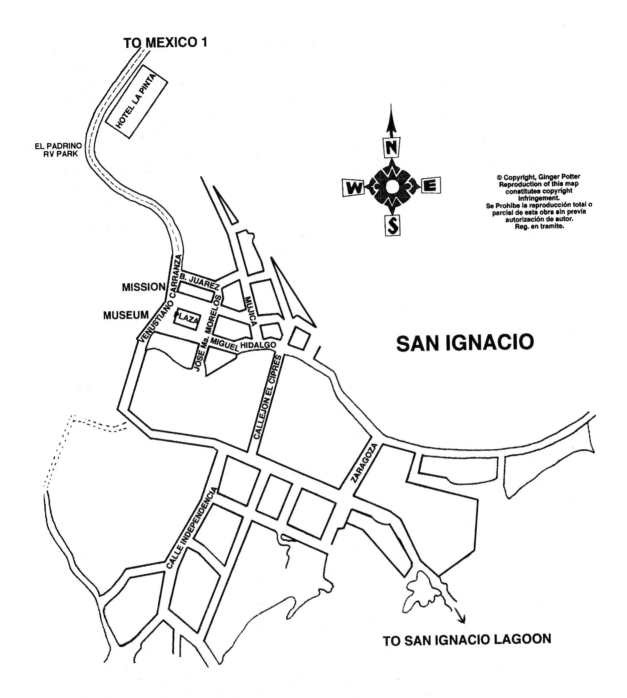

TO MEXICO 1

HOTEL LA PINTA

EL PADRINO
RV PARK

N
W E
S

© Copyright, Ginger Potter
Reproduction of this map
constitutes copyright
infringement.
Se Prohibe la reproducción total o
parcial de esta obra sin previa
autorización de autor.
Reg. en tramite.

MISSION

MUSEUM

B. JUAREZ

VENUSTIANO CARRANZA

PLAZA

JOSE Ma. MORELOS

MIGUEL HIDALGO

MUJICA

CALLEJON EL CIPRES

ZARAGOZA

CALLE INDEPENDENCIA

SAN IGNACIO

TO SAN IGNACIO LAGOON

San Ignacio Lagoon...

Access to Laguna San Ignacio lagoon is from the town of San Ignacio off of México 1. This map shows you how to get through San Ignacio and onto the correct road to the lagoon. For more information on the town of San Ignacio this map is repeated in the section on city maps.

From town arrangements can be made to take you to the lagoon to view the whales with the people at El Padrino Trailer Park or the Hotel La Pinta on your way into town or, in town, with the Fischer family at the Conasupo Market across from the plaza on Miguel Hidalgo. It is an all day trip. If you care to drive to the lagoon yourself it is 38 miles on usually rough, graded dirt. From the edge of the lagoon the boats charge about $50.00 U.S. per boat load (8 people) and usually stay out for 3 hours. Camping is allowed and there are some nice sites. It is usually windy and cool. Fishing and clamming are good at the lagoon.

Humpback Whale

Finback Whale

Grey Whale

Killer Whale

Esp.

93

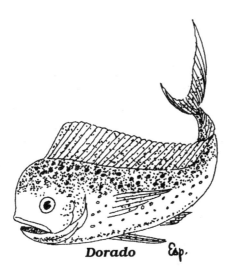

Dorado Esp.

FISHERMAN'S PARADISE

Sportfishing for Baja is her biggest drawing card. Gene Kira has co-authored a best selling book on fishing in Baja. He and his co-author, Neil Kelly, are dedicated Baja fishermen. Their book, "The Baja Catch" is recommended reading, it contains detailed maps and charts to guide you to the best fishing to be found in Baja.

THE MODERN BAJA ANGLER, by Gene Kira

The amazing thing about Baja fishing today is that it is still so very, very good, despite the pressure exerted on it by both sport anglers and commercial fishermen.

In a year's time, you can still probably catch more fish and more species of fish in Baja than any place else in the world. This is true whether you cast from the beach, troll the reefs in a cartop boat, jig deep, drift with live or dead bait, or run far offshore for big game fish.

Admittedly, gill netting, seining, trawling and long-line fishing by commercials - as well as live bait fishing by sport anglers - over the past thirty years, has almost wiped out some species. But even for these, experience has shown that protection can stimulate a recovery of stocks.

Black snook? Totuava? Orange mouth corvina? They are all still there, mixed in a rich fish stew of jacks and snappers and hundreds of other inshore species. Baja's seemingly endless coastline of reefs, rocky points, lagoons and beaches still stretches for two-thousand odd miles, from Ensenada's cold upwellings to the ninety-degree plus waters of San Felipe, and there are still plenty of fish in all of it.

Offshore, big game fish are abundant, in season, mostly along the southern one-third of both coasts, and mostly during the warmer months. Each year, record-breaking game fish are caught in the storied waters within a two-hundred mile radius of Cabo San Lucas. Tuna, sailfish, dorado, and especially striped marlin, are still encountered in those "wide-open" bites of a lifetime. Giant blue marlin and wahoo are plentiful enough to be targeted specifically during the proper seasons.

In the temperate, semi-tropical and tropical waters of today's Baja, the number of fish species that will readily hit an artificial lure is well over one-hundred, and it's difficult even to guess the number of species that can be hooked on live or cut bait.

Nevertheless, there are ominous signs everywhere in Baja that sport anglers and commercial fishing interests must be careful, lest they reduce the world's greatest remaining fishing hole to the status of "just another spot".

Young Baja anglers should consider this sobering thought: No matter how good you think your last trip was, it used to be at least *ten times as good.* No lie. If you can't believe it, just find yourself a weather-beaten old desert rat and listen to the stories...

94

Besides today's critical need for conservation, the other major change in Baja fishing during the past twenty years is the explosive proliferation of Mexican sportsfishing operations.

In the old days, you could land your light plane near one of a handful of fly-in, luxury resorts and you could fish from one of their boats. Or, you could land at a fishing village, such as Bahía de Los Angeles, and fish from a dugout canoe or skiff belonging to one of the local commercials. For a hardy few, equipped with tough hides and even tougher vehicles, a network of boulder strewn tracks - some dating back to the Eighteenth Century - led to adventure and unspoiled fishing that we can only dream about today.

The completion in 1973 of "Mex 1", the blacktopped transpeninsular highway, changed all that forever.

That watershed event caused the trickle of American anglers making the Baja pilgrimage each year, to become first a tide, then a flood. Some brought their own boats. Others came boatless and hired commercial fishermen to take them out. They all brought money, and all along the 1,000 mile length of the transpeninsular highway, signs for Mexican campgrounds, motels,, hotels, RV parks, restaurants and sportsfishing operations of all kinds sprang up faster than you can say, *María, me da la pintura blanca."* (María, give me the white paint.)

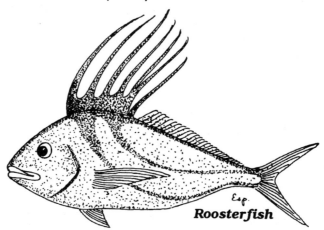

Roosterfish

Today, you can hire a Mexican guide and a *panga* (a fiberglass skiff) on nearly any beach in Baja. Crewed flybridge cruisers will take you out for big game in the La Paz - Cabo San Lucas area. You can reserve your boat by telephone from any number of agents in the U.S. or Baja, and after fishing you can be back at the hotel sipping a cool drink by noon. You can also rent a kayak, get your scuba tanks filled, or find a pretty good cheeseburger darned near any place where Mex 1 touches the coastline. Baja's gotten "sivilized".

Twenty years after the opening of Mex 1, only the more remote parts of Baja's Pacific coast and several short stretches of the Sea of Cortez side remain relatively undeveloped. This is the vestigial remnant of the "old Baja," a place of elemental simplicity and stark beauty, where the drama of the sea is still played out each day as it was in the beginning.

These glimpses of the "old Baja are a nostalgic reminder of a past that we have lost forever. And, we regret that. But, as we carefully load the camper and whip out the credit card for one last run to the tackle shop, we must admit that the good road, the phones, the swimming pools and hot showers, the air conditioning, and the charter boats are awfully nice, too. Most of us old hands, I think, would be forced to admit that we fish Baja more frequently nowadays, thanks to these modern conveniences. And you know what? Maybe we even catch more fish.

Seasons:

Generally, Baja's migrating fish mimic the birds; they head south for the winter and north for the summer in order to follow the seasonal shifts in water temperature.

Migrating fish tend to gather for their "runs" in the spring and fall. For any given point along their route, the "run" occurs as the traveling fish pass you, headed either north or south (or some other direction, due to local conditions).

For non-migrators, "runs" are usually associated with spawning activity, and this can occur at any time of year, depending on species and location.

Whatever the month, you can be sure that something is "running" and something is spawning, somewhere in Baja. But, even if you don't hit a "run" of a particular target species, you can catch fish worthy of your efforts on every trip. In Baja's rich waters, each niche in the ecosystem is constantly occupied by something that eats lures.

Baja summers bring blistering heat and the threat of hurricanes south of Mulegé. Blustery winter storms can make the water rough. In between, the spring months (centered on early May) and the fall months (centered on late October) offer the best combination of good fishing and comfortable conditions.

However, to witness the spectacle of sea life at its most active, there is nothing quite like Baja's mid-summer period of July and August. Yup, it's hot and buggy, and yes a *chubasco* (hurricane) might blow your camp away, but wow! What a show!

The Light Tackle Philosophy:

"Modern" Baja anglers have an outlook vastly different from the meat fisherman of yore.

Strange new terms such as "light tackle", "finesse fishing", "catch-and-release", and even the oxymoronic "salt water fly fishing", have entered our vocabularies. Tarragon and hoisin sauce are pushing beer batter off the trencher boards. Some of us have been seen fishing with our little fingers held in an extended position.

Why all the change?

The bitter, honest truth is that we just can't afford to keep pounding Baja's wonderful fishery the way we have in the past.

No mas.

As we enter the twenty-first century, we must admit that we have reached - and in some cases exceeded - the sustainable limits of the fishery; the time has come to put away the six giant ice chests.

In today's Baja, we see lots of whippy seven- and eight-foot rods, light casting reels, and thread-like line in the 10-25 pound range. Spinning reels and fly fishing tackle are seen everywhere, and nobody is laughing anymore. (Well, almost nobody.)

The emphasis today is on catching just enough for dinner tonight, and releasing the rest. With respect, we give each fish a fighting chance to show us what it can do and thrill us in the process.

With barbless hooks, with lures possibly of our own design and making, and with our senses finely tuned to our quarry and our relationship to it, each fish becomes an entity, each reef a universe, each day a memory etched in time. We weigh our success not in tonnage, but in the richness and intensity of those memories.

If the preceding paragraphs sound suspiciously like borrowed fly fishing writing, the comparison is perhaps unavoidable and a natural consequence of the challenge of maximizing our enjoyment of Baja's incredible fishing without making it go "poof".

Catch and Release:

You will hook up many, many more fish in Baja than you want to keep. Therefore, you need to know how to release them to fight another day.

The odds of a fish surviving for very long with 300 yards of mono hanging out of its mouth can't be very good, so you don't every want to let yourself get spooled. If you feel this happening, it's preferable to raise the drag pressure gradually until the line breaks. And, who knows? You might stop the fish and learn something in the process. Anything is better than getting spooled.

Prolonged battles on light tackle are tough on the larger game fish, especially tuna. It's best to push your skill and your tackle to its absolute limit, risking a break-off, rather than playing it safe.

Other tips for catch-and release fishing:

-Use barbless hooks or hooks with the barbs crimped down with pliers.

-Resist the urge to use bait, which is often swallowed deep.

-Use plain steel hooks. They rust out faster.

-Use long pliers to remove the hook as the tired fish swims beside the boat; no need to take it from the water.

Push groggy fish forward through the water until they wake up and swim out of your hands.

Lures:

Baja fishing is sometimes so productive the challenge is to find a lure that *won't* result in an immediate hookup. During some bites, you can catch fish with bare hooks, pieces of aluminum foil, toy dinosaurs, ball-point pens, and all kinds of odd-ball stuff.

However, when the going gets tough, you need proven lures.

The greatest variety of fish will be caught with wobbling plugs such as jointed Rebels, Rapala Magnums and Bagleys. Virtually all game fish attack these lures on a slow troll.

Outside, you need plastic feathers on weighted trolling heads.

There are a large number of almost indistinguishable brands available. These let you troll much faster than is possible with the plugs.

For casting and jigging you should have a supply of heavy metal lures, or "iron". This can be spoon-shaped, such as the Luhr Jensen Krocodile; candy bar-shaped, such as the Salas jigs; or the skinny, sling jig shape, such as the Stinger. Always carry some sling jigs. They may appear brainlessly simplistic, but they catch fish when nothing else works.

For exploring deep, take some "Lucky Joe" type mackerel flies with light leader loops. Add a couple of big rockcod flies somewhere to the gangion...and brace yourself. There are often big surprises mixed in with the little guys. You will catch more weird species with this rig than by any other method.

Lure Sizes: For blue marlin, you can go up to about fifteen-inches on the plastic feathers. Other billfish like feathers about nine-inches long. For almost *everything else* your lures should be six to seven inches in total length, including diving bills and hooks. The only exception to this rule might be some small lures down to two inches for fooling in the reefs.

Lure Colors: Size and action are much more important than color. However, always try to have blue-and-silver (or white), orange-and-gold, red-and-white, black-and-purple, green-and-black, and black-and-gold.

Wire Leader:

Many of Baja's fish have sharp little teeth that can cut mono with ease, causing you to loose lure after lure, and reducing your tackle box to a disaster area. A common perpetrator of this crime is the sierra mackerel. In a hot bite, sierra will chase after a hooked fish, snapping at the lure in its mouth. Eventually, one of them snips the line by mistake. Cha-Ching! There goes another five bucks. Using dark-colored swivels and dark-colored, six-inch wire leaders will solve this problem For really hot bites, it's also a good idea to double the last five feet of your line with a Bimini twist.

Bait:

Because bait is often swallowed deep, causing injury or death to the fish when the hook is removed, artificial lures with barbless hooks are preferable for catch-and-release.

Live bait, however, does usually catch more fish, and the deep swallowing factor is a plus for charter guides who are under pressure to catch the maximum number of fish for their clients in the least amount of time.

For a charter guide with an inexperienced client, there is nothing like the security of a gut hooked fish on a heavy leader.

For anyone not under such pressure, the use of artificial lures is more sporting and results in a greater survival rate when fish are released. Moreover, in the hands of an expert, artificial lures are perfectly capable of outfishing bait, even live bait.

Live Bait: Making bait can be a problem. Ask around for the best spot and be on it before sunrise. Often, you can buy live bait from a "receiver" converted from a semi-flooded panga. Live baits seen around Baja include various mackerels, sardines, perches, grunts, bass, small jacks, or sometimes, juvenile game fish such as yellowtail, tuna, dorado, etc.

Cut Bait: Only one word is really necessary. "Squid." Buy it frozen at the supermarket and use it for everything from twelve-inch bass to broadbill. It's cheap, it's tough, it keeps forever, and it works. You don't need nothin' else. When you run out of squid, belly strips of almost anything else will usually get the job done.

Rods and Reels:

The following three outfits can handle 95% of the fishing situations you will encounter in Baja:

-An eight-foot rod with 10-pound line (or a ten-foot rod for surf fishing).

-A seven-foot rod with 25-pound line.

-A six-foot rod with 80- pound line.

With practice and some luck, you can whip most inshore fish with 10-pound line. This will become your standard inshore setup, and you will find yourself using it more and more in deep water too.

You'll want to switch to the 25-pound rig for sailfish, larger jacks, dorado, medium tuna, etc.

The 80-pound rig is necessary when using a heavy sinker for deep bottom fishing, for tuna over about 80 pounds, or for larger billfish. You also need it to snub big grouper or yellowtail around rocks. For this work, supplement your 80 pound line with wire leader and a fifteen-foot Bimini twist. Hah!

All three rods should have a "very fast" action and should be a little on the stiff side for the line they carry. Exotic rod blanks are totally unnecessary for this work; fiberglass is all you need. On the two lighter outfits, look for one SIC guide per foot, plus two. Roller guides are preferable for the 80 pound outfit. Only the heavier two rods are normally available off the shelf. You will probably have to have the light rod custom wrapped.

Spinning reels may be used for the two lighter outfits. In that case, buy the very best, salt water reels you can afford. Keep in mind, however, that you will be much better off "in the long run" if you learn to cast properly with a conventional reel.

Boating in The Boonies:

Few things are more satisfying than catching fish from your own boat, and each season Baja's growing list of paved and dirt launch ramps makes it easier to do just that.

However, launching your cartop boat or trailer boat *over-the-beach* in Baja presents a vast array of "challenges" not encountered in ramp launching. "Challenges" here means "getting stuck".

Because of the narrow, soft, rocky trails that lead to the water in many places, and also because of the soft, shallow, steep or rocky beaches that you may find there, it is essential that your boat not be too large for your equipment and skill. Any boat or boat/trailer combination with a total weight over about 500 pounds is cause for serious contemplation of what you are attempting.

Some tips:

-Practice at home first. It's amazing how many boats get taken to Baja for their maiden launch. Do it at a local lake the first couple of times. Iron out the kinks in your system. *Then* head down Mex 1.

The bigger the boat, the better the beach must be. Your canoe you can launch anywhere, but it's a rare beach that can handle a 28-foot sportfisher.

-A 4WD vehicle will let you launch at twice as many locations.

-Launch near Mexican fishermen if possible. They can help if you run into trouble. Try to have a buddy vehicle and tow rope available at all times.

-Do everything in super slow motion, and exercise patience. Wait for the right conditions. High tide is usually much easier to launch into than low tide. Also, it's safer in case you get stuck.

-Tow vehicles should be rated for at least double the weight they are pulling. Tires should be at least three to five sizes larger than standard.

-The boat and tow vehicle should be emptied of excess weight for the launch. Tires, including trailer tires, may be partly deflated for extra flotation.

Boats to about 300 pounds total weight can be rolled into the water on transom-mounted launch wheels.

-Boats to about 600 pounds can be rolled on inflatable rollers made from pairs of boat bumpers tied together to form long tubes.

-Trailer boats can be launched on some otherwise impossible beaches by mounting a spare tire as a rolling nose wheel on the tongue of the trailer. The trailer is unhooked, attached to the tow vehicle by a long safety rope, and rolled independently (and cautiously) into the water.

San Diego's Long Range Fleet:

Unless you own your own 60-foot sportfisher, you're going to have a pretty tough time figuring out a way to fish Baja's fabulous collection of offshore islands, which are home to schools of big wahoo and giant yellowfin tuna ranging up to 400 pounds.

The answer? San Diego's fleet of long-range sport fishing boats that, during the winter months, will whisk you from dockside to the exotic islands off the tip of Baja with all the comforts of home. Think of it as a multi-week luxury cruise with all the fishing action you can handle thrown in.

Shorter trips test the near shore banks around Baja's west coast. The long-range fleet is equipped with freezing equipment to bring your catch home in perfect shape, and the specialized, very heavy duty stand up tackle required for this type of fishing can be rented for the trip.

For phone numbers of the different long range trips see the Resource Guide in the back of this book. For current information, prices and schedules, you can check in *Western Outdoor News* (see below).

Western Outdoor News

The most efficient way to book a fishing trip to Baja is to keep track of the articles and advertisements that appear constantly in the Los Angeles newspaper called "Western Outdoor News", 3197-E Airport Loop Dr., Costa Mesa, CA 92626. Phone 714-546-4370.

This weekly outdoor tabloid contains fresh Baja fishing reports and a constant stream of up-to-date information on airlines, hotels, charter operations, package deals, panga-mother ship trips, long-range schedules, group trips, etc., etc. Fred Hoctor's column is always worth reading. It's all there. Don't leave home without it.

Documentation:

You and everyone with you must have a Mexican fishing license. In addition, your boat must have a Mexican boat permit. If you stay in México longer than 72 hours, you must carry a validated tourist card. You must also have proof of citizenship. Also, you must have Mexican insurance for all of your vehicles, boats, trailers, etc.

Chasing down all this paperwork on your own is a hassle. It's far easier to join one of the travel clubs and let them do it for you. (See: Resources). You will end up saving time and money.

Regulations:

Generally, you are prohibited from taking any shellfish, lobster, shrimp, turtle, etc. Prohibited finfish include totuava and spotted cabrilla.

There are marine reserves at Cabo Pulmo (around the coral reefs), around the mouth of the bay at Cabo San Lucas, and at the extreme northern end of the Sea of Cortez, north of a line drawn between San Felipe and Puerto Peñasco.

Regulations, bag limits and enforcement evolve constantly. It is best to check just before you go at the Mexican Department of Fisheries, 2530 5th Ave, Suite 101, San Diego, CA 92101-6622, phone 619-233-6956.

To order the book "The Baja Catch" send $19.95 plus $3.00 shipping (California residents please add current sales tax) to Apples and Oranges, Inc. P. O. Box 2065, Valley Center, CA 92082.

YOUR BOAT AND BAJA...

The following article is contributed by Mike Bales. Mike is an avid Baja fisherman and he hauls his boat all over the peninsula. He knows where all of the launch ramps are located and probably knows where all of the fish are. He has written a book on the launch ramps, but I don't think he will tell us where all of the fish are. The license plate on his truck reads "I FISH" - need I say more.

TRAILERBOATING IN BAJA, by Mike Bales

The first question that occurs to the neophyte trailerboater who is unfamiliar with driving in México is, ---"is it SAFE"?

Yes, it is safe and practical to tow a boat into Baja. Thousands of trailerboaters cross the border yearly in search of prized gamefish that abound in the Sea of Cortez and the Pacific Ocean. By following a few basic rules that include: no night driving, drive defensively and remember that safe speeds for all vehicles are less than on U.S. Highways, you will find the trip is both enjoyable and adventurous.

The true adventuresome Baja aficionados, the trailer boat anglers, will find over 30 launch ramps between Ensenada and San Felipe on the north and Cabo San Lucas, some 1000 miles to the south. While most of these ramps are not up to stateside standards they will handle the average boat at the proper tide. Weather, tidal action, age of ramp and lack of maintenance affects all the ramps in Baja which have been in service many years. There are also several hard packed dirt ramps located near some untapped fishing grounds that will handle any boat you can tow to Baja.

The trailerboater must be aware of the additional permits, regulations and thorough preparation that is required when towing a boat into México to fish or dive. The following is a brief recap of areas of concern for trailerboaters.

Only Mexican Insurance Policies issued by Mexican companies are accepted as proof of financial responsibility in México. Under Mexican law your insurance coverage is void if your car, truck or RV is towing a trailer, boat or any type of vehicle that is not listed on the Mexican insurance policy.

Under the new Mexican fishing regulations, if there is fishing or diving gear aboard a boat, each person in the boat needs a fishing permit. Also each boat must have a Mexican boating permit. Note: Theses permits are good for one year from the date of purchase. If you are towing a boat into Baja the Mexican border inspectors will ask to see your permits. If you have all the necessary permits readily available you will save yourself a trip into the secondary inspection area.

Recently some people have been cited for not having a red flag tied on the propeller. Avoid the mordida, take a red flag.

Towing a boat into México requires a more thorough preparation of both the towing vehicle and the boat trailer than a similar trip in the U.S. Most vehicles will be loaded past their GVW (Gross Vehicle Weight Rating) due to extra equipment, fuel, ice chests, etc. and rough roads will take their toll on tires, shocks and springs. In fact, trailer boat preparation becomes more important than the tow vehicle. Why? The typical trailerboater spends the time and money keeping his tow vehicle and boat in top running condition throughout the year. He makes a half dozen short trips to the local launch ramps without any problems, therefore, he assumes his rig is ready for a trip down the Baja peninsula, WRONG. If you have not taken your boat trailer to a competent boat trailer shop in the last year, you are asking for trouble. Two items you can not see cause the most headaches, the brakes and the bearings. The bottom line is having your vehicle and boat trailer in top mechanical condition before leaving home. This will give you peace of mind and confidence while driving down the Baja peninsula.

The active Baja boater should carry basic spare parts along with the appropriate tools, service manuals and have sufficient knowledge to repair and/or install the new parts when at sea. Knowing your boat and being able to anticipate what type of problems you might encounter will help you select parts that are most important to you.

When boating, fishing or cruising in Mexican waters a prudent skipper will have a full set of navigation charts aboard for the areas he plans to visit. If you are exploring an area for the first time, use caution. This is especially important when entering anchorages, small coves or passing near offshore islands or a rocky shoreline. Many hazards exist that have not been found or charted.

Tides and currents are a very important consideration for the trailerboater in Baja. The two major areas of concern are: The upper Sea of Cortez from Bahía de Los Angeles north to San Felipe, and the Pacific Coast of Baja. The ramps in the upper gulf are affected by tidal action that can run 20-25 feet, making it nearly impossible to launch except on a high tide. At extreme low tides, that occur during the new and full moon phases, the ramps at San Felipe will be more than 1/4 mile from the water's edge. The tides along the Pacific Coast of Baja are very similar to those found off Southern California. Using a San Diego tide calendar as a reference, the tides along the Pacific coastline of Baja occur from 15 minutes earlier (Ensenada area) to 35 minutes earlier at Magdalena Bay. Most tide charts list exact correction times. Tide times are quite different in the back bays of the lagoons.

Due to the constant changes in Baja weather, tides, and ramp conditions, the final decision and responsibility to launch will rest with the prudent skipper. Only he knows his experience, the experience of his crew and the sea-worthiness of his boat.

Mike Bales is the author of "Launch Ramps of Baja California". Order from Launch Ramp Publications, P. O.. Box 2806-311, Torrance, CA 90509-2806 at $8.95 including shipping and handling.

CAMPING...

Hundreds of beaches, remote and pristine await you. There are many miles of beaches that seemingly belong to no one and offer solitude and sheltered campsites. In the more popular areas you may have to pay $1.00 to $3.00 for the privilege of camping for the night but even this paltry sum is worth it. Campfires are legal, dogs are okay, and the place doesn't close at midnight - it's not like back home. There is a rule against motorcycles and ATC's on the beaches in Baja. It is enforced by people who live nearby and you shouldn't ride near people's homes anyway. Please be polite with these vehicles. You will probably find your campsite clean, please leave it that way. If you bury your trash, the coyotes will dig it up and it will blow all over the desert, so haul your trash with you when you leave.

One of the most terrible things that can happen while you are camped on a beautiful beach is for the DNIW to come up (this is not a typo - spelled backward it means "a very strong breeze"). Since I was a child it has always been a practice to spell this word backwards instead of saying it forward. I believe this tradition started in Easter Camp - it always blew there. If the DNIW does start to blow it's always been the fault of the person who first called the word out loud. It's always nice to have someone to blame.

If you have chosen your campsite appropriately, it is likely you won't be far from a group of Mexican fishermen. During lobster season they may have traps out. Don't hesitate to ask if they will sell you some of their catch; you'll more than likely pay a reasonable price and it certainly will be fresh. You should know that they do not usually bring lobster back in to shore on a daily basis. They remove the lobster from their wire traps daily and put these lobster into wooden, floating, top water holding traps until they have enough to take to market. In this process they sometimes will injure a lobster and these are the ones you will probably be purchasing. These fishermen are members of large cooperatives. They must contribute a sizable catch in order to stay members and to have a good market for their lobster. Don't ask to buy more lobster than you can eat immediately.

With advance notice, usually from the day before, these same fishermen can usually be hired to take you out in their boats to go fishing. Establish the price beforehand. Take fishing gear for them to use too; sometimes they like to use a rod and reel instead of hand lines. Be sure to take enough sodas or beer to share with them. Before releasing fish ask if they need the fish for food for themselves or others. I like to go out with them while they pull their traps and nets. Not only do I get to share in the excitement and disappointment of the adventure, I also like to listen to them sing as they work. I fish the top water as they work. Fishing can be surprisingly lucrative under these circumstances.

For hesitant campers.

Many people love camping in Baja. Once they have gotten over how to handle cooking on a campfire, tea-cup showers, and bush-bathrooms they too, enjoy the peaceful, rugged beauty of Baja's isolated beaches. I am not talking about flying down to Cabo for a week of "good times." I am referring to a person saying "yes" to going south with the kids, spouse, the dog, the tent, sleeping bags and the mountains of gear one tends to haul "just in case."

You will find there is lots more to do than sit on the beach while your spouse is out fishing. You could try learning to fish. It's not difficult. If you're squeamish about handling bait - no problem. We use mostly lures in Baja. You'll need a good lightweight fishing pole that feels just "right" to you. Borrow someone else's on the first trip and upon returning, go to the fishing tackle store (preferably by yourself or you might end up buying your friend another rod) and let the sales people show you what's available.

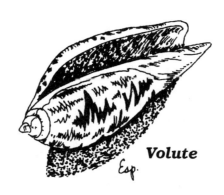

Volute

Learn to tie the knot that holds the lure on the line - it's not difficult. Learn a little about the reel. (You don't need to learn how to take it apart - yet.) Use a pair of pliers to remove the fish from the hook, and if you don't want to touch the fish at all, carry the fish with the same pliers up to wherever your friend will clean it. Don't bother to learn to clean the fish - this is a job to learn a little later. I have caught a lot of fish from the shore while my husband was out in a boat getting skunked (that's fishermen's talk for not getting any fish.) I encourage you to at least try fishing, it can even be fun when *you* get skunked.

Cooking on a campfire? Heaven forbid! But it's not that much more difficult. I suggest you take your favorite cooking utensils with you and also bring along an old barbecue grill to prop on top of the rocks. You will not be able to regulate the fire as easily as at home but you can move the pan to a cooler or warmer spot as needed. Here, too, a pair of pliers is important. Camp stoves are handy to have along if you intend to cook for a whole family. It only takes a minute to learn how to use one. (This should not be done inside a tent.) With either an open fire or camp stove the bottoms of the pans are going to get "pot-black" on them. This stuff stains clothing and everything it touches. It comes off easily with sand and dish soap or, when back at home with oven cleaner. Washing dishes? Use a bucket filled with sea water to place dirty dishes in and add a *few* drops of liquid detergent. When you are ready to wash the dishes add hot water and wash, then rinse with fresh water. Don't use too much soap and be careful to rinse well as soap residue can cause diarrhea.

Tea-cup showers. Take along an extra 5 gallons of fresh water for you to bathe with. Portable "showers in a bag" are available at most sporting goods stores, take up very little space and use very little water. The water bag is heated by the sun and the attached spray nozzle provides a warm fresh water rinse. What more could you ask for?

Bush bathrooms. I bought a fully self-contained camper. My aunt has a camper with a license plate that reads "ZEE BUSH". After many years of bush camping we took the easy way out. Should you find yourself camped out where there are no bathrooms, a roll of toilet paper fits nicely on the handle of an army shovel.

One thing great about camping in Baja is enjoying the star-filled night skies. The Milky Way is so bright that even on nights with no moon there is light. Shooting stars streak the sky. On occasion I have awakened to see the planets appear so large they look like moons. You can lull yourself to sleep counting satellites as they criss-cross across the sky. A pair of regular binoculars will give you an even better look at the heavens. Take a tent to store your gear but take a tarp for a ground cover and sleep outside!

BEACHCOMBING...

The ultimate dream of every true beachcomber is a gently curving beach, remote and uninhabited and generously stocked with man's debris and nature's discards. Baja has it!

Turritella

The great Kiro Siwi current that circles the Pacific Ocean, collecting junk from the whole northern Pacific Ocean, deposits it's accumulation on the beaches of Baja's western coast. From Punta Baja to Punta Eugenia a massive hook of Baja grabs into the current and sifts the flotsam and jetsam onto the beaches. The largest accumulation is on Malarrimo Beach; west of the entrance to Scammon's Lagoon. Getting there is an adventure in itself; the last 26 miles takes at least three hours. But there are other beaches where old whaling ships lie at rest in the sand, their copper bottoms glistening in the sun. One need only to walk the beaches with searching eyes.

I have found that points with a northwest facing beach are particularly fruitful.

Shell collectors will find Baja a generous contributer to their collections. The southwestern coast will, on occasion, have shells generally only found in the southern Pacific Ocean. Large *grinning tuns* and *paper nautilus'* are not uncommon finds. The gulf shores are also abundant with unusual shells. Shell Beach, near Punta Chivato, is a particularly good spot for shelling. Large shiny olive shells, sundials, turbans and a multitude of others have been found there. Each tide deposits new and interesting shells and the amount increases generously with late summer storms. It is surprising how virgin this beach always appears. I know lots of people who like to go there to collect shells, yet there never seems to be a trace of footsteps or tracks - and I always find a few prizes.

Paper Naulitus

Grinning Tun

SEA KAYAKING IN BAJA...

Andromeda Romano-Lax learned to kayak in the Sea of Cortez. Her brief article will give you a taste of sea kayaking in Baja and a feel for the waters of the Sea of Cortez.

Gliding along in a few feet of azure coastal waters, or braving high seas to paddle out to a distant desert isle, the sea kayaker gets a close-up look at a side of Baja that most tourists will never even glimpse. Far from highway noise and the bustle of large resorts, self-propelled and self-sufficient, the sea kayaker is free to explore otherwise inaccessible beaches, rugged coastline, and waters teeming with marine life. Within a day's paddle, the kayaker can bask in the sun and salt air, get a great workout, scout the coast for a hidden campsite, watch for birds and whales, and even tow a fishing line. Best of all, if he or she is conscientious, the kayaker can see much while disturbing little: no garbage, gassy fumes or even footprints need remain behind in his or her wake.

As Baja gains a reputation as one of North America's best paddling spots, the options for sea kayakers are multiplying. Tour groups, outfitters and boat and equipment rentals on both sides of the border have proliferated. You can plan a major expedition, pack all your own gear on top of your car, launch at San Felipe, and paddle south for weeks or months until some 670+ miles later, you reach La Paz. Or you can show up in Bahía Concepción with nothing more than shorts, t-shirt and a willingness to get wet, and be outfitted and initiated into the sport within just a few hours.

Between these two extremes, the adventurous novice or the seasoned paddler can choose from a number of bays and islands well-suited to 2-7 day trips. Keep in mind that since the peninsula has 2000 miles of coastline, these are just a sampling. On the Pacific coast, the Punta Banda peninsula and the Islas de Todos Santos are a good weekend destination within a days drive of San Diego. Bahía San Quintín is a sheltered bay popular among the bird watching crowd. On the Sea of Cortez, the numerous rocky isles that dot Bahía de Los Angeles are great near shore destinations. The Enchanted Island chain south of Puertecitos, the islands Danzante and Carmen near Loreto, and the many-coved western shore of Espíritu Santo Island near La Paz are all popular offshore destinations promising wildlife-watching and remote island camping opportunities. The stretch of coast between Mulegé and Loreto is a challenging choice for a mini-expedition.

A good outfitter or guidebook can brief you on all the Baja kayaking essentials, but in brief...unlike motorboats, kayaks do not currently require a license in Baja. While it is possible to paddle Baja year-round, northerly winds are heaviest from November-May, and (on the hotter Cortez coast) temperatures skyrocket in summer. Many stretches of coast are wild and remote: bring extra supplies, ample food, and sufficient drinking water to last you through unexpected delays or emergency layovers. And, of course, for even the briefest paddle, don't forget your P.F.D.(personal flotation device), sunscreen, and a wide-brimmed hat.

Finally, be aware that the sea kayak's ability to navigate the narrowest channel and land on the most remote beach will demand extra self-restraint from future paddlers. Realize that many small desert islands are fragile, that all island flora and fauna are off-limits to hunters and collectors, and that even the briefest on-land foray can disrupt important bird nesting sites. Knowing more about the areas you are
paddling in advance of an excursion will make your trip more enjoyable, and will alert you to ecologically vulnerable areas.

A list of kayaking outfitters and guided tours for Baja is provided in the back of this book under Resources. Andromeda's book on Kayaking in Baja is highly recommended. For the self-guided paddler, 15 trips with original maps are described in the guidebook.
Sea Kayaking in Baja by Andromeda Romano-Lax (Wilderness Press, $13.95. To order from the publisher call 1-800-443-7227).

SURFING...

I do not surf. But I camp on the beaches of Baja and in some places there are always surfers. I see pick-up trucks with surf boards loaded on top going up and down Mexico 1 all the time. All of the trucks heading north have been off of the highway for quite a distance as evidenced by the layer of dust and salt on their vehicles. Great migrations of surfers head south when late summer hurricanes turn the Pacific Ocean into a giant ripple.

A drive down the dirt road from Punta Canoas to Santa Rosalillita reveals surfers on many of the beaches. This side trip is covered on RL34 in this book. It is not a week-end trip but if you have the time it offers many beautiful isolated beaches with great campsites.

Just below Santa Rosalillita a few miles, an arc of land faces southerly where surfers sometimes enjoy rides of up to a mile or more. They call this place "the wall". Here they have built rock wind-shelters to protect their campsites at the water's edge.

There are always a couple surfers at San Pedrito RV park south of Todos Santos. El Conejo, a few miles off of Mexico 1 (km. 80 south of Constitución on a rugged dirt road) is another spot where surfers seem to be around all of the time. We have seen surfers between Cabo San Lucas and San José del Cabo but some of these beaches have been closed due to new hotels being built. Abreojos and San Hipólito on the southwestern Baja coast are both a good distance from the highway but this doesn't stop the surfers. In the same area, San Juánico (Scorpion Bay) is well-known among the surfing crowd.

The space maps in the Roadlog will show you the more desirable places to find good surf. The surf-board symbols along the coast-line denote where I have seen surfers having a good time.

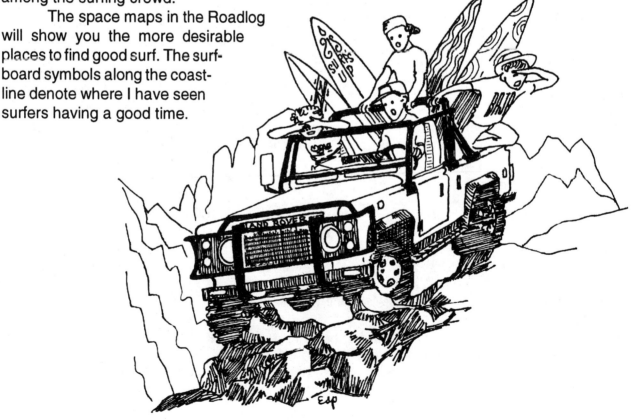

107

WINDSURFING...

The wind used to hurt Baja's economy. Fishermen couldn't fish and people went home. Not any more. Thousands of windsurfers flock to Baja's east cape area every year from mid-December through February to enjoy some of the finest windsurfing in the world. Vela has all the equipment for rent at Hotel Playa del Sol in Los Barriles.

In Los Barriles you can expect good high-wind conditions at least half of the time and there is plenty to do the other half. Sportfishing is world famous in the same area and on days when the wind is down it's the number one thing to do. Explore the area on a rented bicycle. Diving is another choice. Beachcombing is good on the many white sandy beaches in the area.

For the completely self-contained, independent windsurfer there are many other beaches in the East Cape area where the wind comes at the correct angle to the beach. El Sargento, at the northwest side of Bahía de La Ventana south of La Paz, has dry campsites and great winds. Cabo Pulmo has a few nice dry campsites and fairly good winds and when it's not blowing you can snorkel on Baja's only coral reef located there.

Punta Chivato, north of Mulegé is a great place for beginners and advanced too. Inside the huge bay, Bahía de Santa Ines, the water is generally flat and good for learning basics. Nearer the point are better high-wind conditions and occasionally some good swells. The hotel at Punta Chivato at one time provided windsurfing lessons, rental gear and a rescue boat. Whether or not the new managers of the hotel will continue to provide this service remains to be seen.

The northern end of Bahía de Los Angeles can have the correct wind direction and might be a good place to try your skills. When it blows at L.A. Bay - it blows! During the winter the wind here can be very cold.

If you wish you may take your own windsurfing equipment into Baja. One windsurfer per person is allowed without duty.

DIVING...

The warm waters of the gulf provide many unusual and beautiful spots for snorkeling and SCUBA diving. Tropical fish abound in places accessible from shore. Rental gear and air for certified divers are available near all the good areas. If you prefer, the Mexican government will allow you to take your own diving gear into Baja. If you are diving just to enjoy the beauty of nature, no license is required. For spear fishing the diver must have a fishing license. Only rubber band or spring operated spearguns are allowed and you must be using only snorkel gear when taking fish, SCUBA diving equipment is not allowed while taking fish.

Spear fishing is forbidden between the Arch at Cabo San Lucas and Cabesa de Ballena. This area is a refuge, take pictures and leave bubbles.

Spear fishing is also forbidden at Cabo Pulmo reef. This reef, Baja's only true coral reef, is located on the eastern side of the tip of the peninsula. Pepe's Dive Shop is located there; he has rentals, lessons, and air for certified divers. It is a fantastic place to view the myriad of tropical fish existing here. Before Cabo Pulmo was made a marine reserve it was a source for exotic fish for aquariums. Over 300 species of fish inhabit this area.

There are many dive shops in Cabo San Lucas. Most of them are located along the waterfront. Cabo San Lucas also has a recompression Chamber located in the Plaza Las Glorias Hotel complex. The chamber is totally financed by a portion of the tank rentals from all the dive shops in the area. There is also a dive shop with complete rentals at Chileno Bay, Km 15, between San José del Cabo and Cabo San Lucas.

In La Paz impromptu trips go to Isla Espíritu Santo from Palapa Azul at Tecolote Beach 15 miles east of town. They do not have tank rentals. The Hotel La Concha just outside of La Paz (east of town), caters to groups of divers who come in on package trips that include airfare, boats and equipment. Hotel Buena Vista, on the east cape at Buena Vista, has five day divers' packages as does Rancho Leonero.

In Mulegé, Mulegé Divers offers instruction, equipment rentals and trips. Claudia and Miguel, owners of the shop, know the area very well and can take you to some unique and beautiful places. They both speak English.

Chapter 8

RESOURCE GUIDE

If you are planning to drive the Baja Peninsula it is of utmost importance that you have a plan that keeps you from driving at night. Throughout this book I have given the reasons for this but just to refresh your memory: cattle, horses, donkeys and other animals roam free on the roads; pot holes are virtually impossible to see at night; people drive without their headlights on, and the white lines are lacking in many places. Each of your day's travel must allow for some extra time to avoid night driving. In this resource portion of the book I have listed most of the RV parks, a large portion of the hotels and motels, emergency phone numbers and just about all you will need to have a well-planned, enjoyable and safe trip. Some popular places still do not have direct telephone service and must be contacted through U.S. agents or may not have any means of previous contact at all. Most of the RV parks are very basic; a small portion of the parks were built specifically to provide "safe harbor" for the night and provide nothing more than a fenced off area with parking spaces, a bathroom and maybe a shower. Some are at the other end of the scale but these are in the large cities. Plan to take at least 3 days travel time from Tijuana if you are heading for Cabo San Lucas. If you have more time, then you can enjoy a lot more of Baja than most people do. Many people spend a lot of time in Baja cooped up in a trailer park and never see the beauty of the land nor meet any of the wonderful people. We eat in the restaurants and at the taco stands and I only became ill once - from a large fancy American style restaurant in La Paz (this occurred 28 years ago). Venture out and see what Baja can offer you, use your own judgment as to whether to stay or eat in a particular place just like you would do at home.

Hotel and motel phone numbers are provided for you to make reservations. Reservations for RV and trailer parks will only stand up at some places; very few take reservations. It has been our experience that if a park is completely full they will still provide a space for us to park for the night - and a long hose for water and an extension cord for power. The people of Baja will bend over backwards to please.

Regarding the telephone numbers: All of the numbers with the international and country code preceding the actual number (011-52) can be dialed from within Baja by replacing this number with 91. Thus, 01152-113-30616 becomes 91-113-30616 if you are calling from within Baja from one area code to another. If you are calling within the same area code use only the last five digits. To call the U.S. dial 95 + area code + number.

Before entering Mexico it is a good idea to arrange with your long distance carrier for a credit card number and access code for long distance service back to the U.S. AT&T service is recognized everywhere and calls are easily placed with this card. I submitted my MCI bill to AT&T to see if they could meet or beat the prices and they could not so I go to the extra effort to find a special phone for my calls. Knowledgable people will accept either card but MCI is not recognized everywhere yet. Because of theft, credit card calls do not always go through for calls made from within one area code in México to another area code in México. There are many telephone offices where you can make these calls. The AT&T access number is 95-800-462-4240. The MCI access number is 95-800-674-7000.

For those of you who are flying to Baja it is best to make hotel reservations in advance. Many hotels have great package deals that include fishing and other sports activities. If you rent a car I suggest you drive it around town a bit to check it out before taking it out on the highway. If you rented a car in New York and had a problem you could call for help; in Baja there is almost no way to do this.

Enjoy your trip and remember - don't drive at night.

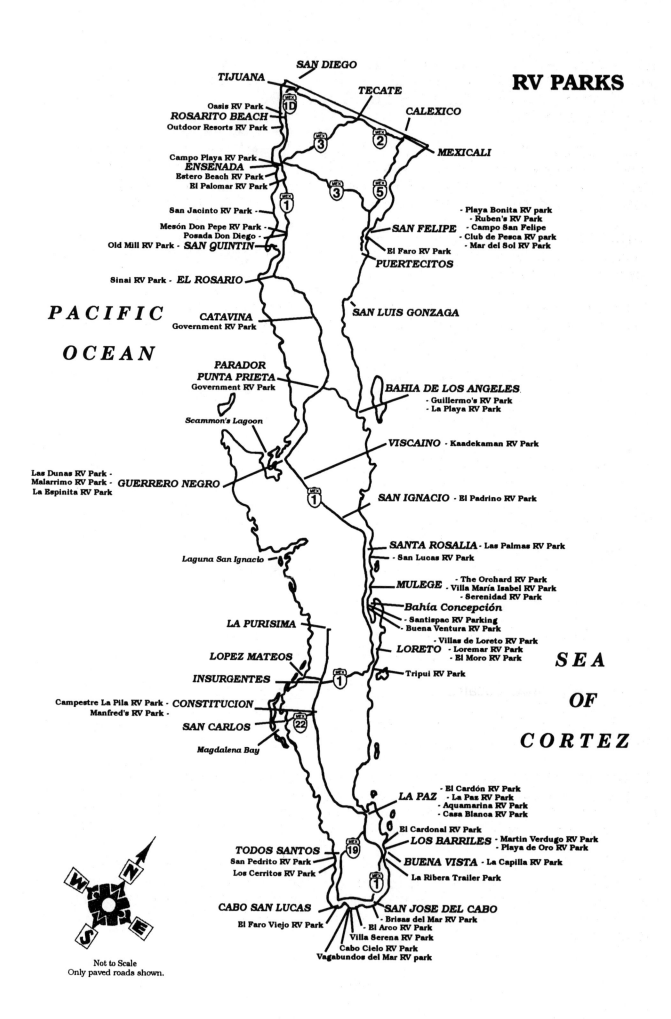

RV PARKS

SAN DIEGO

TIJUANA

Oasis RV Park
ROSARITO BEACH
Outdoor Resorts RV Park

TECATE

CALEXICO

MEXICALI

Campo Playa RV Park
ENSENADA
Estero Beach RV Park
El Palomar RV Park

- Playa Bonita RV park
- Ruben's RV Park
- Campo San Felipe
- Club de Pesca RV park
- Mar del Sol RV Park

SAN FELIPE

San Jacinto RV Park -

Mesón Don Pepe RV Park -
Posada Don Diego -
Old Mill RV Park - **SAN QUINTIN**

El Faro RV Park

PUERTECITOS

Sinai RV Park - **EL ROSARIO**

PACIFIC

OCEAN

CATAVINA
Government RV Park

SAN LUIS GONZAGA

PARADOR
PUNTA PRIETA
Government RV Park

BAHIA DE LOS ANGELES
- Guillermo's RV Park
- La Playa RV Park

Scammon's Lagoon

VISCAINO - Kaadekaman RV Park

Las Dunas RV Park -
Malarrimo RV Park -
La Espinita RV Park - **GUERRERO NEGRO**

SAN IGNACIO - El Padrino RV Park

SANTA ROSALIA - Las Palmas RV Park
- San Lucas RV Park

Laguna San Ignacio

MULEGE
- The Orchard RV Park
- Villa María Isabel RV Park
- Serenidad RV Park

Bahía Concepción
- Santispac RV Parking
- Buena Ventura RV Park

LA PURISIMA

- Villas de Loreto RV Park
LORETO - Loremar RV Park
- El Moro RV Park

SEA

LOPEZ MATEOS

INSURGENTES

Tripui RV Park

OF

Campestre La Pila RV Park - **CONSTITUCION**
Manfred's RV Park -

CORTEZ

SAN CARLOS

Magdalena Bay

- El Cardón RV Park
LA PAZ - La Paz RV Park
- Aquamarina RV Park
- Casa Blanca RV Park

El Cardonal RV Park

LOS BARRILES - Martin Verdugo RV Park
- Playa de Oro RV Park

TODOS SANTOS
San Pedrito RV Park
Los Cerritos RV Park

BUENA VISTA - La Capilla RV Park

La Ribera Trailer Park

CABO SAN LUCAS

SAN JOSE DEL CABO
- Brisas del Mar RV Park

El Faro Viejo RV Park

- El Arco RV Park
Villa Serena RV Park
Cabo Cielo RV Park
Vagabundos del Mar RV park

Not to Scale
Only paved roads shown.

RV Parks are listed in alphabetical order.

Aquamarina RV Park. As you enter La Paz on México 1 from the north turn left on Nayarit street and follow dirt road to water's edge. 19 sites with full hookups. Laundry, pool, boat ramp. Phone 01152-112-23761. Roadlog page 92.

Brisas del Mar RV Park. Located approximately 2 miles southwest of San José del Cabo at kilometer 30 on México 1 between the Cabos on the beach. 80 sites with full hookups, tent sites. Pool, restaurant, bar, store, laundry, bicycle rentals. They do not give reservations and they fill to capacity. Phone 01152-114-23999. Roadlog page 96.

Buena Ventura. Located at kilometer 94.5 south of Mulegé on the shore of Bahía Concepción. No hookups. Toilets and showers, restaurant and bar. Palapas (palm roofed tables). Roadlog page 74.

Cabo Cielo RV Park. A new park located on south side of México 1 at kilometer 4.5 between the Cabos. Number of sites and hookups unknown as they are still building. Roadlog page 96.

Campestre La Pila RV Park. Located at kilometer 210 south of Constitución, 1 mile west of México 1 on graded dirt road. 10 sites with full hookups, lots of tent sites. Large area with lawn around pool, recreation room. Roadlog page 86.

Campo Playa RV Park. Located in Ensenada off the intersection of Lázaro Cárdenas and Calle Agustín Sangines. 60 sites with full hookups, tent sites. Phone 01152-617-62918. Roadlog page 14. DO NOT USE YOUR CREDIT CARD HERE.

Campo San Felipe RV Park. In San Felipe on the shore. 34 sites with full hookups. Tents welcome. Roadlog page 26.

Casa Blanca RV Park. Located on right 3 miles before downtown La Paz on México 1 coming from the north. 33 sites with full hookups. No pull-throughs. Pool, store, laundry. Roadlog page 92.

Club de Pesca RV Park. Located in San Felipe, 1 mile south of town on the beach. 30 sites have electricity and water and there is a dump station. Roadlog page 26.

El Arco RV Park. Located on the north side of México 1 between the Cabos at kilometer 5.5. There are 3 levels to this park and the upper levels have good views. 85 sites with full hookups, tent sites. Pool, laundry, restaurant and bar. Phone and fax 01152-114-31686. Roadlog page 96.

El Cardón RV Park. On the right as you enter La Paz on México 1 from the north. 80 sites with full hookups, most are pull-throughs. Pool, laundry, ice and showers. Each site has a ramada (palm covered shade area) with cement floor. Travel agency and phone on premises. Phone 01152-112-20078. Fax: 01152-112-21261. Roadlog page 92.

El Cardonal RV Park. Located north of Los Barriles and south of Bahía de Los Muertos. Nice clean park; camping, and some sites with full hookups. Accessible by 4WD, jeep type vehicles and possibly small motorhomes. (We have a friend who made it in there in a 30' motorhome.) Fax in México, 01152-114-10040 It is on the map of Roadlog 97.

El Faro Viejo RV Park. Located in town of Cabo San Lucas at Matamoros and Félix Ortega. 49 sites with full hookups. Restaurant, bar, laundry. Roadlog page 94 (also see city map of Cabo San Lucas).

El Moro Trailer Park. Located in the town of Loreto on quiet back street. Follow signs from México 1. Full hookups. Roadlog page 82.

El Oasis RV Park. Located 3 miles north of Rosarito Beach off México 1 between Tijuana and Rosarito Beach at kilometer 25. Access from southbound traffic only; the turnoff is just south of Rancho del Mar off-ramp, there is a large sign for the park. If you are northbound, turn off at Rancho Del Mar, cross over México 1D and head back south to first turnoff. 55 full hookup sites. Restaurant and bar and small store. Phone 800-462-7472, 01152-661-33255. Roadlog page 4.

El Padrino RV Park. Located in the oasis of San Ignacio with palm trees overhead and the river running nearby. About 1.5 miles from México 1 on the paved road into the town of San Ignacio. Full hookups for about 8 rigs. Nice riverside tent sites. Restaurant and bar. Roadlog page 66.

El Palomar RV Park. Located at kilometer 51 south of Ensenada on México 1 in Santo Tomás. 46 Full hookup sites, tent sites. Nice park in an old olive tree orchard. Restaurant, bar, store. Phone 01152-617-70650. Roadlog page 14.

Estero Beach Resort. Turn off at kilometer 15 of México 1 south of Ensenada; follow signs approximately 2 miles on paved road. 74 full hookups at water's edge. Pool, tennis, restaurant, bar, gift shops, museum, watersports. Phone 01152-617-66225. Roadlog page 14.

Guillermo's Trailer Park. Located in Bahía de Los Angeles on the water's edge. 15 sites with full hookups, tent sites. Electricity is not on 24 hours. Boat ramp. Restaurant, bar and gift shop. Roadlog page 48.

Kaadekaman Trailer park. Located in Viscaíno between Guerrero Negro and San Ignacio on the right just after turnoff for the town of Viscaíno. This is a very basic little park but provides shelter and safety for the night. Hookups are planned. Roadlog page 56.

KOA Rosarito. Located 6.5 miles north of Rosarito Beach on the east side of México 1D. Nice ocean view. Turn off at kilometer 22, San Antonio exit. 195 full hookup sites. Tent sites. Phone 01152-661-33305. Roadlog page 4.

La Capilla RV Park. Located 1 mile off kilometer 104+ of México 1 south of Buena Vista. Park has two levels; most of the beach front sites are taken by permanent residents but the upper level has nice ocean breezes. All sites have full hookups. The water comes from artisan wells. Laundry, large clean showers. Each site has a large ramada (palm-covered shade area). Reasonably priced. Roadlog page 98.

La Espinita Trailer Park and Restaurant. Located just north of Guerrero Negro on México 1. Currently the owner allows free parking for the night, he has intentions of putting in full hookups but it will be awhile. He serves good food at a very reasonable price. No phones yet. Roadlog page 46.

La Paz RV Park. As you enter La Paz on México 1 from the north the park is off to your left in a residential area. There is no street sign but there is a sign that says SECOFI; turn left on this street and follow to end. 40 sites with full hookups, tent sites. Laundry. Phone 01152-112-28787. Roadlog page 92.

La Playa RV Park. Located in Bahía de Los Angeles on the edge of the bay. Some electrical hookups, but power is not available 24 hours. Dump station. Roadlog page 48.

La Ribera RV Park. Located 7.5 miles from México 1 at kilometer 93 south of Buena Vista. Access park by going straight on through La Ribera to end of road and turn left, follow road 1/4 mile and turn right. Park has 14 spaces with full hookups and lots of tent sites. The park is almost totally shaded by large mango trees interspersed with papayas. The beach is about 1/4 mile from park. Good surf fishing out front. Roadlog page 98.

Las Dunas Trailer Park. Located just south of the La Pinta Guerrero Negro Hotel north of the town of Guerrero Negro on México 1. 60 sites, some with hookups that work. Fills up during the winter. Restaurant next door at the La Pinta Guerrero Negro. Roadlog page 46.

Las Palmas RV Park. Located just south of Santa Rosalía at kilometer 194. A nice new clean park with 30 sites with full hookups. Roadlog page 68.

Loremar RV Park. Located 1 mile south of the town of Loreto on the water but there is no view of same. Access is through town, turn right on Francisco Madero. 32 sites with full hookups. Roadlog page 82.

Los Cerritos RV Park. Located 2.5 miles off México 1 at kilometer 64 south of Todos Santos. Water and sewer but no electricity yet. Many people camp on the bluff in front of the park overlooking the ocean. The land belongs to the local county members and they have the right to charge for camping there too. Fishing is very good in the little bay. No phone at park. Roadlog page 94.

Malarrimo RV Park, Restaurant and Motel. Located on the paved road into Guerrero Negro on the right as you enter town. 22 Full hookup sites. Tents allowed. Restaurant has very good food. Whale-watching trips arranged here during Jan, Feb. and March. Phone 01152-115-70250. Fax 01152-70020. Roadlog page 46

Manfred's RV Park. Located on east side of México 1 just north of Constitución. 8 sites with full hookups. Roadlog page 78.

Mar del Sol RV Park. Located in San Felipe 1.5 miles south of town on the beach. 85 sites with full hookups. Tent sites. Pool, boat ramp, laundry, store. Reservations: 800-336-5454. Roadlog page 26.

Martín Verdugo Trailer Park. Located in Los Barriles 1/2 mile east of México 1 at kilometer 110, on the beach in town. 70 sites with full hookups. A popular spot for wind-surfers in the winter; they do fill up. Roadlog page 98

Mesón Don Pepe RV Park. Turn off México 1 to west at kilometer 172 of México 1 between Ensenada and San Quintín (4 kilometers past Colonia Guerrero). 30 full hookups sites, tent sites. Restaurant, bar. Roadlog page 22.

Old Mill Motel and RV Park. Turn off to right at kilometer 195 of México 1 south of San Quintín. The park is about 3 miles from México 1. Road is graded but will soon be paved. 28 full hookup sites. Restaurant and bar. Reservations: Baja Outfitter, 223 Via de San Ysidro, San Ysidro, CA 92143, Phone 800-479-7962 (California only) or 619-428-2779. Roadlog page 22.

Outdoor Resorts RV Resort. Located on the beach at kilometer 72 of México 1 south of Rosarito Beach. Easy access for southbound vehicles. Northbound vehicles must go to the next turnoff and return. 134 full hookup sites. Restaurant, bar, store. Phone 01152-662-69255. Roadlog page 4.

Parador Punta Prieta Trailer Park. Located at kilometer 280 between Cataviña and Guerrero Negro at the intersection with the road to Bahía de Los Angeles. No reliable hookups. Fenced. Reasonably priced. Roadlog page 38.

Playa Bonita Trailer Park. Located in San Felipe about 1 mile north of town. 29 sites with full hookups. Roadlog page 26

Playa del Oro RV Park. Located in Los Barriles 1/2 mile east of México 1 at kilometer 110, on the beach north of town. 54 sites with full hookups. Roadlog page 98.

Posada Don Diego RV Park. Take same turnoff as to above park but continue on around for 1/2 mile further. 60 full hookup sites, tent sites. Restaurant, bar. Roadlog page 22.

Punta Chivato. There is no formal RV park here; however, RV's can camp along the shore for a few dollars. Pit toilets and showers. It is really a pretty place. The 20 kilometer graded dirt road from México 1 is maintained but can get very washboard at times. Nearby Shell Beach is great beachcombing. The Hotel Punta Chivato is on the point and has a restaurant, bar and a small store. Roadlog page 68.

Ruben's Trailer Park. Located 1 mile north of San Felipe on the shore. 52 sites with full hookups. Tents welcome, boat ramp, restaurant, bar. Roadlog page 26.

San Jacinto Trailer Park. Turn off of México 1 at kilometer 149 between Ensenada and San Quintín. I have not visited this park. From the highway there is a dirt road leading to the beach (about 3 miles). Roadlog Page 22.

San Lucas RV Park. Located on the beach at San Lucas Cove just south of the town of San Lucas at kilometer 182 of México 1 between Santa Rosalía and Mulegé. Good fishing. No hookups. Dump station. Roadlog page 68.

San Pedrito RV Park. Located 1.5 miles off of México 1 at Km. 58+ south of Todos Santos. 84 sites with full hookups, tent sites, beach camping. All sites are pull-throughs. Sports bar, restaurant, surf fishing, surfing, beautiful wide, white sandy beach that stretches for miles. Gate is locked at night; ask what time if you are going out for the evening. Many restaurants in nearby Todos Santos. No phone at park. Roadlog page 94.

Santispac. Located at kilometer 114+ south of Mulegé just off México 1 at the edge of the waters of Bahía Concepción. A popular spot with RVs, no hookups. Dump station.. Roadlog page 74.

Serenidad Hotel and RV Park. Located at kilometer 131 south of Mulegé about 1 mile from México 1. 10 RV sites with hookups. Restaurant, bar, pool. Dirt landing strip for light planes. Closed month of September. Phone 01152-115-30111. Roadlog page 74.

Sinai Trailer Park. Located in El Rosario at kilometer 55+. A very basic park with full hookups. Tent sites. Restaurant. Roadlog page 22.

The Orchard RV Park. Located 1/2 mile south of Mulegé on México 1 near the river. 46 sites with full hookups, tent sites. Phone 01152-115-30300. Roadlog page 74.

Trailer Park Cataviña. Located at kilometer 174+ of México 1 between San Quintín and Parador Punta Prieta. They say they have full hookups but they don't always work. Fenced off, "safe harbor" for the night at a very reasonable price. Roadlog page 30.

Tripui RV Park. Turn off at kilometer 94 south of Loreto; go 1 mile and turn right into park. 31 full hookup sites. Pool, restaurant, bar, gift shop, grocery store, tennis. Fishing nearby. Phone 01152-113-30818. Fax 01152-113-30828. Roadlog page 82.

Vagabundos del Mar RV Park. Located at km. 2.5 of México 1 east of Cabo San Lucas. 95 sites with full hookups. Pool, restaurant, bar, laundry. Reservations recommended during the winter months. Phone 01152-114-30290. Roadlog page 96.

Villa Maria Isabel RV Park and Bakery. Located 1/2 mile south of Mulegé on México 1. 25 pull-through sites with electricity and water. Dump station. Bakery goods are highly recommended. Phone: 01152-115-30246. Roadlog page 74.

Villa Serena RV Park. Located off kilometer 7.5 of México 1 between the two Cabos, this park overlooks the tip of Baja. 50 sites with full hookups. Pool, gym, laundry, restaurant, bar. Reservations needed during the winter months. Phone 800-932-5599; 01152-114-30509; 408-848-2226. Roadlog page 96.

Villas de Loreto. Located south of the town of Loreto, access through town, turn right on Francisco Madero. A new RV park on the site of the old Flying Sportsmen's Lodge at the water's edge. Pool and laundry. 12 full hookup sites, 20 campsites. Roadlog page 82.

Vista del Mar RV Park. Located in San Felipe about 1 mile north of town on Mar de Cortez. 20 sites with full hookups. Tents welcome. Roadlog page 26.

Sports packages can be booked from the following numbers. Many of these places provide everything for your trip including hotel and airfare. Some will require you to get there on your own. Call or write for brochures.

DIVING

Dive Palmilla Hotel Palmilla P.O. Box 37 Cabo San Lucas, BCS 800-637-2226 01152-114-32986	Cabo San Lucas Diving Plaza Marina Local F-5 Marina Blvd. S/N Cabo San Lucas, BCS 714-728-1026 01152-114-34004	Baja Diving Service La Concha Hotel Carretera a Pichilingue La Paz, BCS 800-999-2252 01152-112-26544
Pacific Coast Adventures 1323 Lincoln Blvd., Ste. 101 Santa Monica, CA 90401 800-491-3483	Tio Watersports P.O. Box 37 Cabo San Lucas, Baja CA Sur 800-336-3542 01152-114-32986	Mulegé Divers Trips from Mulegé Gral. Martinez S/N Mulegé, Baja CA Sur 01152-115-30059

WINDSURFING - SURFING

Baja Air Adventures 386 East "H" Street Chula Vista, CA 91910 619-691-8551	Baja Surf Adventures P.O. Box 1381 Vista, CA 92085 800-428-7873	Baja Surf Club PO Box 9016 Calabasas, CA 91372 800-551-8844
Excursions Extraordinaire P.O. Box 5766 Eugene, OR 97405 800-678-2252	Mr. Bill's Windsurfing Adv. 1635 Avalon Ct. Hood River OR 97031 800-533-8452	Vela 351 C Foster City Blvd. Foster City, CA 94404 800-223-5443

KAYAKING

Ecosummer Expeditions 1516 Duranleau Vancouver, BC V6H 3F4 800-688-8605	Elekah! Expeditions P.O. Box 4092 Bellingham, WA 98227 206-734-7270	Mar Y Aventuras Interior Topeté #564 E/5 de Feb. y Navarro La Paz, BCS 406-848-7550
Paddling South 4510 Silverado Trail Calistoga, CA 94515 707-942-4550 in U.S. 01152-113-50142 in Mex	Ron Yarnell Wilderness 1231 Sundance Loop Fairbanks, Alaska 99709 907-497-8203	Seaquest/Zodetic P.O. Box 2424 Friday Harbor, WA 92424 206-378-5767
Solo Sports 78 Blazewood Foothill Ranch, CA 92610 714-837-1396	Southwest Sea Kayaks 2590 Ingram Ave. San Diego, CA 92109 619-222-3616	Baja Tropicales Mulegé Kayaks S.A.de C.V. Mulegé, Baja Calif Sur, Mexico fax 01152-115-30190

WHALEWATCHING

Baja Expeditions, Inc. 2625 Garnet Ave. San Diego, CA 92109 800-843-6967	Oceanic Society Expeditions Fort Macon Center, BLD E San Francisco, CA 94123 415-441-1106	Pacific Sea Fari Tours 2803 Emerson St. San Diego, 92106 619-226-8224
Special Expeditions, Inc. 720 5th Ave. New York, NY 10019 212-765-7740	Malarrimo Motel, Cafe & RV Park. Guerrero Negro 01152-115-70250	Discover Baja Travel Club 3065 Clairemont Drive San Diego, CA 92117 800-727-2252 619-275-4225

Sportfishing and Baja go together. Most of these places have complete travel packages and will send you brochures on request.

SPORTFISHING

Arturo's Sportfishing Loreto, Baja CA Sur 800-451-6997 01152-113-50409 fax 01152-113-50022	Baja California Tours 6986 La Jolla Blvd, Ste 204 La Jolla, CA 92037 619-454-7166	Baja Fishing Adventures 2221 Palo Verde, Ste 1D Long Beach, CA 90815 310-594-9441
Baja Fishing Resorts East Cape Hotels P.O. Box 9016 Calabasas, CA 91372 800-368-4334	Baja Outfitters Old Mill - San Quintín 223 Via de San Ysidro San Ysidro, CA 92173 619-428-6946	Captain Villegas Sportfishing San Felipe 133 So Yorba St. Orange, CA 92669 714-538-9300
Cass Tours P.O. Box 218 Placentia, CA 92670 800-593-6510	Costamar Sportfishing 22565 Ventura Blvd Woodland Hills, CA 91364 800-347-2760	Fish With Me 9140 Gramercy Dr. San Diego, CA 92123 800-347-4963
Fritz's Boat House Ensenada Sport Boats P.O. Box 553 Ensenada, Baja CA Norte 01152-617-40294	Gaviota Fleet 404 Tennant Station, Ste B Morgan Hill, CA 95037 800-932-5599	Gordo's Sport Fishing Ensenada Sport Boats Waterfront, Ensenada 01152-617-83515
Jig Stop Tours 34186 Pacific Coast Highway Dana Point, CA 92629 800-521-2281	Mexican Resorts International 4216 Bonita Road Bonita, CA 91902 800-336-5454 Local 619-470-3475	Pisces Fleet Blvd Marina & Madero, #2 Apdo Postal 137 Cabo San Lucas, BCS 23410 800-946-2252 Local 01152-114-31288
Sea of Cortez Sportfishing P.O. Box 5303 Hacienda Heights, CA 91745 818-333-9012	Tony Reyes Tours San Felipe 133 So Yorba St. Orange, CA 92669 714-538-8010	Williams & Associates P.O. Box 223240 Carmel, CA 93922 800-777-2664
Lee Palm Sportfishers Long Range Fishing Trips 2801 Emerson, San Diego, CA 92106 619-224-3857	Fishermen's Landing Long Range Fishing Trips 2838 Garrison St. San Diego, CA 92106 619-221-8500	Point Loma Sportfishing Long Range Fishing Trips 1403 Scott St. San Diego, CA 92106 619-223-1627
H & M Landing Long Range Fishing Trips 2803 Emerson St. San Diego, CA 92106 619-222-1144	Rancho Leonero 8689 El Rancho Fountain Valley, CA 92681 800-334-2252 714-375-3720	Hotel Cabo San Lucas Km. 15+ Carretera Transp. Cabo San Lucas, BCS 800-733-2226 From CA 213-665-2323 01152-114-33457

TIDE TABLES

Tidelines Pacific Side tables & calendars 800-345-8524	University of Arizona Sea of Cortez tables Printing & Reproduction Dept. Tucson, AZ 85721	Baja Outfitters Jan & Dan Williams 223 Via de San Ysidro San Ysidro, CA 92173 619-428-6946

TRAVEL CLUBS

Discover Baja Travel Club 3065 Clairemont Dr. San Diego, CA 92117 800-727-2252 619-275-4225	Vagabundos Del Mar 33 N. 2nd St. Rio Vista, CA 94571 800-474-2252	Cabo Assoc. of Boat Owners "The CABO Club" 213-587-2523
Flight Log - Private Pilots P.O. Box 2465 Fullerton, CA 92633 310-391-4464-714-521-2531	Mexican Hunting Assoc. Hunting Assistance 6840 El Salvador St. Long Beach, CA 90815 310-430-3256	

INSURANCE

Instant México Auto Insur. 223 Via de San Ysidro San Ysidro, CA 92073 800-345-4701 619-428-4714	MacAfee & Edwards Airplanes & Autos 260 So. Los Robles, Ste 303 Pasadena, CA 91101 800-334-7950	Mex-Insur 99 Bonita Road Chula Vista, CA 91910 619-425-2390
Oscar Padilla Insurance 1660 Hotel Circle North San Diego, CA 92108 800-258-8600	Sanborn's Box 310 McAllen, TX 78505-0310	Aeromedevac air ambulance 800-462-0911 in Baja 95-800-832-5087

RV CARAVANS

Baja Winters 1024 SW 354th St. Federal Way, WA 98023 206-239-1793	Carr's RV Tours 11781 Hunter Ave. Yuma, AZ 95367 800-526-6469	Fantasy Caravans P.O. Box 95605 Las Vegas, NV 89193-5605 800-952-8496
Point South RV Tours 11313 Edmonson Ave. Moreno Valley, CA 92555 800-421-1394	Tracks to Adventure 2811 Jackson El Paso, TX 79930 800-351-6053	Caravanas Voyagers 1155 Larry Mahan Hwy. El Paso, TX 79925 800-933-9332 fax 915-592-1293

AIRLINES

Aero California 1960 E. Grand Ave. Ste 1200 El Segundo, CA 90245 800-237-6225 in Los Cabos 95-114-30848	AeroMexico 800-237-6639	Alaska Airlines 800-426-0333 In Los Cabos 95-114-21015
Mexicana Airlines 800-531-7921		

CAR RENTALS

AMCA - in the U.S. P.O. Box 19216 San Diego, CA 92159 800-832-9529	AMCA - Cabo San Lucas Ave. Revolución/Pemex Cabo San Lucas, BCS 01152-114-32515	AMCA - La Paz 1715 Madero St. La Paz, Baja Ca Sur 01152-112-30335
AMCA - San José del Cabo Km 33, Col. Rosarito San José del Cabo, BCS 01152-114-21314	Baja Rent-A-Car 9245 Jamacha Blvd. Spring Valley, CA 619-470-7368	Budget Rent-A-Car Paseo de Los Heroes 77 Tijuana, Baja Ca Norte 01152-663-43303
M & M Jeeps 2200 El Cajon Blvd. San Diego, CA 92104 619-297-1615	National Car Rental (International Reservations) 800-227-3876	National Car Rental Cabo San Lucas 01152-114-31414
National Car Rental San José del Cabo 01152-114-20160	Avis (International Reservations) 800-331-1212	Budget Worldwide Reservations 800-527-0700
Dollar Rent-A-Car They rent vehicles that can be taken into Baja. U.S. 800-800-4000		

FERRY RESERVATIONS

La Paz - Pichilingue office La Paz to Mazatlán or La Paz to Topolobampo 01152-112-53833 in Baja 95-112-53833	Santa Rosalía Office Santa Rosalía to Guaymas 01152-115-20013 in Baja 95-115-20013	

There is an exceptional magazine now available on Baja. It should be at any large newstand or you can order direct from:
Baja Life Magazine
23172 Alcalde Dr. "B"
Laguna Hills, CA 92653
714-470-9086

The BAJA SUN, an English language newspaper covering all of Baja, is a good source for current information on Baja. For subscription rates and information write to:
Baja Sun
 P.O. Box 8530
Chula Vista, CA 91912-8530.

Note: Hotel and motel accommodations are listed in order of area as you travel down the peninsula with Mexicali and San Felipe listed at the end. Read left to right. For obvious reasons not all hotels and motels are listed here.

ACCOMMODATIONS

Tijuana Fiesta Americana Hotel Blvd. Agua Caliente 4500 Tijuana, BCN 01152-668-17000	**Tijuana** Holiday Inn - Tijuana 800-465-4329	**Tijuana** Lucerna Hotel 10902 Paseo De Los Heroes Tijuana, Baja Ca Norte 800-582-3762
Tijuana Paraíso Radisson Hotel 53 Cuspide, Col. Tijuana, Baja Ca Norte 800-333-3333	**Tijuana** Premier Hotel Paseo del Centenario 60 Esq. Zona Rio, Tijuana, BCN 01152-668-42710	**Rosarito Beach** Brisas del Mar - Rosarito Beach Benito Juarez 22 Rosarito, BCN 800-697-5223
Rosarito Beach Los Pelícanos Calle 113 Rosarito, BCN 01152-661-20445	**Rosarito Beach** Rosarito Beach Hotel Benito Juarez 31 Rosarito, BCN 800-343-8582	**So. of Rosarito Beach** Bajamar Resort Km 77.5 Carretera Ensenada Ensenada, BCN 800-222-1191
Ensenada Joker Hotel - Ensenada Km 12.5 Carretera Trans. Ensenada, BCN 800-225-6537	**Ensenada** La Pinta - Ensenada Loreto Y Bucaneros Ensenada, BCN 800-336-5454	**East of Ensenada** Meling Ranch Mountains east of Ensenada 619-758-3526
East of Ensenada Mike's Sky Ranch Mountains each of Ensenada P.O. Box 1948 Imperial Beach , CA 01152-668-15514	**South of Ensenada** Estero Beach Resort & RV Pk 6 Miles So of Ensenada P.O. Box 86 Ensenada, BCN 01152-667-66225	**South of Ensenada** Santo Tomás Hotel (El Palomar) Located in Santo Tomás 01152-617-40301
San Quintín 7 mi so. Cielito Lindo Motel San Quintín P.O. Box 7 San Quintín, BCN No Phone	**San Quintín 7 mi so.** La Pinta - San Quintín Km 206+ South of Town San Quintín, BCS 800-336-5454 01152-617-52878	**San Quintín 3 mi. west** Old Mill Motel & RV Park On the Bay - San Quintín Reservations: 619-428-2779
San Quintín Quintín Rest, Bar & Motel Km 190 San Quintín BCS 01152-616-52376	**San Quintín** Villa Serena Bed & Breakfast 1.5 Miles South of town San Quintín, BCN 909-982-7087	**Bahía de Los Angeles** Villa Vita Hotel P.O. Box 462701 Escondido, Ca 92046 619-741-9583
Cataviña La Pinta Hotel Km 174 Carretera Trans. Cataviña, BCN 800-336-5454	**Guerrero Negro** Malarrimo Motel & RV Park 01152-115-70250 Fax 01152-115-70020	**Guerrero Negro** La Pinta Hotel Km 128 Carretera Trans. Guerrero Negro, BCS 800-336-5454
San Ignacio Hotel La Pinta Km 74 Carretera Transpenin. San Ignacio, BCS 800-336-5454	**Santa Rosalía** El Morro Hotel Km. 195 Carretera Trans. Santa Rosalía, BCS 01152-115-20414	**Mulegé** Hacienda Hotel Center of Town across from Plaza. P.O. Box 16392, Irvine, CA 92713 01152-115-30021
Mulegé Serenidad Hotel Km 131 Carretera Transpen. Mulegé, BCS 01152-115-30111	**Loreto** La Pinta Hotel Km 0 Carretera Transpenin. Loreto, Baja Ca Sur 800-336-5454	**Loreto** Loreto Inn Km 111 Nopoló, Loreto, BCS 01152-113-30700

Loreto Misión de Loreto Hotel P.O. Box 49 Loreto, BCS 01152-113-50048	**Loreto** Oasis Hotel Apdo Postal No 17 Loreto, BCS 01152-113-50112	**La Paz** La Concha Hotel Km. 5 Carr. a Pichilingue La Paz, BCS 800-999-2252
La Paz La Perla Hotel Alvaro Obregón 1570 La Paz, BCS 01152-112-20777	**La Paz** La Posada de Engelbert Nueva Performa y Playa Sur, La Paz, BCS 01152-112-24011	**La Paz** Los Arcos Hotel 18552 MacArthur Blvd Irvine, CA 92715 800-347-2252
La Paz Club El Morro Apdo. Postal 357 La Paz, BCS 01152-112-24084	**La Paz** La Concha 7860 Mission Center Crt #202 San Diego, CA 92108 800-999-2252	**La Paz** Marina Suites Hotel Carretera a Pichilingue La Paz, BCS
Todos Santos California Hotel Domocilio Conocido Todos Santos, BCS 01152-114-50002	**East Cape** Bahía Los Frailes 819 12th St. Paso Robles, CA 93446 800-762-2252	**East Cape** Buena Vista Hotel 16211 E. Whittier Whittier, CA. 90603 800-752-3555
East Cape El Cardonal Resort El Cardonal, BCS Fax 01152-114-10040	**East Cape** Palmas de Cortez Hotel Buena Vista, BCS 800-368-4334	**East Cape** Playa Del Sol Hotel Los Barriles, BCS 800-368-4334
East Cape Punta Pescadero Hotel 24831 Alicia Parkway Laguna Hills, CA 92656 800-426-2252 01152-114-10101	**East Cape** Rancho Buena Vista P.O. Box 1408 Santa María, Ca 93456 800-258-8200	**East Cape** Rancho Leonero 8689 El Rancho Fountain Valley, CA 92681 800-334-2252 714-375-3720
Los Cabos Cabo San Lucas Hotel Km 15+ Carr. Trans. Cabo San Lucas, BCS 800-733-2226 From CA 213-655-2323 01152-114-33457	**Los Cabos** Casa Madre Bed and Breakfast 63 Finisterra Blvd. San José del Cabo, BCS 23400 01152-114-20869	**Los Cabos** Finisterra Hotel Land's end - Cabo San Lucas. 800-347-2252 01152-114-30000
Los Cabos Hacienda Beach Hotel Cabo San Lucas 6523 Wilshire Blvd, Los Angeles, CA 90048 800-733-2226	**Los Cabos** Intercontinental Presidente Paseo San José, San José del Cabo, BCS México 23410 800-327-0200 01152-114-20211	**Los Cabos** Melía Cabo Real Km 19.5 Carretera Trans. San José del Cabo 800-336-3542
Los Cabos Melía Los Cabos Cabo San Lucas 800-336-3542	**Los Cabos** Palmilla Hotel Km. 27 Carr. Trans. 800-637-2226	**Los Cabos** Plaza Las Glorias Cabo San Lucas 800-342-AMIGO
Los Cabos Posada Real Hotel Blvd. Malecón San José del Cabo 800-528-1234 01152-114-20155	**Los Cabos** Solmar Hotel Land's end, Cabo San Lucas, BCS23410 México 800-326-2252	**Los Cabos** Twin Dolphins Hotel Km 12 Carretera Trans. Reservations in U.S. 800-421-8925

Los Cabos	Mexicali	Mexicali
Westin Regina Resort Km 24 Carretera Trans. 800-228-3000 01152-114-29000	Lucerna Hotel Blvd Benito Juarez 2151 Mexicali, BCN 800-LUCERNA	San Juan Capistrano Hotel Reforma 646, Zona Central 01152-655-24104
San Felipe	San Felipe	San Felipe
El Cortez Motel P.O. Box 1227 Calexico, CA 92232 01152-656-18324	Las Misiones Hotel 148 Ave. Misión de Loreto San Felipe, BCN 800-6-MISIONES	Riviera Hotel Ave. Mar Baltico S/N San Felipe, BCN 01152-655-36616
San Felipe	Bahía de Los Angeles	
San Felipe Marina Resort Km. 4.5 Carr. a aeropuerto San Felipe, BCN 21850 800-777-1700	Villa Vita Hotel P.O. Box 462701 Escondido, CA 92046 Fax 619-489-5687	

EMERGENCY NUMBERS:

Attorney General, Protection of Tourists, Tijuana, 01152-668-80555
American Consulate in Tijuana, 01152-668-17400
American Consulate in Cabo San Lucas, 01152-114-33566
Bi-National Emergency Medical Care, Chula Vista, 619-425-5080
Canadian Consulate in Tijuana, 01152-668-40461
Mexican Consulate, Los Angeles, 213-341-6818
Mexican Consulate, San Diego, 619-231-8414
Mexican Consulate, Colorado, 303-830-6702
Mexican Consulate, Florida, 305-441-8780
Mexican Consulate, Illinois, 312-855-1380
Mexican Consulate, New York, 212-689-0456
Mexican Consulate, Texas, 214-522-9741
Mexican Department of Fisheries, 619-233-6956
Mexican Tourist Office, Los Angeles, 213-203-8191
National Tourism Hotline, from anywhere in Baja, 91-800-90392
Sect of Tourism, Assistance office, Tijuana, 01152-668-19492
Sect of Tourism, Bahía de Los Angeles, 01152-665-03206
Sect of Tourism, Ensenada, 01152-617-23000
Sect of Tourism, Los Cabos, 01152-114-20446
Sect of Tourism, Loreto, Felipe Davis, 01152-113-50573
Sect of Tourism, La Paz, 01152-112-40199
Sect of Tourism, Mexicali, 01152-655-72561
Sect of Tourism, Rosarito, 01152-661-20200
Sect of Tourism, San Felipe, 01152-657-71155
Sect of Tourism, Tecate, 01152-665-41095
Sect of Tourism, Tijuana, office 01152-668-19492
Sect of Tourism, Vicente Guerrero, 01152-666-62216
Sect of Tourism, La Paz, 01152-112-40100
Vehicle Importation Permit Information, 900-452-8277

Quién no se aventura no pasa la mar.
Nothing ventured, nothing gained.

BIBLIOGRAPHY...

This bibliography is provided for your further reading enjoyment. Many of the books listed here are out of print. The library at University of California at San Diego has an extensive collection of books on Baja California. Many of these books can be requested at your local library. Some very fine literature has been written about Baja but, sadly, the better books were only printed in small quantities. The current publications on Baja are available from Baja Source. A complete list of these books with prices and ordering information is at the back of this book.

Aschmann, Homer. *The Central Desert of Baja California: Demography and Ecology.* Ibero-Americana, No 42. Berkeley and Los Angeles: University of California. Riverside: Manessier reprint, 1967.

Automobile Club of Southern California. *Baja California.* Los Angeles: 1994.

Automobile Club of Southern California. *Log of Baja California, México.* Los Angeles: 1961.

Baegert, Johann J. *Observations in Lower California.* Berkeley and Los Angeles: University of California Press, 1952.

Bales, Mike. *Launch Ramps of Baja California.* Torrance, CA: Launch Ramp Publications, 1992.

Barco, Miguel del. *The Natural History of Baja California.* Baja California Travels Series, No. 43, Dawson's Book Shop. Los Angeles, 1980.

Cannon, Ray. *How To Fish The Pacific Coast.* A Sunset Book. Menlo Park, California: Lane Publishing Co., 1967.

Cannon, Ray. *The Sea of Cortez.* Menlo Park, California: Lane Magazine and Book Co., 1966.

Clavigero, Francisco J. *The History of Lower California.* Translated by Sara E. Lake. Palo Alto: Stanford University Press, 1937. Riverside: Manessier Reprint, 1971.

Crosby, Harry W. *Antigua California: Mission and Colony on the Peninsular Frontier.* Albuquerque: University of New Mexico Press, 1994.

Crosby, Harry W. *The Cave Paintings of Baja California.* Salt Lake City: Copley Books, 1975.

Crosby, Harry W. *The Kings Highway in Baja California.* Salt Lake City: Copley Books, 1974.

Dunne, Peter M. *Black Robes in Lower California.* Berkeley and Los Angeles: University of California Press, 1952.

Ellsberg, Helen. *Doña Anita of El Rosario.* Glendale: La Siesta Press, 1974.

Englehart, Fr. Zephyrn. *The Missions and Missionaries of California.* Second Edition, Volume I. Chicago: Franciscan Herald Press, 1929.

Gardner, Erle Stanley. *Hovering over Baja.* New York: William Morrow & Co., 1961.

Gardner, Erle Stanley. *Hunting the Desert Whale.* New York: William Morrow & Co., 1960.

Gardner, Erle Stanley. *The Hidden Heart of Baja.* New York: William Morrow & Co., 1962.

Gerhard, Peter, and Gulick, Howard E. *Lower California Guidebook.* Glendale: The Arthur H. Clark Co. 1958.

Gerhard, Peter. *Pirates on the West Coast of New Spain 1575-1742.* Glendale: The Arthur H. Clark Co., 1960.

Gilmore, Raymond M. *Bubbles and Other Pilot Whales.* Del Mar, California: Barley Brae Printers, 1962.

Gilmore, Raymond M. *The Story of the Grey Whale.* 2nd edition, revised. San Diego: 1961

Gilmore, Raymond M. *The Story of the Grey Whale.* San Diego: Yale Printing Co. 1958.

Gohier, Francois. *A Pod of Grey Whales.* San Luis Obispo, CA: Blake Books 1988.

Goldbaum, David. *Towns of Baja California, A 1918 Report.* Glendale: La Siesta Press, 1971.

Goodson, Gar. *Fishes of The Pacific Coast.* Stanford: Stanford University Press, 1988.

Gotshall, Daniel W. *Marine Animals of Baja California.* Second Edition. Monterey, CA: Sea Challengers, 1987.

Hancock, Ralph, with Ray Haller, Mike McMahan, and Frank Alvarado. *Baja California.* Los Angeles: Academy Publishers, 1953.

Henderson, David A. *Men and Whales.* Baja California Travels Series No 29. Dawson's Book Shop. Los Angeles, 1972.

Henderson, David. *Scammon's Lagoon: Focus in the Desert.* Paper written for the VIII Symposium of Baja California.

Jones, Fred and Gloria. *Baja Camping.* San Francisco: Foghorn Press, 1994,

Kelly, Neil, and Gene Kira. *The Baja Catch.* Valley Center, California: Apples & Oranges, Inc., 1988.

Krutch, Joseph W. *The Forgotten Peninsula: A Naturalist in Baja California.* New York: William Sloane Associates, 1961.

Lewis, Leyland R. *Baja Sea Guide, Vol. II.* San Francisco: Miller Freeman, 1971.

Mathes, W. Michael. *The Conquistador in California, 1535.* Baja California Travels Series No. 31, Dawson's Book Shop. Los Angeles, 1973.

Mathes, W. Michael. *The Mission of Baja California 1683 - 1849.* La Paz, Baja California Sur, México: Editorial Aristos, 1977.

Mathes, W. Michael. *The Pearl Hunters in the Gulf of California 1668..* Baja California Travels Series No. 4, Dawson's Book Shop. Los Angeles, 1966.

McMahan, Mike. *Adventures in Baja.* Los Angeles: Stephens Press, 1973.

McMahan, Mike. *There It Is: Baja!.* Riverside: Manessier Publishing Co., 1973.

Meighan, Clement W., et al. *Seven Rock Art Sites in Baja California.* Socorro, New México: Ballena Press, 1978.

Miller, Tom, and Hoffman, Carol. *The Baja Book III.* 16th edition. Huntington Beach, California: Baja Trails Publications, 1992.

Miller, Tom. *Angler's Guide to Baja California.* Huntington Beach, California: Baja Trails Publications, 1984.

Minch, John, and Thomas Leslie. *The Baja Highway.* San Juan Capistrano: John Minch and Associates, Inc., 1991.

Nelson, Edward W. *Lower California and It's Natural Resources.* Memoirs of the National Academy of Sciences, Vol. XVI, Washington D.C., 1921. Riverside: Manessier Publishing Co. Reprint, 1966.

Orr, Robert T. *Marine Mammals of California.* California Natural History Guides Vol. XXIX. Berkeley, Los Angeles and London: University of California Press, 1972.

Peterson, Walt. *The Baja Adventure Book.* Berkeley: Wilderness Press, 1987.

Peyton, John Dennis. *How to Buy Real Estate in Mexico.* San Diego: Law Mexico Publishing, 1994.

Rice, Dale W. and Allen A. Wolman. *The Life History and Ecology of the Grey Whale,.* No. 3. Seattle: The American Society of Mammologists, 1971.

Roberts, Norman C. *Baja California Plant Field Guide.* San Diego: Natural History Publishing Co. 1989.

Romano-Lax, Andromeda. *Sea Kayaking in Baja.* Berkeley: Wilderness Press, 1993.

Scammon, Charles M. *Marine Mammals and the American Whale Fishery.* San Francisco: John H. Carmany & Co., 1874. Riverside, Ca: Manessier Reprint, 1969.

Scammon, Charles M. *The Marine Mammals of the Northwestern Coast of North America.* New York, Dover Publications reprint. 1968.

Scammon, Charles M. *Journal of the Ocean Bird, 1858-1859.* Bancroft Library. Annotated by David A. Henderson, Vol. 21. Los Angeles: Dawson's Book Shop, 1970.

Steinbeck, John, and Edward F. Ricketts. *Sea of Cortez,* New York: Viking Press, 1941.

Walker, Theodore J. *Whale Primer.* 6th revised edition. San Diego: Cabrillo Historical Association, 1975.

Wibberley, Leonard. *Yesterday's Land: A Baja California Adventure.* New York: Ives Washburn, Inc., 1961.

INDEX

Entries in **bold** text reference the Roadlog.

Abreojos, 107, **61, 62, 64**
Achoy, Enrique, 52, 64
Agave, 43
Agricultural inspection, 31, **46, 90**
Agua Caliente race track, 58, **6**
Agua Caliente Resort, **15, 16**
Agua Caliente, **97**
Airlines, commercial, 17
Alfonsinas, **31, 35, 37**
Alfredo's sportfishing, 72, 73
Algodones, **11**
Almejas Bay, **84**
Alphonsinas, **36**
Anthropology museum, La Paz, 75
Aquamarina RV Park, 112, **92**
Aquarios Hotel, 75
Arroyo Calamajué, **36**
Aserradero, **17**
Asunción, **51, 52, 56, 62**
Auto parts, 26
Bahía Agua Verde, **80, 81**
Bahía Almejas, **51, 83, 86**
Bahía Asunción, **51**
Bahía Ballenas, **61**
Bahía Blanca, **33**
Bahía Chileno, **93, 95**
Bahía Concepción, 70, **73, 74**
Bahía Coyote, **73, 74**
Bahía de Calamajué, **39**
Bahía de La Ventana, 108, **91**
Bahía de Los Angeles,106, 108, **38, 47, 48, 49, 60**
Bahía de Los Muertos, **91, 92, 97**
Bahía de San Cristobal, **51**
Bahía de Sebastian Viscaíno, **43**
Bahía Las Animas, **47, 49**
Bahía Los Frailes, **97**
Bahía Magdalena, **75, 78, 83, 84**
Bahía Refugio, **39, 50**
Bahía Remedios, **39**
Bahía San Basillio, **73**
Bahía San Carlos, **57, 87**
Bahía San Francisquito, **60**
Bahía San Hipólito, **52**
Bahía San Hipólito, **61**
Bahía San Juan Bautista, **57**
Bahía San Juanico, **69**
Bahía San Lucas, **93, 95**
Bahía San Luis Gonzaga, **38, 39**
Bahía San Pablo, **51**
Bahía San Quintín, 106
Bahía San Raphael, **49, 60**
Bahía Santa Inez, **67, 73**
Bahía Santa María, **75**
Bahía Santa Teresa, **57, 59**
Bahía Tordilla, **74**
Bahía Tortugas, **41, 52, 56**

Bait, 98
Baja 1000, 17
Baja Malibu, **4**
Baja Outfitter, 62
Baja Winters Caravans, 21
Bajamar, **3, 4, 5**
Beach Club Patty, **26**
Beachcombing, 86, 105, 108, 115, **44, 60, 76,**
Benito Juarez, **77**
Black snook, 70, 94
Boat permits, 27
Boca de Las Animas, **77**
Boca de Marrón, **33, 34, 45**
Boca de Santo Domingo, **77**
Boca de Solidad, **75**
Boca de Tule, **97**
Brisas del Mar RV Park, 112, **96, 98**
Brown, Kirk and Jan, 21
Buena Ventura RV Park, 112, **74**
Buena Ventura, **73, 74**
Buena Vista Hotel, 109
Buena Vista, **93, 95, 97, 98**
Burkhart, John and Terry, 18
Bus travel, 27
Cabo Cielo RV Park, 112, **96**
Cabo Falso, **93, 95**
Cabo Pulmo, 95, 107, 109, **97, 98**
Cabo San Lázaro, **75**
Cabo San Lucas city map, 81
Cabo San Lucas Hotel, **96**
Cabo San Lucas, 11, 32, 80, 94, 107, 109, **92, 93, 95, 94, 96**
Cabo San Miguel, **57**
Cabo Thurloe, **41**
Cabo Vírgenes, **67**
Calamajué, **35, 36, 37, 38**
Caleta San Juanico, **73**
Calexico, **9, 10**
Camalú, **21, 22**
Cameras, 28, 32
Camper dump stations, 20
Campestre La Pila RV Park, 112, **86**
Camping, 75, 86, 89, 90, 91, 92, 102, 103, 106, **4, 8, 14, 26, 32, 46, 68, 74, 76, 82, 92, 94**
Campo Cadena, **32**
Campo Cielito Lindo, **32**
Campo Cristina, **32**
Campo Diamante, **32**
Campo Don Abel, **26**
Campo El Consuelo, **32**
Campo El Paraíso, **26**
Campo Esmeralda, **26**
Campo Feliz, **32**
Campo Garcia, **32**
Campo Hawaii, **26**

Campo Jimenez, **32**
Campo La Jolla, **26**
Campo Los Amigos, **26**
Campo Los Burritos, **32**
Campo Los Pulpos, **32**
Campo Lupita, **26**
Campo Mayma, **26**
Campo Padilla, **32**
Campo Pee Wee, **26**
Campo Playa RV Park, 61
Campo Playa RV Park, 112, **14**
Campo Punta Bufeo, **31**
Campo Rene, **61, 62**
Campo San Felipe RV Park, 112, **26**
Campo San Fernando, **26**
Campo San Francisco, **32**
Campo San José, **32**
Campo San Martín, **32**
Campo San Pedro, **26**
Campo Santa Fe, **32**
Campo Santa María, **26**
Campo Santa Teresa, **32**
Campo Toba, **32**
Campo Turistico Vallarta, **32**
Campo Villa Del Mar, **32**
Canal de San Lorenzo, **91**
Cancún, **83, 86**
Candelaria, **65, 93, 95**
Cantamar, **3, 4, 5**
Cantú grade, **10**
Cantú Palms, **9**
Caravans, 21
Cardón, 39
Casa Blanca RV Park, 112, **92**
Casas de cambio, 15
Cataviña Trailer Park, 116, **30**
Cataviña, 22, 24, **29, 30, 34, 38**
Catch and release, 97
Cave paintings, 66
CCC Market, 31
Cedros Island, **41, 42, 54**
Chileno Bay, 109, **93, 95, 96**
Cielito Lindo Motel, 53, 62, 63, **22**
Cinco de Mayo, 51
Cirio, 41
Climate, 32
Clothing, 32
Club de Pesca RV Park, 112, **26**
Coahuila, **11, 19**
Cochimí Indians, 44
Cócopah Indians, 44
Colonet, **13, 14**
Colonia Elias Calles, **93, 95**
Colonia Guerrero, 21, **21, 22**
Colonia Nunez, **85**
Colonia Progreso, **9**
Colonia Zaragoza, **9**
Colorado River, **10**
Comitán, **89**
Constitución city map 74
Constitución, 21, 24,, 74, 91, **76, 77, 78, 85**

Copper Canyon, 22
Cortés, Hernán, 75
Cortés, Juanita, 53
Coyote Lagoon, **73**
Credit cards, 16
Creeping devil cactus, 43
Crucero del Pacifico, **63**
Crucero Trinidad, **17, 18**
Customs regulations, 27, 28, 29, 30
Damiana, 78
Día de Los Muertos, 51
Día de Los Reyes, 51
Día de Todos Santos, 51
Diesel fuel, 24
Dinosaurs, 36
Discover Baja Travel Club, 33
Diving, 68, 70, 75, 80, 101, 117, 109, **38, 48, 60, 84, 86**
Dogs, 33
Domecq Winery, **8**
Don Pepe RV Park, **22**
Drinking water, 32
Duties, 28, 29
East cape, 11, 108
Easter Camp, 98
Eiffel church, 69
Ejido Benito Juarez, **55**
Ejido Cárdenas, **15**
Ejido Chula Vista, **8**
Ejido de Los Heroes, **15,**
Ejido Eréndira, **13**
Ejido Francisco Villa, **70, 77**
Ejido Francisco Zarco, **8**
Ejido Guillermo Prieto, **55**
Ejido Morelos, **45**
Ejido San Matías, **15, 17**
Ejido Uruapan, **13, 15**
Ejido Viscaíno, **56**
Ejido Zaragoza, **7**
El Alamo, **16, 63**
El Arco RV Park, 112, **96**
El Arco, **55, 56**
El Barril, **57, 59, 60**
El Boleo bakery, 69
El Boleo Mining Company, 68
El Bombedor, **73**
El Cardón RV Park, 112, **96**
El Cardón, **63**
El Cardonal RV Park, 112, **97**
El Cardonál, **97, 98**
El Carricito, **66**
El Centenario, **89, 92**
El Cien, 24, **85, 86, 89**
El Coloradito, **32**
El Comitán, **91, 92**
El Condor, **7**
El Conejo, 94, **89, 90**
El Consuelo, **21, 27**
El Coro, **98**
El Crucero, **25, 26**
El Dátil, **83**
El Doctor, **19**

El Faro Beach, **26**
El Faro RV Park, 113, **94**
El Golfo, 86
El Hongo, **7, 8**
El Juncalito, **82**
El Major, **9, 19**
El Mármol, **29, 30, 31**
El Mesquital, **65**
El Metate, **29**
El Migrino, **93, 95**
El Mirador, **3, 4, 5**
El Mogote, **91**
El Moro Trailer Park, 113, **82**
El Morro Motel, **68**
El Muertito, **45**
El Oasis Hotel, 72
El Oasis RV park, 113, **4**
El Oasis, **7**
El Padrino RV Park, 66, 67, 92, 113, **66**
El Palomar RV park, 58, 113, **14**
El Papalote, **22**
El Pescadero, **92**
El Progreso, **29, 30**
El Requesón, **73, 74**
El Rincón, **15, 17**
El Rodeo, **15**
El Rosario, 24, 36, 53, **21, 22, 27**
El Rosarito, **45, 46**
El Sargento, 108, **91, 92**
El Sauzal, **3, 4, 5**
El Soccoro, **21, 22**
El Testerazo, **7**
El Tomatal, **46**
El Triunfo, 40,**91, 92, 93, 97**
El Vergel, **26**
El Volcán, **29, 31**
Electricity, 20
Elephant tree, 42
Ensenada Blanca, **81, 82**
Ensenada city map, 60
Ensenada El Aterrizaje, 67
Ensenada, 21, 60, **3, 4, 5, 8, 10, 13,
    14, 15, 16, 42, 62**
Eréndira, **13, 14**
Ernesto's Trailer Park, **22**
Escondido, **15**
Espinosa, Doña Anita, 53
Espíritu Santo Island, 106, 109
Estero Beach Resort, 58, 60, **3, 5, 14**
Estero Coyote, **61**
Exchange rates, 15, 16
Ferries, 15
Finisterra Hotel, 80, 81
Fishing license, 13, 109
Fishing limits, 13
Fishing, 95, 60, 70, 72, 75, 80, 86, 101
Flight Log, 18
Flying Samaritans, 53
FM-3, 12
Gardner, Erle Stanley, 17
Gasoline, 23, 24
Geology, 35

Gilmore, Dr. Raymond, 88
Gold Coast, 11
Golf, 72, **4, 82, 96,**
Green angels, 14, 19
Grey whale, 87, **42, 54, 56**
Guadalupe Canyon, **9, 10**
Guadalupe, **3, 5**
Guayaquil, **29, 30**
Guaycura Indians, 44
Guerrero Negro area map, 89
Guerrero Negro city map, 65
Guerrero Negro Lagoon, **54**
Guerrero Negro, 11, 21, 22, 24, 31, 51,
    64, 89, **34, 43, 45, 46, 53**
Guillermo's Trailer Park, 113, **48**
Guns, 28
Hacienda Beach Resort, 80, 81
Hadrosaur, 36
Hamilton Ranch, **21**
Heroes de la Independencia, **16**
Hoctor, Fred, 100
Holidays, 51
Hot springs, **16, 78**
Hunting licenses, 13, **10**
Immigration , 12, 61, **4, 68**
Insurance, 14, 19, 33
Insurgentes, 24, **70, 77, 78, 80**
Isla Angel De La Guarda, 4, **39, 49, 50**
Isla Carmen, 106, **81, 82**
Isla Cedros, **41**
Isla Cerralvo, **91**
Isla Coronado, **81**
Isla Cresciente, **83**
Isla Danzante, 106, **81**
Isla El Huerfanito, **31**
Isla El Piojo, **47**
Isla Espíritu Santo, 109, **91**
Isla Estanque, **49**
Isla Ildefonso, **73**
Isla Las Animas, **49, 59**
Isla Magdalena, **75, 76, 83**
Isla Monserrate, **81**
Isla Natividad, **41**
Isla Partida, **49, 91**
Isla Raza, **49, 50**
Isla Salsipuedes, **49, 59**
Isla San Diego, **87**
Isla San Esteban, **59**
Isla San Francisco, **87**
Isla San Geronimo, **27**
Isla San José, **87**
Isla San Lorenzo, **49, 59**
Isla San Marcos, **67**
Isla San Martín, **26**
Isla San Pedro Martír, **59**
Isla San Roque, **52**
Isla Santa Catalina, **81**
Isla Santa Cruz, **87**
Isla Santa Inez, **73**
Isla Santa Margarita, **83, 84**
Isla Smith, **47, 49**
Isla Tortuga, **67**

Islote Partida, **87**
IVA tax, 16
Jacumé, **7**
Jai Alai, 58
Jaraquay, **38**
Jatay, **4**
Jesús María, 24, **45, 46**
Juncalito, **81**
Kaadekaman Trailer Park, 113, **56**
Kayaking, 75, 106, 117, **78**
Kelly, Neil, 101
Kira, Gene, 94
Kiro Siwi current, 105
KOA Rosarito RV Park, 113, **4**
Kumihay Indians, 44
L. A. Cetto Winery, **8**
La Almeja restaurant, 70
La Bachata, **38**
La Banqueta, **77**
La Bocana, **14, 61**
La Bufadora, 60, **3, 5, 13, 14**
La Candelaria, **94**
La Capilla RV park, 113, **97, 98**
La Concha Hotel 109
La Costilla, **32**
La Espinita RV Park, 113, **46**
La Fonda, **4**
La Gringa, **47, 49**
La Mesa, **3, 5**
La Misión, **3, 4, 5**
La Pasión, **85, 87**
La Paz city map, 76-77
La Paz International Airport, **92**
La Paz RV Park, 114, **92**
La Paz, 12, 21, 31, 72, 75, 109 **91, 92,
   94, 96, 98**
La Perla Hotel, 75
La Pinta Hotel, Guerrero Negro, **46**
La Pinta Hotel, San Ignacio, 67
La Pinta Hotel, San Quintín, 62, 63
La Playa RV Park, 114, **48**
La Poza Grande, **77, 79**
La Purísima, **71, 72, 80, 82**
La Quinta, **6**
La Ribera RV Park, 114, **98**
La Ribera, **97, 98**
La Roca, **26**
La Rumorosa, **8, 9, 16**
La Salina, **3, 4, 5**
La Turquesa, **30**
La Ventana, 91
La Ventana, **91, 92**
La Vinorama, **97**
La Virgencita, **53**
Laguna Chapala, **35, 37, 38**
Laguna Guerrero Negro, **43, 45, 53**
Laguna Hansen, **7, 16, 17**
Laguna Manuela, **45, 46**
Laguna Ojo de Liebre, 89, **43, 53, 54,
   5 6**
Laguna Salada, **9**
Laguna San Ignacio, **64, 66**

Las Animas, **47, 49**
Las Arrastras, **35, 36, 37**
Las Barrancas, **70**
Las Brisas, **22**
Las Casitas Hotel, 70
Las Cruces, **91**
Las Dunas Trailer Park, 114, **46**
Las Juntas, **7**
Las Palmas RV park, 68, 114, **68**
Las Parras, **81**
Las Vírgenes, **30**
Ledón, **19**
Leonero, **97**
Leslie, Thomas, 35
Liguí, **81, 82**
Liquor, 28
Lobster season, 30
Longline fishing, 75
Lopez Mateos city map, 90
Lopez Mateos, 90, **75, 76, 77, 78, 84**
Lopez Mateos, see Puerto
Loremar RV Park, 114, **82**
Loreto city map, 72
Loreto, 24, 35, 54, 72, 73, **70, 74, 81,
   8 2**
Los Arcos Hotel, 75
Los Barriles, 108, **97, 98**
Los Cabos, 11, 21
Los Cabos Fishing Center, 80
Los Cerritos RV Park, 114, **94**
Los Equipales restaurant, 70
Los Frailes, **97, 98**
Los Gavilanes, **7**
Los Laguneros, **56**
Los Mapaches, **47, 49, 57**
Los Muertos, **92**
Los Naranjos, **74**
Los Planes, **91, 98**
Los Pozos, **93, 95**
Ludwig, Daniel K., 64
Lures, 97
Magdalena Plain, **82**
Malarrimo Beach, 3, 105, **43, 51, 52,
   53, 56**
Malarrimo RV Park, 52, 64, 89, 114, **46**
Maneadero, **13, 14, 15**
Manfred's Trailer Park, 114, **78**
Mangoes, 31
Manila galleon, **54**
Mapaches, **58**
Maps of cities, 58-82
Mar del Sol RV Park, 114, **26**
Martín Verdugo Trailer Park, 114, **98**
Mathis, Dr. W. Michael, 44
Matomí wash, **32**
Mazatlán ferry, 15
McMahan, Mike, 3
Melía Cabo Real Hotel, **96**
Melía Los Cabos Hotel, 81
Meling Ranch, **22, 24**
Mercado La Ballena, 64
Mesón Don Pepe RV Park, 114, **22**

Mexicali, **6, 8, 9, 10, 18, 26**
Mexican Department of Fisheries, 13
Mexican Hunting Association, 13
Midriff, 11
Migrino, **93, 95**
Mike's Sky Ranch, **16, 23**
Miller's Landing, **45**
Minch, John, 35
Miraflores, **93, 95, 97, 98**
Misión Calamajué, **36**
Misión de Loreto Hotel, 72, 73
Misión El Descanso, 44, **4**
Misión La Purísima Concepción de
    Cadegomó, 47, **80**
Misión Nuestra Señora de Guadalupe de
    Huasinapí, 45, 47, **8, 74**
Misión Nuestra Señora de Loreto
    Conchó, 48, 72, **82**
Misión Nuestra Señora de los Dolores
    Apaté, 49, **86**
Misión Nuestra Señora del Pilar de La Paz
    Airapí, 49, **92**
Misión Nuestra Señora del Rosario de
    Viñadarco, 45 , **22**
Misión San Fernando Rey de España de
    Velicatá, 45, **30**
Misión San Francisco de Borja Adac, 46,
    4 6
Misión San Francisco Javier de Biaundó,
    48, 72, **70, 82**
Misión San Ignacio de Kadakaaman, 47,
    66, **66**
Misión San José de Comondú, 48, **80**
Misión San José del Cabo Añuití, 49, **96**
Misión San Luis Gonzaga Chiriyaqui, 48,
    7 8
Misión San Miguel Arcángel del la
    Frontera, 44, **4**
Misión San Pedro Mártir de Verona, 45
Misión Santa Catalina Vírgen y Mártir, 45,
    1 6
Misión Santa Gertrudis la Magna de
    Cadacamán, 46, **56**
Misión Santa María de Los Angeles, 45,
    3 0
Misión Santa Rosalía de Mulegé, 47, 70,
    7 4
Misión Santiago el Apóstol Aiñiní, 49, **98**
Misión Santo Domingo de la Frontera, 45,
    2 2
Misión Santo Tomás, **14**
Missions, 44
Mitsubishi, 64
Money exchange, 15
Mordida, 28, 101
Morro Hermoso, **51**
Motel Chavez, **22**
Muelle Viejo, **22**
Mulegé city map, 71
Mulegé Divers, 70, 71, 109
Mulegé, 24, 70, **70, 73, 74**

Museums, 4, 45, 48, 60, 66, 72, 75, **8,**
    22, 48, 82,
Nacho's camp, **32**
Napoleonic code, 14
Nopoló, 72, **81, 82**
Notrí, **81, 82**
Nueva Chapala, **35, 37**
Nuevo Leon, **11**
Nuevo Mazatlán, **26**
Oasis Hotel, 72, 73
Observatories, 68, **18, 24**
Ocotillo, 39
Ojos Negros, **7, 8, 15, 16**
Old Mill Motel & RV Park, 62, 63, 115, **22**
Orchard RV Park, 70, 71, 116, **74**
Osprey, **54**
Otay Mesa, **6**
Outdoor Resorts RV park, 115, **4**
Padilla, Oscar, insurance, 14
Pai Pai Indians, 44
Palm Beach, **93, 94, 95**
Palmas de Cortez Hotel, **98**
Palmilla Hotel, **96**
Panchos Place, **26**
Papa Diaz, 4
Papa Fernandez' camp, **32**
Parador Punta Prieta Trailer Park, 115, **38**
Parador Punta Prieta, **35, 37, 38**
Parque Nacional de Observatorio, **23**
Parque National Constitución de 1857,
    1 6
Parque National San Pedro Martír, **16,**
    2 2
Passports, 27
Pearls, 75
Pedrogoso, 80
Pénjamo, **85, 86**
Pepe's Dive Shop, 109
Percebú, **26**
Pericú Indians, 44
Permits, 12
Pescadero, **93, 94, 95**
Pesos, 15,
Pete's Camp, **26**
Pets, 33
Picacho del Diablo, **18, 24, 28**
Pichilingue, 15, **91**
Pilots, 18
Pitaya, 40, **92**
Plants, 38
Playa Adriana, **32**
Playa Armenta, **74**
Playa Blanca, **26, 34**
Playa Bonita Trailer Park, 115, **26**
Playa Buena Ventura, **73**
Playa del Oro RV Park, 115, **98**
Playa del Sol Hotel, 108
Playa Dorada, **32**
Playa Hermosa Hotel, **98**
Playa Linda, **26**
Playa Los Cerritos, **94**
Playa María Bay, **34**

Playa México, **32**
Playa Punta Loma, **32**
Playa Saldamando, **4**
Playa San Antonio, **32**
Playa San Juanico, **82**
Playa San Rafael, **57**
Playa Santa Inéz, **74**
Playa Santa María, **21, 68**
Playa Sol y Mar, **32**
Playa Xanic, **32**
Playas de Tijuana, **4**
Plaza Las Glorias, 80, 81, 109
Polo Blanco, **79**
Popotla, **3, 5**
Porvenir, **29**
Posada Concepción, **73, 74**
Posada Don Diego RV Park, 115, **22**
Pozo Salado, **7**
Presa de Santa Inez, **93, 95**
Presa Vieja, **79**
Prescription drugs, 30
Propane, 21, **46, 68, 96**
Puebla Bonita Hotel, 81
Puertecitos, **31, 32**
Puerto Chale, **83, 86**
Puerto Escondido, **81, 82**
Puerto Lopez Mateos, 90, **75, 76, 77, 78, 80, 84**
Puerto Magdalena, **83**
Puerto Nuevo, **3, 4, 5**
Puerto San Carlos city map, 91
Puerto San Carlos, 74, **28, 78**
Puerto Santa Catarina, **27, 30**
Puerto Santo Tomás, **14**
Puerto Viejo, **83**
Punta Arena de la Ventana, **91**
Punta Arena de la Ventana, **91**
Punta Arena, **73, 74**
Punta Asunción, **51**
Punta Baja, 105, **32, 67, 81**
Punta Ballena, **59**
Punta Banda, 35, 60, 106, **3, 5**
Punta Blanca, **34**
Punta Bronaugh, **61, 63**
Punta Bufeo, **32**
Punta Calabozo, **87**
Punta Canoas, 107, **27, 33, 34**
Punta Chivato, 105, 108, 115, **67, 68, 73**
Punta Colorada Hotel, **98**
Punta Colorada, **97**
Punta Concepción, **73**
Punta Conejo, **89**
Punta Cono, **33, 34**
Punta Coyote, **91**
Punta Entrada, **83**
Punta Estrella, **26**
Punta Eugenia, 105
Punta Eugenio, **41**
Punta Final, **36, 39**
Punta Holcombe, **63, 61**
Punta Hughes, **75**

Punta Lobos, **91**
Punta Mangles, **73**
Punta Marquez, **89**
Punta Montalvo, **87**
Punta Negra, **33**
Punta Palmilla, **93, 95**
Punta Pescadero Hotel, **98**
Punta Pescadero, **97**
Punta Prieta, **34, 35, 37, 38, 51**
Punta Pulpito, **73**
Punta Redondo, **83**
Punta Rocosa, **45, 49**
Punta Rompiente, **41**
Punta San Basillio, **73**
Punta San Carlos, **27**
Punta San Francisquito, **59**
Punta San Hipólito, **61**
Punta San Pablo, **51**
Punta San Roque, **51**
Punta San Telmo, **87**
Punta Santa Teresa, **73**
Punta Santo Domingo, **69**
Punta Soledad, **49**
Punta Sudeste, **91**
Punta Thurloe, **51**
Punta Tosca, **83**
Punta Trinidad, **57**
Rancho Banchetti, **8**
Rancho Buena Vista Hotel, **98**
Rancho El Consuelo, **22**
Rancho El Mesquital, **66**
Rancho Leonero, 109, **97, 98**
Rancho María Teresa, **8**
Rancho Ojai, **8**
Rancho Percebú, **26**
Rancho San Juan de Dios, **15**
Rancho Santa Catarina, **34**
Rancho Santa Inés, **38**
Rancho Sereno Bed and Breakfast, **22**
Real del Mar, **4**
Recipes, 52
Recompression chamber, 109
Red Cross, 86
Remedios, **39, 48**
Resource Guide, 114
Revolution of 1910, 51
Riíto, **11, 19**
Rio Hardy, **9, 10, 19**
Road conditions, 22
Road signs, 99
Roadlog quick reference guide, 85
Roadlog, 86
Roberts, Norman, 38
Rodriquez Dam, **6**
Rods and reels, 98
Romano-Lax, Andromeda, 106
Rosa de Costilla, **15**
Rosarito Beach, 11, **3, 4, 5**
Rosarito, **73**
Rubin's Trailer Park, 115, **26**
RV caravans to Baja, 21
RV parks, 19

RV travel tips, 19
Saguaro, 40
Salsipuedes, **3, 4, 5**
San Agustín, **29, 30**
San Andrés, **45**
San Antonio de Las Minas, **8**
San Antonio del Mar, **3, 4, 5, 13, 14**
San Antonio, **91, 97, 98**
San Bartolo, **97, 98**
San Borja, **47**
San Borjitas, **68**
San Bruno, **67, 68**
San Carlos, 91, **28, 75, 76, 78, 83**
San Evaristo, **87, 90**
San Faustino, **7**
San Felipe city map, 83
San Felipe, 24, 82, 86, **8, 10, 16, 18, 25, 26, 36, 40**
San Francisco de La Sierra, **64**
San Francisquito, **59**
San Hipólito, 107, **51, 61**
San Ignacio city map, 67, 92
San Ignacio lagoon, 92
San Ignacio, 24, 66, **38, 42, 64, 65, 66, 79**
San Ignacito, **47**
San Isidro, **13, 71, 72, 87, 82**
San Jacinto Trailer Park, 115, **22**
San Jorge, **77**
San José Comondú, **71, 72, 79**
San José de Castro, **44, 52**
San José de Las Palomas, **46**
San José de Magdalena, **68**
San José del Cabo city map, 79
San José del Cabo, 11, 107, 78, **93, 95, 96, 97, 98**
San José del Castro, **51**
San José Viejo, **93, 95, 97**
San Juan de Dios, **29**
San Juan de La Costa, **90**
San Juan de Los Planes, **92, 98**
San Juan, **13, 73**
San Juanico, 107, **69, 70, 73**
San Lino, **65**
San Lucas Cove, **67, 68**
San Lucas RV park, 115, **68**
San Lucas, **67**
San Luis, **11, 89, 93, 95**
San Miguel Comondú, **71, 72**
San Miguel, **4**
San Nicolas, **73**
San Pedrito RV park, 107, 115, **93, 94, 95**
San Pedro de la Presa, **85**
San Pedro, **89, 91, 92**
San Quintín area map, 63
San Quintín, 24, 62, **14, 21, 22, 34, 38**
San Rafael, **49, 57, 59**
San Roque, **51, 52**
San Sebastian, **65, 73**
San Simon, **21**

San Telmo, **13, 16, 21, 22**
San Vicente, **13, 14, 15**
San Ysidro, **3, 5**
San Zacarias, **63**
Santa Agueda, **68**
Santa Anita, **93. 95, 96, 97**
Santa Catarina (mission), **15**
Santa Catarina, 36, **30, 34**
Santa Clara Mountains, **56**
Santa Gertrudis, **57**
Santa Inez, **29, 35, 37**
Santa María, **21**
Santa Marta orphanage, **14**
Santa Martha, **66**
Santa Rita, **83, 85, 86**
Santa Rosa, **65, 97**
Santa Rosalía city map, 69
Santa Rosalía ferry, 15
Santa Rosalía, 12, 21, 24, 68, **46, 67, 68**
Santa Rosalillita, 107, **34, 38, 45, 46**
Santiago, **97, 98**
Santispac, **73, 74**
Santo Domingo, **45, 70, 77**
Santo Tomás, 58, 60, **13, 14, 15**
Scammon's Lagoon, 64, 87, 89, **42, 43, 53, 56**
Scammon, Charles, M., 87
Scorpion Bay, 107, **69**
Scuba diving
SCUBA, 109
Sea kayaking, 75, 106
SEDESOL, 88
Semana Santa, 51
Sematur, 15
Serenidad Hotel & RV Park, 70, 71, 116, **74**
Shell Beach, 105, **68, 73**
Shopping, 29, 31, 64, **14**
Sierra de La Giganta, **82**
Sierra San Pedro Martír, 13
Sinai Trailer Park, 116, **22**
Sol Mar Hotel, 80, 81
Sombrerito Point, 70
Spa Buena Vista Hotel, **98**
Speedy's Camp, **32**
Surf fishing, 13, 82, 98, 114, 115, **14, 22, 28, 52, 60, 90, 92, 94**
Surfing, 86, 107, 117, **34, 38, 52, 62, 84, 107, 117**
Tecate, **4, 7, 6, 8**
Tecolote Beach, 109, **91**
Telephones, 110
The Wall, **45**
Tiburón, **50**
Tides, 86
Tijuana Airport, **6**
Tijuana city map, 59
Tijuana, 58, **3, 4, 5, 6**
Tipping, 34
Todos Santos, 49, 55, 107, **93, 94, 95**
Tomatal, 55, **45**

Totuava, 13, 82, 94, **36, 40**
Tourist card, 12
Trailerboating, 101
Travelers checks, 16
Tres Pozos, **7**
Tres Vírgenes, **65, 67**
Tripui RV park, 116, **82**
Tropic of Cancer, 78, **98**
Twin Dolphins Hotel, **96**
U.S. Customs, 30
Vagabundos del Mar RV park, 116, **81,
     96**
Vagabundos del Mar Travel Club, 33
Valle de Guadalupe, **8**
Valle de Las Palmas, **7, 8**
Valle de Trinidad, **16**
Valle Trinidad, **15**
Vaquita porpoise, 82
Vehicle permits, 12, 15
Victoria, **11**
Video cameras, 28
Villa María Isabel RV Park, 71, 116, **74**
Villa Morelos, **85, 86**
Villa Serena RV Park, 116, **96**
Villa Vita Hotel, 4
Villas de Loreto RV Park, 116, **82**
Vírgenes grade, **66**
Visas, 12
Viscaíno, 24, **52, 55, 56**
Visita de Calamajué, 45, **38**
Vista del Mar RV Park, 116, **26**
Vista Hermosa, **26**
Water for drinking, 20, 32
Water for motorhomes, 19
Western Outdoor News, 100
Westin Regina Hotel, **96**
Whale bones, 30
Whale-watching, 86, 87-93
Windsurfing, 86, 108, 117, **48, 92**
Wineries, **8**
Yucca, 5, **18**

MEXICAN ROAD SIGNS

Stop

Escuela
School

Puente Angosto
Narrow Bridge

Ganado
Cattle

Yield right of way

Vado
Dip

Hombres Trabajando
Men Working

Zona de Derrumbes
Slide Area

Camino Sinuoso
Winding Road

Curva Peligrosa
Dangerous Curve

One Way

Keep to the right

NO VOLTEAR EN U
No U Turn

No Parking
8 a.m. to 9 p.m.

PROHIBIDO
ESTACIONARSE
No Parking

One Hour Parking

Speed Limit
(in kilometers)

Two Way Street

Left Turn Only

Rest Room

Telephone

Mechanic

Gas Station

DESVIACION
Detour

NO HAY PASO
Road Closed

POBLADO
PROXIMO
Town Nearby

DESPACIO
Slow

Parking

Trailer Park

PARADA
Bus Stop

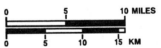

Hospital

Restaurant

Airport

LITERS TO GALLONS

Gallons	Liters	Gallons	Liters
1	3.8	16	60.6
2	7.6	17	64.4
3	11.4	18	68.1
4	15.1	19	71.9
5	18.9	20	75.7
6	22.7	21	79.5
7	26.5	22	83.3
8	30.3	23	87.1
9	34.1	24	90.8
10	37.9	25	94.6
11	41.6	30	113.6
12	45.4	35	132.5
13	49.2	40	151.4
14	53.0	45	170.3
15	56.8	50	189.3

0   5   10 MILES

0   5   10   15 KM

KILOMETERS TO MILES*

Kilometers	Miles	Kilometers	Miles
1	0.62	20	12.43
3	1.86	40	24.85
4	2.49	50	31.07
7	4.35	60	37.28
9	5.59	80	49.71
10	6.21	90	55.92
15	9.32	100	62.14

★ NOTE: To convert kilometers into miles
divide by two and add 25%. Thus, 40
kilometers would be 20 plus 5 or 25 miles.
1 mile = 1.61 km.

BAJA BOOKS AVAILABLE FROM BAJA SOURCE
Your #1 source for all of the books on Baja.

A POD OF GREY WHALES, F. Gohier. Whale-watching, petting and touching at its finest. Photographs taken in the lagoons of Baja. Characteristics of the California gray whale described and what to expect when you are actually out there among the whales yourself. $7.95

ADVENTURES IN BAJA, Mike McMahan. Mike, one of the early pioneers of Baja, recounts what Baja was like before the highway was built. This book is filled with a lifetime of captivating experiences, first time discoveries, fishing, hunting, diving, campfire tales, history of the land and the people. $6.95

ANGLER'S GUIDE TO BAJA, Tom Miller. Where and when to fish in Baja by Baja's most avid fisherman. Includes maps, tales of the best fishing to be found anywhere, stories about special places and people. Fish identification. Fishing calendars. 4th edition, revised. $7.95

ANTIGUA CALIFORNIA: Mission and Colony on the Peninsular Frontier, 1697-1768. Harry Crosby. Travel nearly 300 years back into Baja's history. Learn about the family and social life of Baja's first colony, the building of Jesuit missions and artifacts revealing untold stories of this time. Hard bound limited edition of 2000 copies. $39.95

AUTO CLUB GUIDE TO BAJA CALIFORNIA, Automobile Club of Southern California. Roads, mileages, restaurants and everything you would expect to find in a good tour book. These people have been mapping Baja longer than anyone. (Restrictions prohibit the sale of this book in certain areas.) $7.95

BACKROAD BAJA, Patti and Tom Higginbotham. 20 backroad Baja trips for either 2 wheel or 4 wheel drive vehicles. Maps, logs, and thorough detailed descriptions. Available January, 1996.

BAJA ADVENTURE BOOK, Walt Peterson. Lots of photos of the authors first hand experiences in Baja. Road logs, side trips, city maps. Very entertaining to read at home or use as one of your guide books on your next trip down the peninsula. $19.95

BAJA ADVENTURES BY LAND, SEA AND AIR, Marvin Patchen. They did it - they had access to boats, kayaks, helicopters, airplanes, 4WD vehicles and all the rest of it - and - they used it to explore Baja - in detail. Book recounts these trips. Printed in 1981 - a few copies available at the original price of $9.95.

BAJA BOOK IV, Ginger Potter. A completeupdate and revision of Tom Miller's best seller. New road maps superimposed on satellite Spacemaps®. Mile-by-mile roadlog of the Baja peninsula. Fishing, camping, whale watching, all watersports, boating, customs regulations entering and leaving, 60 plus maps, permits, licenses, laws, this book covers it all. $19.95

BAJA CAMPING, Fred & Gloria Jones. Gives details on the campgrounds of Baja that are highway accessible. Includes maps showing campground locations. Loaded with travel info, things to do, requirements for preparation as well as historical anecdotes. $12.95

BAJA CATCH, Kelly & Kira. The Baja fisherman's guide by *the* Baja fisherman himself. Maps, tips on boat ramps, tackle, vehicles, permits and fish identification. Detailed maps show where to go for specific types of fishing. Travel and camping information. $19.95

BAJA FEELING, Ben Hunter. Recounts the trials and joys of building a home in Los Barriles along with other interesting Baja escapades. Out of print. Limited supply. $11.95.

BAJA HIGHWAY, John Minch & Thomas Leslie. A thorough geological and botanical work on the Baja Peninsula. Complete descriptions referenced by the kilometer markers along the road. Great to have your passenger read aloud as you drive. Includes where to find petrified sharks teeth, agatized shells, dinosaur bones and much more. $19.95

BUSINESS OPPORTUNITIES AND RETIREMENT GUIDE, Tom and Mary Lou Magee. The Baja California culture and how it differs from ours, business opportunities, banking, real estate, NAFTA, the legal system, employment and investing. $19.95

DICTIONARY. Pocket sized basic dictionary. English to Spanish and Spanish to English. $4.50

EATING YOUR WAY THROUGH BAJA, Tom Miller. A reference to the restaurants of Baja. Organized by area. Includes prices, favorite dishes and comments. $4.95

FISHES OF THE PACIFIC COAST, Gar Goodson. Alaska to Peru including the Sea of Cortez and Galapagos Islands. 507 color paintings, range, habits, where you might catch them and edibility. Diving tips and maps. $8.95

FOR THE LOVE OF BAJA, Kay Choat. A seafood cookbook for Baja. Includes basic fish cleaning, shucking clams and oysters, cooking lobster and many of the other edible animals that come from the sea around Baja. Good recipes. $14.95

HOW TO BUY REAL ESTATE IN MEXICO, Dennis Peyton. A good guide to understanding what has to take place when you buy property in Mexico. Well defined, easy to understand. Covers every aspect of the laws affecting foreigners. Don't buy or lease land in Mexico without reading this book first. $19.95

KING OF THE MOON: A Novel of Baja California, Gene Kira. By the co-author of <u>The Baja Catch</u>. A vivid, action-packed story, set in the 1960's, follows the exploits of the Abundio Rodriguez family in the tiny fishing hamlet of Agua Amargosa. Publication date: March 1996.

LAUNCH RAMPS OF BAJA CALIFORNIA, Mike Bales. A trailer-boaters guide to the launching places in Baja. Complete and comprehensive with detailed information and photographs of each launch ramp. $6.95

LONG WALK TO MULEGE, Howard Hale. In 1924 two adventurous young men set out on foot to walk more than half of the Baja Peninsula. Their experiences, the people they met, the trials they encountered. Rugged adventure - a most enjoyable book. $12.95

MARINE ANIMALS OF BAJA CALIFORNIA, Dan Gotshall. For divers, tidepoolers and fishermen. Fantastic color photos. Descriptions of common fishes and invertebrates. $20.95

MEXICO WEST BOOK, Tom Miller. The first road and recreation guide to Mexico's west coast. Covers Arizona to Guatemala with over 5,000 miles of road logs, 100+ maps, 160 drawings, 200 beaches. Detailed descriptions of places to stay and places to eat. Fishing, surfing, artisan centers, retirement, fiestas, camping and more. $15.95

PLANT FIELD GUIDE TO BAJA CALIFORNIA, Norman Roberts. Color photos identify the unique and interesting plants of Baja. Botanical, common, English and Spanish names. Uses of plants as herbs, poultices, teas and food. Very well done by a dedicated Baja traveler. $22.95

SEAFOOD BAJA-STYLE, Patti Higginbotham. 19 unique and delicious recipes printed on spiral-bound postcards to save or send to your friends. $7.95

SEA KAYAKING IN BAJA, Andromeda Romano-Lax. Kayaking has become very popular in the Sea of Cortez and around the lagoons of the Pacific side of Baja. 15 complete trips, equipment suggestions, preparation tips. Maps, good area descriptions. Where to rent kayaks and gear to take. $13.95

SOMETHIN'S FISHY IN BAJA, Patti Higginbotham. A seafood cookbook with 220 Baja tested recipes. Cleaning and preparation included. $14.95

THERE IT IS: BAJA!, Mike McMahan. Discoveries of two previously unknown Indian pictograph and petroglyph sites, first-hand fishing experiences, Malarrimo Beach, recipes and history all written in the *macho manner*. Hard bound. Original issue price was $6.95, out of print for 22 years. Limited supply at $14.95

BAJA SOURCE SPECIALTY MERCHANDISE

THE BAJA MAP, Mike McMahan & Ginger Potter. Beautiful 4 color map of Baja printed on tear-resistant Dupont Tyvek®. This is the one you have seen in all the hotels and restaurants in Baja and on the back cover of this book. 5th edition updated. Size 34" x 59". $34.50. Laminated, $44.50.

MINI BAJA MAP, 7th edition of the above beautiful four-color Baja map now comes in a smaller size to fit apartments and RV's. Measuring just 21" x 36" this completely updated map is printed on special pre-laminate paper and then professionally laminated on both sides. $24.00

SATELLITE MAP OF BAJA. So detailed and clear you can even pick out some of the roads. Black and white, 53" x 20". Originally printed in 1975, these are out of print and we only have a few left at $10.00 each.

PHOTO ALBUM, by Baja Source. Quality photo album covered with the Baja map and a smaller Baja map sewn into the front. Holds 80 4" x 6" photos on two flip-up pages. $28.00

BAJA ROAD MAP by Automobile Club of Southern California. The most accurate road map of Baja. These people have been mapping Baja for 30+ years. Now available to non-members at $3.95. (Restrictions prohibit the sale of this book in certain areas.)

BAJA ROAD MAP by International Travel Maps. Fold-up travel map. 5 colors, printed on one side. Interesting historical insets to read as you travel. Updated. $6.95

MEXICO ROAD MAP by International Travel Maps. Covers all of Mexico and Baja. 4 color, printed on one side. Scale: 1:3,300,00. $6.95

MEXICO SOUTH ROAD MAP by International Travel Maps. Covers Mexico City to Guatemala. Scale: 1:1,000,000. $7.95

BAJA SOURCE, from time to time, sells out of print and rare books on Baja. If you are looking for a title that is out of print, give us a call.

Baja Source
1945 Dehesa Road
El Cajon, CA 92019
619-442-7061
Phone & fax orders accepted
Visa & Mastercard

BAJA SOURCE - ORDER FORM

1945 DEHESA RD, EL CAJON, CA 92019 - 619-442-7061 fax & phone

QTY	ITEM DESCRIPTION	PRICE	TOTAL
	A POD OF GREY WHALES	7.95	
	ADVENTURES IN BAJA	6.95	
	ANGLER'S GUIDE TO BAJA	7.95	
	ANTIGUA CALIFORNIA	39.95	
	AUTO CLUB GUIDE TO BAJA	7.95	
	BACKROAD BAJA	*	
	BAJA ADVENTURE BOOK	19.95	
	BAJA ADVENTURES BY LAND, SEA & AIR	9.95	
	BAJA BOOK IV	19.95	
	BAJA CAMPING	12.95	
	BAJA CATCH	19.95	
	BAJA FEELING	12.95	
	BAJA HIGHWAY	19.95	
	BUSINESS OPPORTUNITIES & RETIREMENT GUIDE	19.95	
	DICTIONARY, POCKET, ENGLISH-SPANISH	4.50	
	EATING YOUR WAY THROUGH BAJA	4.95	
	FISHES OF THE PACIFIC COAST	8.95	
	FOR THE LOVE OF BAJA, COOKBOOK	14.95	
	HOW TO BUY REAL ESTATE IN MEXICO	19.95	
	KING OF THE MOON	*	
	LAUNCH RAMPS OF BAJA CALIFORNIA	6.95	
	LONG WALK TO MULEGE	12.95	
	MARINE ANIMALS OF BAJA CALIFORNIA	20.95	
	MEXICO WEST BOOK	15.95	
	PLANT FIELD GUIDE TO BAJA CALIFORNIA	22.95	
	SEAFOOD BAJA-STYLE	7.95	
	SEA KAYAKING IN BAJA	13.95	
	SOMETHIN'S FISHY IN BAJA	14.95	
	THERE IT IS: BAJA!	14.95	
	PHOTO ALBUMS	28.00	
	MINI-WALL MAP, 4 COLOR, LAMINATED 21" X 36"	24.00	
	WALL MAP, 4-COLOR, TYVEK 34" X 59"	34.50	
	WALL MAP, 4-COLOR, TYVEK, LAMINATED 34" X 59"	44.50	
	ROAD MAP OF BAJA by Automobile Club of So. Calif.	3.95	
	ROAD MAP OF BAJA by Intl. Travel Maps	6.95	
	TOTAL		
	Calif residents add current sales tax		
	Shipping and handling. (See note below)		
	FINAL TOTAL		

*Pricing not available. At time of publication, please call for price.
Shipping & handling $4.00 first item & $1.00 each additional. Road maps, $1.50. All orders sent UPS, street address required. Orders must be prepaid, credit cards okay, please make checks payable to Baja Source. Foreign orders will be charged appropriate additional freight.

NAME_____DATE_____

STREET ADDRESS_____

CITY_____STATE____ZIP_____

CREDIT CARD #_____EXP DATE_____

PHONE NUMBER_____

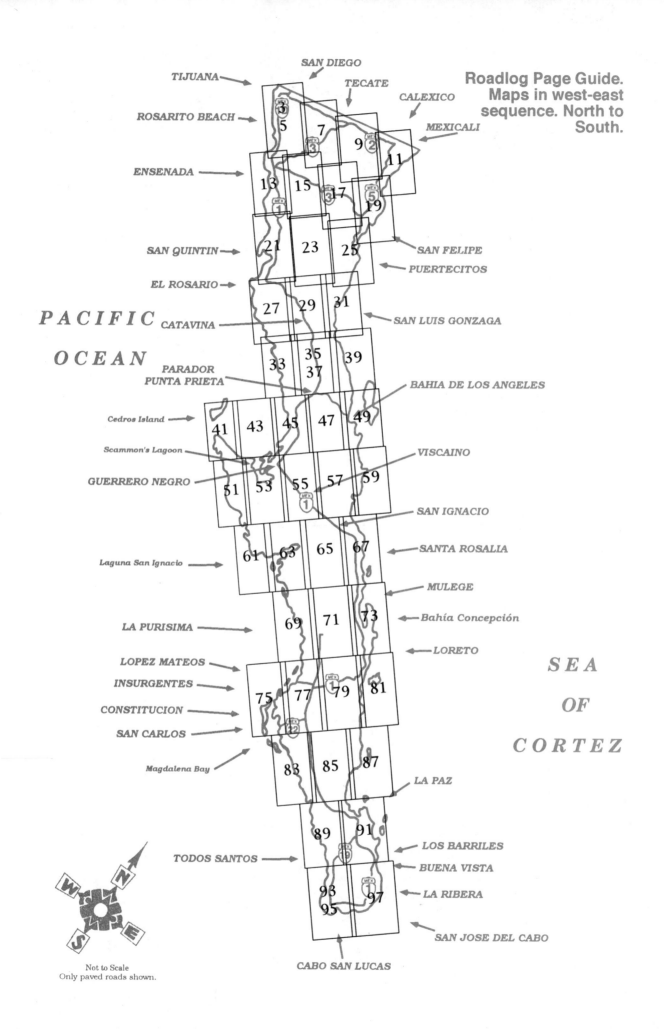